HIS LIFE

manuscript

OPTIMUM VIZH-AN

Order this book online at www.trafford.com
or email orders@trafford.com

Most Trafford titles are also available at major online book retailers.

Printed in the United States of America.

ISBN: 978-1-4269-7881-4 (sc)
ISBN: 978-1-4269-7882-1 (e)

Trafford rev. 07/29/2011

www.trafford.com

North America & international
toll-free: 1 888 232 4444 (USA & Canada)
phone: 250 383 6864 ✦ fax: 812 355 4082

Table of Contents

Dedication

This book is dedicated to
Jesus Christ for becoming human,
exposing himself to us
and enduring extreme temptations;
to earn the right to be our
mediator, elder brother and co-heir
versus choosing to have a distant
relationship with us.
JOHN 1:1-14

We stand in awe,
with our praises to you,
for the rest of our lives!

Thank you!
Jesus Christ

Author

Dedication II

This book is dedicated to the following people:
My parents: Richard and Sally, for assisting God in bringing me into this world, putting up with me in all my seasons and reminding me from time to time, I am really human.
My children: Kezia, Rakkal and Aron for giving me the honor and privilege of being your father and a mother when none availed. Your lives were the beginning of my life in realizing how truly wise God was, in designing family, so that we could understand the depth of unconditional love, faith and hope, between us as a family.
My children by marriage: for giving me the experience of embracing you like you were my very own.
My grand children: Dakota, Isabella, Ashton, Madison and Adin; for giving me the honor and privilege of seeing my children become parents themselves. Your lives were the beginning of my life in realizing how truly wise God was, in allowing us to remember, how important it is, to always embrace life like a child.
My future children and grand children by birth and marriage: for giving me the honor and privilege of enjoying and celebrating life as a legacy.
The two men in my life, that are like brothers, sons, friends, fathers, men, mentors, entrepreneurs, philosophers, confidantes, comrades and kings to me: Aron and Nicholas, for giving me the honor and

privilege of knowing what is like to sincerely enjoy all these roles as a man. Time itself will reveal to all what this really means.

My special and dear friend Mackenzie: for healing all those human relationship scares I subconsciously accumulated through out all my life.

My furry friend – Cooper: for assisting me in writing this book; by waking me up in the morning when my alarm clock wouldn't, waking me up when I fell asleep in the chair writing and taking all those play breaks from writing. Your timing was implacable. You put a smile on my face every time I think about it. Thank you Cooper!

You all have made me realize how good God is, in allowing us to enjoy His Life together, to the fullest!

I forever thank you all.

Habakkuk

Then the LORD replied:
"Write down the revelation
and make it plain on tablets
so that a herald may run with it.
For the revelation awaits
an appointed time;
it speaks of the end
and will not prove false.
Though it linger,
wait for it;
it will certainly come
and will not delay.

Habakkuk 2:2-3

Disclaimer

Weaving the Books;
Matthew, Mark, Luke and John
into one account is based on
the author's logistics choice.

The author also chose to
include additional references
to Christ, as documented in
the books of Isaiah, Acts and Revelation,
to give a more complete
account of His Life.

The author's choice of sequencing
the events of His Life was based on
cross checking and comparing each account's
documented sequence events. Then
determined the more than likely best
sequence of events, into
one combined compilation
account.

It is not the intention of the author
to replace the above
individual accounts with this
one woven account version.

Preface

Imagine if we could all sit together in the same place, at the same time, having all the time in the world. We would all witness for the first time in history, every ones opinions, debates and testimonies about his life. We would see and hear each other taking sides on all sides. Be it wrong or right, involved or not involved, everyone seems to be effected by his story, every time it's told. Some will die by it. Some will die trying to stop his story from ever being told again. Both young and old, age doesn't seem to matter. His story either moves people closer to him or further away. Why is his story so motivating; when it's just a fable, when he's just a man? Or maybe he is truly God in the flesh? If he is, how could a God with everything, convince himself that becoming human, is the best thing for himself and the humans he made, in his image. What could that possibly prove or even accomplish? How could a God justify allowing pain to run chaotically across the perfect paradise he made, and then choose to die in that pain. Couldn't he of just as easily continued to live with us in that paradise without the pain? No matter how many questions we ask or answer, we are still asking and answering the same questions. Over and over, every generation is plagued with the same predictable debates, that have same predictable out comes.

His story has been told countless of times, by countless of people that have produced countless of stories, about whom he is and who he isn't. We change our life styles, our careers and our beliefs to mimic his life. We will go to extremes to eliminate his story from history, change our careers and forsake our loved ones. How can his story make insane people sane and sane people insane?

I have wondered myself about who he is. I have read the accounts of his story in all four gospels, to the point I don't want to read them anymore. But I feel like I have over looked something. Something that's fresh. Something that captivates me to read his story again, from the beginning to the end, without putting it down, until I'm done – good. But how could I gain a new revelation from an old story? Then I thought, hmm...what if I read his story with all the perspectives woven together into one account? That sounds complex. Let alone messy. Could it be heresy? It can't be. Nothing's distorted. Nothing's added or subtracted. It would be woven just like fabric. The colors are separated or in different patterns, either way, it's the same fabric. Makes sense to me. I'm hooked. Now, which books should be woven together. In respect to traditional Christendom, I sould start with the widely accepted four gospels; Matthew, Mark, Luke, John. Still sounds like something's missing. Need some kickers. Aah! How about adding the references of Christ, when he's interacting with mankind, in the books of Acts and Revelations. I like it. I like it a lot. My curiosity is intriguing me. I can't wait no more. I want to read this new one woven account about his life...now!

This book is the result of those questions, I asked a little more than twenty years ago. I hope you find His Life as enlightening as I did, when I read my first copy. Enjoy!

Construction Notes

The following notes are the behind the scenes, to the core logistics on how the four gospels of Matthew, Mark, Luke and John were woven together.

Which of the four gospel accounts of Matthew, Mark, Luke and John would be the best account, to weave the other accounts to?

Luke? Was strongly considered based on Luke starting his account with documenting that he had carefully investigated, verified and then wrote an orderly account, of the events that took place. Plus Luke was considered a doctor. But when it came time to weave his documented events together, Luke had the events in chaotic groups. Those groups had to be broken up, to be in better alignment with the other accounts.

Matthew? Matthew was a tax collector. This makes more sense, because he had to keep track of who owes what and when they didn't, he had to make sure they did.

Mark? John? When studying Mark, the least publicized account; it was surprising to know, that he had more details per event listed then the other accounts. And John has a ton more of details on Christ the night he was betrayed.

Each account had their fair share of new revelations about the individual event or events, as well as being repeated in the other accounts.

It was decided that Matthew would be the over all framework to weave the four accounts to. Then based on the individual details of each event, would determine which account, would be the framework used to weave the other accounts to based on their individual focal points.

How were the other event references to Christ, in the other Books, considered?

Any event that had mentioned of Christ interacting with mankind was considered and added to this book. The other references were considered and added to this book were in the books of Isaiah, Acts and Revelations.

In the book of Isaiah, the reference considered and added was the description of what Christ looked like at his crucifixion.

In the book of Acts, the references considered and added were after Christ's resurrection from the dead, his ascension, his encounter with Paul and Herod's death.

In the book of Revelations, the references considered and added were who Christ is, what Christ looks like, his message to each angel over each of the seven churches, his throne, his worthy, his rest, his reign forever, his bride, his new heaven and new earth, and his invitation.

How was each woven event referenced?

The account with the most details would be the framework of that documented event. Then the next reference, with the most details was woven within the major reference framework. The same thing for the next reference, and the same again until all the references were woven together. Example: if Matthew had the most details, then Mark, then Luke and then John; it was listed like this, after each woven account details. Matthew CH:VS. Mark CH:VS. Luke CH:VS. John CH:VS. CH equals chapter and VS equals verse.

If the next event was better described by Mark, then John, then Luke then Matthew; it was referenced as, Mark CH:VS. John CH:VS. Luke CH:VS. Matthew CH:VS.

This pattern was more than likely adhered to, majority of the time. However when warranted, due to the flow of events, the framework reference would be chosen based on continuity.

Four examples on how the before and after actual individual event accounts where woven together:

1. Christ's Water Baptism. Before:

16 As soon as Jesus was baptized, he went up out of the water. At that moment heaven was opened, and he saw the Spirit of God descending like a dove and lighting on him. Matthew 3:16.

10 As Jesus was coming up out of the water, he saw heaven being torn open and the Spirit descending on him like a dove. Mark 1:10.

21b And as he was praying, heaven was opened 22a and the Holy Spirit descended on him in bodily form like a dove. Luke 3:21b-22a.

1. Christ's Water Baptism. After:

16 As soon as Jesus was baptized, as he was coming up out of the water he was praying and at that moment he saw heaven being torn opened and the Spirit of God descended on him in bodily form like a dove and lighting on him. Matthew 3:16. Mark 1:10. Luke 3:21b-22a.

Summary of weaving the accounts together as one:

For this event, we discovered there was no reference in the book of John on this event pertaining to his life.

Matthew's reference brings to the one woven account: "lighting on him." Mark's reference brings to the one woven account: "heaven being torn open." Luke's reference brings to the one woven account: "as he was praying."

2. Seed Sown on Good Soil. Before:

23 But the one who received the seed that fell on good soil is the man who hears the word and understands it. He produces a crop, yielding a hundred, sixty or thirty times what was sown." Matthew 13:23.

15 But the seed on good soil stands for those with a noble and good heart, who hear the word, retain it, and by persevering produce a crop. Luke 8:15.

20 Others, like seed sown on good soil, hear the word, accept it, and produce a crop-thirty, sixty or even a hundred times what was sown." Mark 4:20.

2. Seed Sown on Good Soil. After:

23 But the other ones who received the sown seed that fell on good soil, stands for those with a noble and good heart who hear the word, accepts it, understands it and retains it. And by persevering they produce a crop, yielding a hundred, sixty or thirty times what was sown." Matthew 13:23. Luke 8:15. Mark 4:20.

Summary of weaving the accounts together as one:

For this event, we discovered there was no reference in the book of John on this event pertaining to his life.

Matthew's reference brings to the one woven account: "understands it." Luke's reference brings to the one woven account: "with a noble and good heart," "retain it," "persevering." Mark's reference brings to the one woven account: "accept it."

3. Christ's Encounter with Demons. Before:

1 They went across the lake to the region of the Gerasenes. 2 When Jesus got out of the boat, a man with an evil spirit came from the tombs to meet him. 3 This man lived in the tombs, and no one could bind him any more, not even with a chain. 4 For he had often been chained hand and foot, but he tore the chains apart and broke the irons on his feet. No one was strong enough to subdue him. 5 Night and day among the tombs and in the hills he would cry out and cut himself with stones. Mark 5:1-5.

26 They sailed to the region of the Gerasenes, which is across the lake from Galilee. 27 When Jesus stepped ashore, he was met by a demon-possessed man from the town. For a long time this man had not worn clothes or lived in a house, but had lived in the tombs. Luke 8:26-27.

28 When he arrived at the other side in the region of the Gadarenes, two demon-possessed men coming from the tombs met him. They were so violent that no one could pass that way. Matthew 8:28.

3. Christ's Encounter with Demons. After:

1 They sailed across the lake to the region of the Gerasenes which is across the lake from Galilee. 2 When they arrived at the other side, Jesus got out of the boat and stepped ashore, two men with an evil demon-possessed spirits came from the town tombs to meet him. They were so violent that no one could pass that way. 3 For a long time these men had not worn clothes or lived in a house, but lived in the tombs, and no one could bind them any more, not even with a chain. 4 For many times it had seized them,

and though they had often been chained hand and foot and kept under guard; they tore the chains apart, broke the irons on their feet and had been driven by the demons into solitary places. No one was strong enough to subdue them. 5 Night and day among the tombs and in the hills they would cry out and cut themselves with stones. Mark 5:1-5. Luke 8:26-27. Matthew 8:28.

Summary of weaving the accounts together as one:

For this event, we discovered there was no reference in the book of John on this event pertaining to his life.

Mark's reference brings to the one woven account: brings most of the details to this event, as stated above. Luke's reference brings to the one woven account: "For a long time this man had not worn clothes or lived in a house." Matthew's reference brings to the one woven account: "two demon-possessed men," "so violent that no one could pass that way."

4. Christ with Pilate. Before:

33 Pilate then went back inside the palace, summoned Jesus and asked him, "Are you the king of the Jews?" 34 "Is that your own idea," Jesus asked, "or did others talk to you about me?" 35 "Am I a Jew?" Pilate replied. "It was your people and your chief priests who handed you over to me. What is it you have done?" 36 Jesus said, "My kingdom is not of this world. If it were, my servants would fight to prevent my arrest by the Jews. But now my kingdom is from another place." 37 "You are a king, then!" said Pilate. Jesus answered, "You are right in saying I am a king. In fact, for this reason I was born, and for this I came into the world, to testify to the truth. Everyone on the side of truth listens to me." 38 "What is truth?" Pilate asked. John 18:33-38a.

11 Meanwhile Jesus stood before the governor, and the governor asked him, "Are you the king of the Jews?" "Yes, it is as you say," Jesus replied. Matthew 27:11.

2 "Are you the king of the Jews?" asked Pilate. "Yes, it is as you say," Jesus replied. Mark 15:2.

3 So Pilate asked Jesus, "Are you the king of the Jews?" "Yes, it is as you say," Jesus replied. Luke 23:3.

43. Christ with Pilate. After:

33 Pilate then went back inside the palace, summoned Jesus and Jesus stood before the governor and the governor asked him, "Are you the king of the Jews?" 34 "Yes, it is as you say," "Is that your own idea," Jesus asked, "or did others talk to you about me?" 35 "Am I a Jew?" Pilate replied. "It was your people and your chief priests who handed you over to me. What is it you have done?" 36 Jesus said, "My kingdom is not of this world. If it were, my servants would fight to prevent my arrest by the Jews. But now my kingdom is from another place." 37 "You are a king, then!" said Pilate. Jesus answered, "You are right in saying I am a king. In fact, for this reason I was born, and for this I came into the world, to testify to the truth. Everyone on the side of truth listens to me." 38a "What is truth?" Pilate asked. John 18:33-38a. Matthew 27:11. Mark 15:2. Luke 23:3.

Summary of weaving the accounts together as one:

For this event, we discovered all the individual accounts had reference to this event.

John's reference brings to the one woven account: All of the details except for the minor details in Matthew, Mark and Luke. See above. Matthew's reference brings to the one woven account: "Jesus stood before the governor," "Yes, it is as you say." Mark's reference brings to the one woven account: "Yes, it is as you say." Luke's reference brings to the one woven account: verifies the same reference as Mark's.

Construction Notes Summary:

Based on weaving all four accounts together as one account, it leads us to believe, that each separate account potentially has missing details. When these missing details are added together they enhance the event even more. Without weaving the four accounts together, we would have to take time to read the other references and then some how combined them in our minds. Let a lone, try to remember which account reference detail is located. This version allows us to enjoy reading the enhance events, without thinking about how to sequence each event.

Construction Notes Mystery:

After going through the mechanics, in putting this all together, it felt like his story was originally one account to begin with. It's like Matthew, Mark, Luke and John were sitting around the camp fire one night, discussing how they should break his life story up into separate accounts, for the purpose of increasing the odds in preserving it for generations to come. It's like they reasoned, protecting four accounts had a better chance of surviving all the famines, floods, pestilences and tyrannies it might have to go through versus protecting one account. Three out of four accounts could be lost and there would still be one account to refer to. If the only one account was lost, then there would be no hope of preserving it. One account would be harder to prove as authentic, as would four accounts. Since there are four different people who wrote an account on his story, maybe there's a better chance of his story being true. It's like they took this original puzzle, broke it apart, mixed up the pieces and then randomly divided them up into four groups. Each would organize their allotted pieces and call it their account. And then by chance somehow, twenty centuries later, God in his grace, decided to put the "his life story" puzzle back together again.

Chapter One

HIS ORIGIN

His Origin

1 The beginning of the gospel about Jesus Christ, the Son of God. Mark 1:1.

1 Many have undertaken to draw up an account of the things that have been fulfilled among us, 2 just as they were handed down to us by those who from the first were eyewitnesses and servants of the word.

3 Therefore, since I myself have carefully investigated everything from the beginning, it seemed good also to me to write an orderly account for you, most excellent Theophilus, 4 so that you may know the certainty of the things you have been taught. Luke 1:1-4.

1 In the beginning was the Word, and the Word was with God, and the Word was God. 2 He was with God in the beginning. 3 Through him all things were made; without him nothing was made that has been made. 4 In him was life, and that life was the light of men. 5 The light shines in the darkness, but the darkness has not understood it. John 1:1-5.

9 The true light that gives light to every man was coming into the world. John 1:9.

His Preparer's Origin

5 In the time of Herod king of Judea there was a priest named Zechariah, who belonged to the priestly division of Abijah; his wife Elizabeth was also a descendant of Aaron. 6 Both of them were upright in the sight of God, observing all the Lord's commandments and regulations blamelessly. 7 But they had no children, because Elizabeth was barren; and they were both well along in years.

8 Once when Zechariah's division was on duty and he was serving as priest before God, 9 he was chosen by lot, according to the custom of the priesthood, to go into the temple of the Lord and burn incense. 10 And when the time for the burning of incense came, all the assembled worshipers were praying outside.

11 Then an angel of the Lord appeared to him, standing at the right side of the altar of incense. 12 When Zechariah saw him, he was startled and was gripped with fear. 13 But the angel said to him: "Do not be afraid, Zechariah; your prayer has been heard. Your wife Elizabeth will bear you a son, and you are to give him the name John. 14 He will be a joy and delight to you, and many will rejoice because of his birth, 15 for he will be great in the sight of the Lord. He is never to take wine or other fermented drink, and he will be filled with the Holy Spirit even from birth. 16 Many of the people of Israel will he bring back to the Lord their God. 17 And he will go on before the Lord, in the spirit and power of Elijah, to turn the hearts of the fathers to their children and the disobedient to the wisdom of the righteous-to make ready a people prepared for the Lord." 18 Zechariah asked the angel, "How can I be sure of this? I am an old man and my wife is well along in years." 19 The angel answered, "I am Gabriel. I stand in the presence of God, and I have been sent to speak to you and

to tell you this good news. 20 And now you will be silent and not able to speak until the day this happens, because you did not believe my words, which will come true at their proper time."

21 Meanwhile, the people were waiting for Zechariah and wondering why he stayed so long in the temple. 22 When he came out, he could not speak to them. They realized he had seen a vision in the temple, for he kept making signs to them but remained unable to speak.

23 When his time of service was completed, he returned home. 24 After this his wife Elizabeth became pregnant and for five months remained in seclusion. 25 "The Lord has done this for me," she said. "In these days he has shown his favor and taken away my disgrace among the people." Luke 1:5-25.

His Earthly Mother

26 In the sixth month, God sent the angel Gabriel to Nazareth, a town in Galilee, 27 to a virgin pledged to be married to a man named Joseph, a descendant of David. The virgin's name was Mary. 28 The angel went to her and said, "Greetings, you who are highly favored! The Lord is with you." 29 Mary was greatly troubled at his words and wondered what kind of greeting this might be. 30 But the angel said to her, "Do not be afraid, Mary, you have found favor with God. 31 You will be with child and give birth to a son, and you are to give him the name Jesus. 32 He will be great and will be called the Son of the Most High. The Lord God will give him the throne of his father David, 33 and he will reign over the house of Jacob forever; his kingdom will never end." 34 "How will this be," Mary asked the angel, "since I am a virgin?" 35 The angel answered, "The Holy Spirit will come upon you, and the power of the Most High will overshadow you. So the holy one to be born will be called the Son of God. 36 Even

Elizabeth your relative is going to have a child in her old age, and she who was said to be barren is in her sixth month. 37 For nothing is impossible with God." 38 "I am the Lord's servant," Mary answered. "May it be to me as you have said." Then the angel left her. Luke 1:26-38.

18 This is how the birth of Jesus Christ came about: His mother Mary was pledged to be married to Joseph, but before they came together, she was found to be with child through the Holy Spirit. 19 Because Joseph her husband was a righteous man and did not want to expose her to public disgrace, he had in mind to divorce her quietly.

20 But after he had considered this, an angel of the Lord appeared to him in a dream and said, "Joseph son of David, do not be afraid to take Mary home as your wife, because what is conceived in her is from the Holy Spirit. 21 She will give birth to a son, and you are to give him the name Jesus, because he will save his people from their sins." 22 All this took place to fulfill what the Lord had said through the prophet: 23 "The virgin will be with child and will give birth to a son, and they will call him Immanuel"-which means, "God with us."

24 When Joseph woke up, he did what the angel of the Lord had commanded him and took Mary home as his wife. 25 But he had no union with her until she gave birth to a son. And he gave him the name Jesus. Matt 1:18-25

39 At that time Mary got ready and hurried to a town in the hill country of Judea, 40 where she entered Zechariah's home and greeted Elizabeth. 41 When Elizabeth heard Mary's greeting, the baby leaped in her womb, and Elizabeth was filled with the Holy Spirit. 42 In a loud voice she exclaimed: "Blessed are you among women, and blessed is the child you will bear! 43 But why am I so favored, that the mother of my Lord should come to me? 44 As soon as the sound of your greeting reached my ears, the baby in my womb leaped for joy. 45 Blessed is she who has believed

that what the Lord has said to her will be accomplished!" 46 And Mary said: "My soul glorifies the Lord 47 and my spirit rejoices in God my Savior, 48 for he has been mindful of the humble state of his servant. From now on all generations will call me blessed, 49 for the Mighty One has done great things for me- holy is his name. 50 His mercy extends to those who fear him, from generation to generation. 51 He has performed mighty deeds with his arm; he has scattered those who are proud in their inmost thoughts. 52 He has brought down rulers from their thrones but has lifted up the humble. 53 He has filled the hungry with good things but has sent the rich away empty. 54 He has helped his servant Israel, remembering to be merciful 55 to Abraham and his descendants forever, even as he said to our fathers."

56 Mary stayed with Elizabeth for about three months and then returned home. Luke 1:39-56.

His Preparer's Birth

57 When it was time for Elizabeth to have her baby, she gave birth to a son. 58 Her neighbors and relatives heard that the Lord had shown her great mercy, and they shared her joy.

59 On the eighth day they came to circumcise the child, and they were going to name him after his father Zechariah, 60 but his mother spoke up and said, "No! He is to be called John." 61 They said to her, "There is no one among your relatives who has that name." 62 Then they made signs to his father, to find out what he would like to name the child. 63 He asked for a writing tablet, and to everyone's astonishment he wrote, "His name is John." 64 Immediately his mouth was opened and his tongue was loosed, and he began to speak, praising God. 65 The neighbors were all filled with awe, and throughout the hill country of Judea people were talking about all these things. 66 Everyone who heard this

wondered about it, asking, "What then is this child going to be?" For the Lord's hand was with him.

67 His father Zechariah was filled with the Holy Spirit and prophesied: 68 "Praise be to the Lord, the God of Israel, because he has come and has redeemed his people. 69 He has raised up a horn of salvation for us in the house of his servant David 70 (as he said through his holy prophets of long ago), 71 salvation from our enemies and from the hand of all who hate us- 72 to show mercy to our fathers and to remember his holy covenant, 73 the oath he swore to our father Abraham: 74 to rescue us from the hand of our enemies, and to enable us to serve him without fear 75 in holiness and righteousness before him all our days.

76 And you, my child, will be called a prophet of the Most High; for you will go on before the Lord to prepare the way for him, 77 to give his people the knowledge of salvation through the forgiveness of their sins, 78 because of the tender mercy of our God, by which the rising sun will come to us from heaven 79 to shine on those living in darkness and in the shadow of death, to guide our feet into the path of peace." Luke 1:57-79.

His Earthly Birth

1 In those days Caesar Augustus issued a decree that a census should be taken of the entire Roman world. 2 (This was the first census that took place while Quirinius was governor of Syria.) 3 And everyone went to his own town to register.

4 So Joseph also went up from the town of Nazareth in Galilee to Judea, to Bethlehem the town of David, because he belonged to the house and line of David. 5 He went there to register with Mary, who was pledged to be married to him and was expecting a child. 6 While they were there, the time came for the baby to be

born, 7 and she gave birth to her firstborn, a son. She wrapped him in cloths and placed him in a manger, because there was no room for them in the inn. Luke 2:1-7

14 The Word became flesh and made his dwelling among us. We have seen his glory, the glory of the One and Only, who came from the Father, full of grace and truth. John 1:14.

8 And there were shepherds living out in the fields nearby, keeping watch over their flocks at night. 9 An angel of the Lord appeared to them, and the glory of the Lord shone around them, and they were terrified. 10 But the angel said to them, "Do not be afraid. I bring you good news of great joy that will be for all the people. 11 Today in the town of David a Savior has been born to you; he is Christ the Lord. 12 This will be a sign to you: You will find a baby wrapped in cloths and lying in a manger." 13 Suddenly a great company of the heavenly host appeared with the angel, praising God and saying, 14 "Glory to God in the highest, and on earth peace to men on whom his favor rests." 15 When the angels had left them and gone into heaven, the shepherds said to one another, "Let's go to Bethlehem and see this thing that has happened, which the Lord has told us about."

16 So they hurried off and found Mary and Joseph, and the baby, who was lying in the manger. 17 When they had seen him, they spread the word concerning what had been told them about this child, 18 and all who heard it were amazed at what the shepherds said to them. 19 But Mary treasured up all these things and pondered them in her heart.

20 The shepherds returned, glorifying and praising God for all the things they had heard and seen, which were just as they had been told.

21 On the eighth day, when it was time to circumcise him, he was named Jesus, the name the angel had given him before he had been conceived. Luke 2:8-21.

His Earthly Father's Genealogy

1 A record of the genealogy of Jesus Christ the son of David, the son of Abraham: 2 Abraham was the father of Isaac, Isaac the father of Jacob, Jacob the father of Judah and his brothers, 3 Judah the father of Perez and Zerah, whose mother was Tamar, Perez the father of Hezron, Hezron the father of Ram, 4 Ram the father of Amminadab, Amminadab the father of Nahshon, Nahshon the father of Salmon, 5 Salmon the father of Boaz, whose mother was Rahab, Boaz the father of Obed, whose mother was Ruth, Obed the father of Jesse, 6 and Jesse the father of King David. David was the father of Solomon, whose mother had been Uriah's wife, 7 Solomon the father of Rehoboam, Rehoboam the father of Abijah, Abijah the father of Asa, 8 Asa the father of Jehoshaphat, Jehoshaphat the father of Jehoram, Jehoram the father of Uzziah, 9 Uzziah the father of Jotham, Jotham the father of Ahaz, Ahaz the father of Hezekiah, 10 Hezekiah the father of Manasseh, Manasseh the father of Amon, Amon the father of Josiah, 11 and Josiah the father of Jeconiah and his brothers at the time of the exile to Babylon. 12 After the exile to Babylon: Jeconiah was the father of Shealtiel, Shealtiel the father of Zerubbabel, 13 Zerubbabel the father of Abiud, Abiud the father of Eliakim, Eliakim the father of Azor, 14 Azor the father of Zadok, Zadok the father of Akim, Akim the father of Eliud, 15 Eliud the father of Eleazar, Eleazar the father of Matthan, Matthan the father of Jacob, 16 and Jacob the father of Joseph, the husband of Mary, of whom was born Jesus, who is called Christ.

17 Thus there were fourteen generations in all from Abraham to David, fourteen from David to the exile to Babylon, and fourteen from the exile to the Christ. Matthew 1:1-17.

His Earthly Mother's Genealogy

23b He was the son, so it was thought, of Joseph, the son of Heli, 24 the son of Matthat, the son of Levi, the son of Melki, the son of Jannai, the son of Joseph, 25 the son of Mattathias, the son of Amos, the son of Nahum, the son of Esli,the son of Naggai, 26 the son of Maath, the son of Mattathias, the son of Semein, the son of Josech, the son of Joda, 27 the son of Joanan, the son of Rhesa, the son of Zerubbabel, the son of Shealtiel, the son of Neri, 28 the son of Melki, the son of Addi, the son of Cosam, the son of Elmadam, the son of Er, 29 the son of Joshua, the son of Eliezer, the son of Jorim, the son of Matthat, the son of Levi, 30 the son of Simeon, the son of Judah, the son of Joseph, the son of Jonam, the son of Eliakim, 31 the son of Melea, the son of Menna, the son of Mattatha, the son of Nathan, the son of David, 32 the son of Jesse, the son of Obed, the son of Boaz, the son of Salmon, the son of Nahshon, 33 the son of Amminadab, the son of Ram, the son of Hezron, the son of Perez, the son of Judah, 34 the son of Jacob, the son of Isaac, the son of Abraham, the son of Terah, the son of Nahor, 35 the son of Serug, the son of Reu, the son of Peleg, the son of Eber, the son of Shelah, 36 the son of Cainan, the son of Arphaxad, the son of Shem, the son of Noah, the son of Lamech, 37 the son of Methuselah, the son of Enoch, the son of Jared, the son of Mahalalel, the son of Kenan, 38 the son of Enosh, the son of Seth, the son of Adam, the son of God. Luke 3:23b-38.

Chapter Two

HIS EARTHLY CHILDHOOD

His Consecration

22 When the time of their purification according to the Law of Moses had been completed, Joseph and Mary took him to Jerusalem to present him to the Lord 23 (as it is written in the Law of the Lord, "Every firstborn male is to be consecrated to the Lord"), 24 and to offer a sacrifice in keeping with what is said in the Law of the Lord: "a pair of doves or two young pigeons."

25 Now there was a man in Jerusalem called Simeon, who was righteous and devout. He was waiting for the consolation of Israel, and the Holy Spirit was upon him. 26 It had been revealed to him by the Holy Spirit that he would not die before he had seen the Lord's Christ. 27 Moved by the Spirit, he went into the temple courts. When the parents brought in the child Jesus to do for him what the custom of the Law required, 28 Simeon took him in his arms and praised God, saying: 29 "Sovereign Lord, as you have promised, you now dismiss your servant in peace. 30 For my eyes have seen your salvation, 31 which you have prepared in the sight of all people, 32 a light for revelation to the Gentiles and for glory to your people Israel." 33 The child's father and mother marveled at what was said about him. 34 Then Simeon blessed them and said to Mary, his mother: "This child is destined to cause the falling and rising of many in Israel, and to be a sign that will be spoken against, 35 so that the thoughts of many hearts will be revealed. And a sword will pierce your own soul too."

36 There was also a prophetess, Anna, the daughter of Phanuel, of the tribe of Asher. She was very old; she had lived with her husband seven years after her marriage, 37 and then was a widow until she was eighty-four. She never left the temple but worshiped night and day, fasting and praying. 38 Coming up to them at that very moment, she gave thanks to God and spoke about the child to all who were looking forward to the redemption of Jerusalem.

39 When Joseph and Mary had done everything required by the Law of the Lord, they returned to Galilee to their own town of Nazareth. Luke 2:22-39.

His Magi

1 After Jesus was born in Bethlehem in Judea, during the time of King Herod, Magi from the east came to Jerusalem 2 and asked, "Where is the one who has been born king of the Jews? We saw his star in the east and have come to worship him."

3 When King Herod heard this he was disturbed, and all Jerusalem with him. 4 When he had called together all the people's chief priests and teachers of the law, he asked them where the Christ was to be born. 5 "In Bethlehem in Judea," they replied, "for this is what the prophet has written: 6 "'But you, Bethlehem, in the land of Judah, are by no means least among the rulers of Judah; for out of you will come a ruler who will be the shepherd of my people Israel.'"

7 Then Herod called the Magi secretly and found out from them the exact time the star had appeared. 8 He sent them to Bethlehem and said, "Go and make a careful search for the child. As soon as you find him, report to me, so that I too may go and worship him." 9 After they had heard the king, they went on their way, and the star they had seen in the east went ahead of them until it

stopped over the place where the child was. 10 When they saw the star, they were overjoyed. 11 On coming to the house, they saw the child with his mother Mary, and they bowed down and worshiped him. Then they opened their treasures and presented him with gifts of gold and of incense and of myrrh. 12 And having been warned in a dream not to go back to Herod, they returned to their country by another route. Matthew 2:1-12.

His Escape to Egypt

13 When they had gone, an angel of the Lord appeared to Joseph in a dream. "Get up," he said, "take the child and his mother and escape to Egypt. Stay there until I tell you, for Herod is going to search for the child to kill him." 14 So he got up, took the child and his mother during the night and left for Egypt, 15 where he stayed until the death of Herod. And so was fulfilled what the Lord had said through the prophet: "Out of Egypt I called my son."

16 When Herod realized that he had been outwitted by the Magi, he was furious, and he gave orders to kill all the boys in Bethlehem and its vicinity who were two years old and under, in accordance with the time he had learned from the Magi. 17 Then what was said through the prophet Jeremiah was fulfilled: 18 "A voice is heard in Ramah, weeping and great mourning, Rachel weeping for her children and refusing to be comforted, because they are no more." Matthew 2:13-18.

His Return to Israel

19 After Herod died, an angel of the Lord appeared in a dream to Joseph in Egypt 20 and said, "Get up, take the child and his mother and go to the land of Israel, for those who were trying to take the child's life are dead." 21 So he got up, took the child and his mother and went to the land of Israel. 22 But when he heard that Archelaus was reigning in Judea in place of his father Herod, he was afraid to go there. Having been warned in a dream, he withdrew to the district of Galilee, 23 and he went and lived in a town called Nazareth. So was fulfilled what was said through the prophets: "He will be called a Nazarene." Matthew 2:19-23.

His Childhood

40 And the child grew and became strong; he was filled with wisdom, and the grace of God was upon him.

41 Every year his parents went to Jerusalem for the Feast of the Passover. 42 When he was twelve years old, they went up to the Feast, according to the custom.

43 After the Feast was over, while his parents were returning home, the boy Jesus stayed behind in Jerusalem, but they were unaware of it. 44 Thinking he was in their company, they traveled on for a day. Then they began looking for him among their relatives and friends.

45 When they did not find him, they went back to Jerusalem to look for him. 46 After three days they found him in the temple courts, sitting among the teachers, listening to them and asking them questions. 47 Everyone who heard him was amazed at his understanding and his answers.

48 When his parents saw him, they were astonished. His mother said to him, "Son, why have you treated us like this? Your father and I have been anxiously searching for you." 49 "Why were you searching for me?" he asked. "Didn't you know I had to be in my Father's house?" 50 But they did not understand what he was saying to them.

51 Then he went down to Nazareth with them and was obedient to them. But his mother treasured all these things in her heart. 52 And Jesus grew in wisdom and stature, and in favor with God and men. Luke 2:40-52.

His Preparer's Childhood

80 And the child (John the Baptist) grew and became strong in spirit; and he lived in the desert until he appeared publicly to Israel. Luke 1:80.

Chapter Three

His Preparer's Ministry

1 In the fifteenth year of the reign of Tiberius Caesar-when Pontius Pilate was governor of Judea, Herod tetrarch of Galilee, his brother Philip tetrarch of Iturea and Traconitis, and Lysanias tetrarch of Abilene- 2a during the high priesthood of Annas and Caiaphas, Luke 3:1-2a.

6 There came a man who was sent from God; his name was John. 7 He came as a witness to testify concerning that light, so that through him all men might believe. 8 He himself was not the light; he came only as a witness to the light. John 1:6-8.

2b the word of God came to John son of Zechariah in the desert. Luke 3:2b.

6 John wore clothing made of camel's hair, with a leather belt around his waist, and his food was locusts and wild honey. Mark 1:6. Matthew 3:4.

3:1 In those days John the Baptist came, preaching in the Desert of Judea Matthew 3:1.

3 He went into all the country around the Jordan, preaching a baptism of repentance for the forgiveness of sins. Luke 3:3.

2 and saying, "Repent, for the kingdom of heaven is near." Matthew 3:2.

4a This is he who was spoken of and as it is written in the book of the words of Isaiah the prophet: Luke 3:4a. Matthew 3:3a. Mark 1:2a.

2b "I will send my messenger ahead of you, who will prepare your way"- Mark 1:2b.

3b "A voice of one calling in the desert, 'Prepare the way for the Lord, make straight paths for him.'" Matthew 3:3b. Mark 1:3. Luke 3:4b.

5 Every valley shall be filled in, every mountain and hill made low. The crooked roads shall become straight, the rough ways smooth. 6 And all mankind will see God's salvation.'" Luke 3:5-6.

5 People went out to him from Jerusalem and all Judea and the whole region of the Jordan. 6 Confessing their sins, they were baptized by him in the Jordan River. Matthew 3:5-6.

19 Now this was John's testimony when the Jews of Jerusalem sent priests and Levites to ask him who he was. 20 He did not fail to confess, but confessed freely, "I am not the Christ." 21 They asked him, "Then who are you? Are you Elijah?" He said, "I am not." "Are you the Prophet?" He answered, "No." 22 Finally they said, "Who are you? Give us an answer to take back to those who sent us. What do you say about yourself?" 23 John replied in the words of Isaiah the prophet, "I am the voice of one calling in the desert, 'Make straight the way for the Lord.'"

24 Now some Pharisees who had been sent 25 questioned him, "Why then do you baptize if you are not the Christ, nor Elijah, nor the Prophet?" John 1:19-25.

7 But when John saw the crowds and many of the Pharisees and Sadducees coming to where he was baptizing, he said to them: "You brood of vipers! Who warned you to flee from the coming wrath? 8 Produce fruit in keeping with repentance. 9 And do not

think you can say to yourselves, 'We have Abraham as our father.' I tell you that out of these stones God can raise up children for Abraham. 10 The ax is already at the root of the trees, and every tree that does not produce good fruit will be cut down and thrown into the fire. Matthew 3:7-10. Luke 3:7-9.

10 "What should we do then?" the crowd asked. 11 John answered, "The man with two tunics should share with him who has none, and the one who has food should do the same." 12 Tax collectors also came to be baptized. "Teacher," they asked, "what should we do?" 13 "Don't collect any more than you are required to," he told them. 14 Then some soldiers asked him, "And what should we do?" He replied, "Don't extort money and don't accuse people falsely-be content with your pay." 15 The people were waiting expectantly and were all wondering in their hearts if John might possibly be the Christ. Luke 3:10-15.

16 John answered them all with this message, "I baptize you with water for repentance. But among you stands one you do not know; one more powerful than I will come after me, the thongs of whose sandals I am not worthy to carry and untie. He will baptize you with the Holy Spirit and with fire. Luke 3:16. Matthew 3:11. Mark 1:7-8. John 1:26-27.

12 His winnowing fork is in his hand, and he will clear his threshing floor, gathering his wheat into the barn and burning up the chaff with unquenchable fire." Matthew 3:12. Luke 3:17.

18 And with many other words John exhorted the people and preached the good news to them. Luke 3:18.

28 This all happened at Bethany on the other side of the Jordan, where John was baptizing. John 1:28.

4 And so John came, baptizing in the desert region and preaching a baptism of repentance for the forgiveness of sins. 5 The whole Judean countryside and all the people of Jerusalem went out

to him. Confessing their sins, they were baptized by him in the Jordan River. Mark 1:4-5.

29 The next day John saw Jesus coming toward him and said, "Look, the Lamb of God, who takes away the sin of the world! 30 This is the one I meant when I said, 'A man who comes after me has surpassed me because he was before me.' 31 I myself did not know him, but the reason I came baptizing with water was that he might be revealed to Israel." John 1:29-31.

9 At that time Jesus came from Nazareth in Galilee and was baptized by John in the Jordan. Mark 1:9. Matthew 3:13.

14 But John tried to deter him, saying, "I need to be baptized by you, and do you come to me?" 15 Jesus replied, "Let it be so now; it is proper for us to do this to fulfill all righteousness." Then John consented. Matthew 3:14-15.

15 John testifies concerning him. He cries out, saying, "This was he of whom I said, 'He who comes after me has surpassed me because he was before me.'" 16 From the fullness of his grace we have all received one blessing after another. 17 For the law was given through Moses; grace and truth came through Jesus Christ. 18 No one has ever seen God, but God the One and Only, who is at the Father's side, has made him known. John 1:15-18.

21a When all the people were being baptized, Jesus was baptized too. Luke 3:21a.

16 As soon as Jesus was baptized, as he was coming up out of the water, he was praying and at that moment he saw heaven being torn opened and the Spirit of God descended on him in bodily form like a dove and lighting on him. Matthew 3:16. Mark 1:10. Luke 3:21b-22a.

11 And a voice came from heaven: "You are my Son, whom I love; with you I am well pleased." Mark 1:11. Matthew 3:17. Luke 3:22b.

32 Then John gave this testimony: "I saw the Spirit come down from heaven as a dove and remain on him. 33 I would not have known him, except that the one who sent me to baptize with water told me, 'The man on whom you see the Spirit come down and remain is he who will baptize with the Holy Spirit.' 34 I have seen and I testify that this is the Son of God." John 1:32-34.

His Ministry's Beginning

23a Now Jesus himself was about thirty years old when he began his ministry. Luke 3:23a

1 Jesus, full of the Holy Spirit, returned from the Jordan and was at once led by the Spirit in the desert, 2a where for forty days he was tempted by the devil. Luke 4:1-2a. Matthew 4:1. Mark 1:12-13a.

13b He was with the wild animals, Mark 1:13b.

2 After fasting forty days and forty nights, he was hungry. Matthew 4:2. Luke 4:2b.

3 The tempter came to him and said, "If you are the Son of God, tell these stones to become bread." Matthew 4:3. Luke 4:3.

4 Jesus answered, "It is written: 'Man does not live on bread alone, but on every word that comes from the mouth of God.'" Matthew 4:4. Luke 4:4.

5 Then the devil led and took him to the holy city Jerusalem and had him stand on the highest point of the temple. 6 "If you are the Son of God," he said, "throw yourself down. For it is written: "'He will command his angels concerning you, to guard you carefully;

they will lift you up in their hands, so that you will not strike your foot against a stone.'" Matthew 4:5-6. Luke 4:9-11.

7 Jesus answered him, "It is also written: 'Do not put the Lord your God to the test.'" Matthew 4:7. Luke 4:12.

8 Again, the devil took him to a very high mountain place and showed him in an instant all the kingdoms of the world and their splendor. Matthew 4:8. Luke 4:5.

6 And he said to him, "I will give you all their authority and splendor, for it has been given to me, and I can give it to anyone I want to. 7 So if you bow down and worship me, it will all be yours." Luke 4:6-7. Matthew 4:9.

10 Jesus said to him, "Away from me, Satan! For it is written: 'Worship the Lord your God, and serve him only.'" Matthew 4:10. Luke 4:8.

13 When the devil had finished all this tempting, he left him until an opportune time. Luke 4:13. Matthew 4:11a.

11b and angels came and attended him. Matthew 4:11b. Mark 1:13c.

His Preparer's Proclamation

35 The next day John was there again with two of his disciples. 36 When he saw Jesus passing by, he said, "Look, the Lamb of God!" 37 When the two disciples heard him say this, they followed Jesus. 38 Turning around, Jesus saw them following and asked, "What do you want?" They said, "Rabbi" (which means Teacher), "where are you staying?" 39 "Come," he replied, "and you will

see." So they went and saw where he was staying, and spent that day with him. It was about the tenth hour.

40 Andrew, Simon Peter's brother, was one of the two who heard what John had said and who had followed Jesus. 41 The first thing Andrew did was to find his brother Simon and tell him, "We have found the Messiah" (that is, the Christ). 42 And he brought him to Jesus. Jesus looked at him and said, "You are Simon son of John. You will be called Cephas" (which, when translated, is Peter).

43 The next day Jesus decided to leave for Galilee. Finding Philip, he said to him, "Follow me." 44 Philip, like Andrew and Peter, was from the town of Bethsaida. 45 Philip found Nathanael and told him, "We have found the one Moses wrote about in the Law, and about whom the prophets also wrote-Jesus of Nazareth, the son of Joseph." 46 "Nazareth! Can anything good come from there?" Nathanael asked. "Come and see," said Philip. 47 When Jesus saw Nathanael approaching, he said of him, "Here is a true Israelite, in whom there is nothing false." 48 "How do you know me?" Nathanael asked. Jesus answered, "I saw you while you were still under the fig tree before Philip called you." 49 Then Nathanael declared, "Rabbi, you are the Son of God; you are the King of Israel." 50 Jesus said, "You believe because I told you I saw you under the fig tree. You shall see greater things than that." 51 He then added, "I tell you the truth, you shall see heaven open, and the angels of God ascending and descending on the Son of Man." John 1:35-51.

His Ministry's First Miracle

1 On the third day a wedding took place at Cana in Galilee. Jesus' mother was there, 2 and Jesus and his disciples had also been invited to the wedding. 3 When the wine was gone, Jesus' mother said to him, "They have no more wine." 4 "Dear woman, why do

you involve me?" Jesus replied. "My time has not yet come." 5 His mother said to the servants, "Do whatever he tells you." 6 Nearby stood six stone water jars, the kind used by the Jews for ceremonial washing, each holding from twenty to thirty gallons. 7 Jesus said to the servants, "Fill the jars with water"; so they filled them to the brim. 8 Then he told them, "Now draw some out and take it to the master of the banquet." They did so, 9 and the master of the banquet tasted the water that had been turned into wine. He did not realize where it had come from, though the servants who had drawn the water knew. Then he called the bridegroom aside 10 and said, "Everyone brings out the choice wine first and then the cheaper wine after the guests have had too much to drink; but you have saved the best till now."

11 This, the first of his miraculous signs, Jesus performed at Cana in Galilee. He thus revealed his glory, and his disciples put their faith in him.

12 After this he went down to Capernaum with his mother and brothers and his disciples. There they stayed for a few days. John 2:1-12.

His Zeal

13 When it was almost time for the Jewish Passover, Jesus went up to Jerusalem. 14 In the temple courts he found men selling cattle, sheep and doves, and others sitting at tables exchanging money. 15 So he made a whip out of cords, and drove all from the temple area, both sheep and cattle; he scattered the coins of the money changers and overturned their tables. 16 To those who sold doves he said, "Get these out of here! How dare you turn my Father's house into a market!" 17 His disciples remembered that it is written: "Zeal for your house will consume me." 18 Then the Jews demanded of him, "What miraculous sign can you show us

to prove your authority to do all this?" 19 Jesus answered them, "Destroy this temple, and I will raise it again in three days." 20 The Jews replied, "It has taken forty-six years to build this temple, and you are going to raise it in three days?" 21 But the temple he had spoken of was his body. 22 After he was raised from the dead, his disciples recalled what he had said. Then they believed the Scripture and the words that Jesus had spoken.

23 Now while he was in Jerusalem at the Passover Feast, many people saw the miraculous signs he was doing and believed in his name. 24 But Jesus would not entrust himself to them, for he knew all men. 25 He did not need man's testimony about man, for he knew what was in a man. John 2:13-25.

His Born of the Spirit

1 Now there was a man of the Pharisees named Nicodemus, a member of the Jewish ruling council. 2 He came to Jesus at night and said, "Rabbi, we know you are a teacher who has come from God. For no one could perform the miraculous signs you are doing if God were not with him." 3 In reply Jesus declared, "I tell you the truth, no one can see the kingdom of God unless he is born again." 4 "How can a man be born when he is old?" Nicodemus asked. "Surely he cannot enter a second time into his mother's womb to be born!" 5 Jesus answered, "I tell you the truth, no one can enter the kingdom of God unless he is born of water and the Spirit. 6 Flesh gives birth to flesh, but the Spirit gives birth to spirit. 7 You should not be surprised at my saying, 'You must be born again.' 8 The wind blows wherever it pleases. You hear its sound, but you cannot tell where it comes from or where it is going. So it is with everyone born of the Spirit." 9 "How can this be?" Nicodemus asked. 10 "You are Israel's teacher," said Jesus, "and do you not understand these things? 11 I tell you the truth, we speak of what we know, and we testify to what we have

seen, but still you people do not accept our testimony. 12 I have spoken to you of earthly things and you do not believe; how then will you believe if I speak of heavenly things? 13 No one has ever gone into heaven except the one who came from heaven-the Son of Man. 14 Just as Moses lifted up the snake in the desert, so the Son of Man must be lifted up, 15 that everyone who believes in him may have eternal life. 16 "For God so loved the world that he gave his one and only Son, that whoever believes in him shall not perish but have eternal life. 17 For God did not send his Son into the world to condemn the world, but to save the world through him. 18 Whoever believes in him is not condemned, but whoever does not believe stands condemned already because he has not believed in the name of God's one and only Son. 19 This is the verdict: Light has come into the world, but men loved darkness instead of light because their deeds were evil. 20 Everyone who does evil hates the light, and will not come into the light for fear that his deeds will be exposed. 21 But whoever lives by the truth comes into the light, so that it may be seen plainly that what he has done has been done through God." John 3:1-21.

His Ministry vs His Preparers

22 After this, Jesus and his disciples went out into the Judean countryside, where he spent some time with them, and baptized. 23 Now John also was baptizing at Aenon near Salim, because there was plenty of water, and people were constantly coming to be baptized.

24 (This was before John was put in prison.) 25 An argument developed between some of John's disciples and a certain Jew over the matter of ceremonial washing. 26 They came to John and said to him, "Rabbi, that man who was with you on the other side of the Jordan-the one you testified about-well, he is baptizing, and everyone is going to him." 27 To this John replied, "A man can

receive only what is given him from heaven. 28 You yourselves can testify that I said, 'I am not the Christ but am sent ahead of him.' 29 The bride belongs to the bridegroom. The friend who attends the bridegroom waits and listens for him, and is full of joy when he hears the bridegroom's voice. That joy is mine, and it is now complete. 30 He must become greater; I must become less. 31 "The one who comes from above is above all; the one who is from the earth belongs to the earth, and speaks as one from the earth. The one who comes from heaven is above all. 32 He testifies to what he has seen and heard, but no one accepts his testimony. 33 The man who has accepted it has certified that God is truthful. 34 For the one whom God has sent speaks the words of God, for God gives the Spirit without limit. 35 The Father loves the Son and has placed everything in his hands. 36 Whoever believes in the Son has eternal life, but whoever rejects the Son will not see life, for God's wrath remains on him." John 3:22-36.

His Preparer is Jailed

19 But when John rebuked Herod the tetrarch because of Herodias, his brother's wife, and all the other evil things he had done, 20 Herod added this to them all: He locked John up in prison. Luke 3:19-20.

His Ministry Gains

1 The Pharisees heard that Jesus was gaining and baptizing more disciples than John, 2 although in fact it was not Jesus who baptized, but his disciples. 3 When the Lord learned of this, he left Judea and went back once more to Galilee. John 4:1-3.

His Living Water

4 Now he had to go through Samaria. 5 So he came to a town in Samaria called Sychar, near the plot of ground Jacob had given to his son Joseph. 6 Jacob's well was there, and Jesus, tired as he was from the journey, sat down by the well. It was about the sixth hour. 7 When a Samaritan woman came to draw water, Jesus said to her, "Will you give me a drink?" 8 (His disciples had gone into the town to buy food.) 9 The Samaritan woman said to him, "You are a Jew and I am a Samaritan woman. How can you ask me for a drink?" (For Jews do not associate with Samaritans.) 10 Jesus answered her, "If you knew the gift of God and who it is that asks you for a drink, you would have asked him and he would have given you living water." 11 "Sir," the woman said, "you have nothing to draw with and the well is deep. Where can you get this living water? 12 Are you greater than our father Jacob, who gave us the well and drank from it himself, as did also his sons and his flocks and herds?" 13 Jesus answered, "Everyone who drinks this water will be thirsty again, 14 but whoever drinks the water I give him will never thirst. Indeed, the water I give him will become in him a spring of water welling up to eternal life." 15 The woman said to him, "Sir, give me this water so that I won't get thirsty and have to keep coming here to draw water." 16 He told her, "Go, call your husband and come back." 17 "I have no husband," she replied. Jesus said to her, "You are right when you say you have no husband. 18 The fact is, you have had five husbands, and the man you now have is not your husband. What you have just said is quite true." 19 "Sir," the woman said, "I can see that you are a prophet. 20 Our fathers worshiped on this mountain, but you Jews claim that the place where we must worship is in Jerusalem." 21 Jesus declared, "Believe me, woman, a time is coming when you will worship the Father neither on this mountain nor in Jerusalem. 22 You Samaritans worship what

you do not know; we worship what we do know, for salvation is from the Jews. 23 Yet a time is coming and has now come when the true worshipers will worship the Father in spirit and truth, for they are the kind of worshipers the Father seeks. 24 God is spirit, and his worshipers must worship in spirit and in truth." 25 The woman said, "I know that Messiah" (called Christ) "is coming. When he comes, he will explain everything to us." 26 Then Jesus declared, "I who speak to you am he." John 4:4-26.

His Food

27 Just then his disciples returned and were surprised to find him talking with a woman. But no one asked, "What do you want?" or "Why are you talking with her?"

28 Then, leaving her water jar, the woman went back to the town and said to the people, 29 "Come, see a man who told me everything I ever did. Could this be the Christ?" 30 They came out of the town and made their way toward him.

31 Meanwhile his disciples urged him, "Rabbi, eat something." 32 But he said to them, "I have food to eat that you know nothing about." 33 Then his disciples said to each other, "Could someone have brought him food?" 34 "My food," said Jesus, "is to do the will of him who sent me and to finish his work. 35 Do you not say, 'Four months more and then the harvest'? I tell you, open your eyes and look at the fields! They are ripe for harvest. 36 Even now the reaper draws his wages; even now he harvests the crop for eternal life, so that the sower and the reaper may be glad together. 37 Thus the saying 'One sows and another reaps' is true. 38 I sent you to reap what you have not worked for. Others have done the hard work, and you have reaped the benefits of their labor." John 4:27-38.

39 Many of the Samaritans from that town believed in him because of the woman's testimony, "He told me everything I ever did." 40 So when the Samaritans came to him, they urged him to stay with them, and he stayed two days. 41 And because of his words many more became believers. 42 They said to the woman, "We no longer believe just because of what you said; now we have heard for ourselves, and we know that this man really is the Savior of the world." John 4:39-42.

His Light has Dawned

14 After Jesus heard that John was put in prison, Jesus returned to Galilee, proclaiming the good news of God. Mark 1:14. Matthew 4:12.

13 Leaving Nazareth, he went and lived in Capernaum, which was by the lake in the area of Zebulun and Naphtali- 14 to fulfill what was said through the prophet Isaiah: 15 "Land of Zebulun and land of Naphtali, the way to the sea, along the Jordan, Galilee of the Gentiles- 16 the people living in darkness have seen a great light; on those living in the land of the shadow of death, a light has dawned." Matthew 4:13-16.

17 From that time on Jesus began to preach, "The time has come, repent, for the kingdom of heaven is near and believe the good news." Matthew 4:17. Mark 1:15.

14 Jesus returned to Galilee in the power of the Spirit, and news about him spread through the whole countryside. 15 He taught in their synagogues, and everyone praised him. Luke 4:14-15.

His Ministry's Second Miracle

43 After the two days he left for Galilee. 44 (Now Jesus himself had pointed out that a prophet has no honor in his own country.) 45 When he arrived in Galilee, the Galileans welcomed him. They had seen all that he had done in Jerusalem at the Passover Feast, for they also had been there. John 4:43-45.

46 Once more he visited Cana in Galilee, where he had turned the water into wine. And there was a certain royal official whose son lay sick at Capernaum. 47 When this man heard that Jesus had arrived in Galilee from Judea, he went to him and begged him to come and heal his son, who was close to death. 48 "Unless you people see miraculous signs and wonders," Jesus told him, "you will never believe." 49 The royal official said, "Sir, come down before my child dies." 50 Jesus replied, "You may go. Your son will live." The man took Jesus at his word and departed.

51 While he was still on the way, his servants met him with the news that his boy was living. 52 When he inquired as to the time when his son got better, they said to him, "The fever left him yesterday at the seventh hour." 53 Then the father realized that this was the exact time at which Jesus had said to him, "Your son will live." So he and all his household believed. 54 This was the second miraculous sign that Jesus performed, having come from Judea to Galilee. John 4:46-54.

His Proclamation

16 He went to Nazareth, where he had been brought up, and on the Sabbath day he went into the synagogue, as was his custom. And he stood up to read. 17 The scroll of the prophet Isaiah was handed to him. Unrolling it, he found the place where it is written: 18 "The Spirit of the Lord is on me, because he has anointed me to preach good news to the poor. He has sent me to proclaim freedom for the prisoners and recovery of sight for the blind, to release the oppressed, 19 to proclaim the year of the Lord's favor." 20 Then he rolled up the scroll, gave it back to the attendant and sat down. The eyes of everyone in the synagogue were fastened on him, 21 and he began by saying to them, "Today this scripture is fulfilled in your hearing." 22 All spoke well of him and were amazed at the gracious words that came from his lips. "Isn't this Joseph's son?" they asked. 23 Jesus said to them, "Surely you will quote this proverb to me: 'Physician, heal yourself! Do here in your hometown what we have heard that you did in Capernaum.'" 24 "I tell you the truth," he continued, "no prophet is accepted in his hometown. 25 I assure you that there were many widows in Israel in Elijah's time, when the sky was shut for three and a half years and there was a severe famine throughout the land. 26 Yet Elijah was not sent to any of them, but to a widow in Zarephath in the region of Sidon. 27 And there were many in Israel with leprosy in the time of Elisha the prophet, yet not one of them was cleansed-only Naaman the Syrian."

28 All the people in the synagogue were furious when they heard this. 29 They got up, drove him out of the town, and took him to the brow of the hill on which the town was built, in order to throw him down the cliff. 30 But he walked right through the crowd and went on his way. Luke 4:16-30.

His First Disciples

18 As Jesus was walking beside the Sea of Galilee, he saw two brothers; Simon called Peter and his brother Andrew. They were casting a net into the lake, for they were fishermen. Matthew 4:18. Mark 1:16.

19 "Come, follow me," Jesus said, "and I will make you fishers of men." 20 At once they left their nets and followed him. Matthew 4:19-20. Mark 1:17-18.

21 Going on a little farther from there, he saw two other brothers, James son of Zebedee and his brother John. They were in a boat with their father Zebedee, preparing their nets. Without delay Jesus called them, 22 and immediately they left the boat and their father in the boat with the hired men and followed him. Matthew 4:21-22. Mark 1:19-20.

His Authority

31 Then they went down to Capernaum, a town in Galilee, and when the Sabbath began, Jesus went into the synagogue and began to teach the people. Luke 4:31. Mark 1:21.

22 The people were amazed at his teaching, because he taught them as one who had authority, not as the teachers of the law. Mark 1:22. Luke 4:32.

33 Just then a man in their synagogue who was possessed by a demon, an evil spirit, cried out at the top of his voice, 34 "Ha! What do you want with us, Jesus of Nazareth? Have you come to destroy us? I know who you are-the Holy One of God!" Luke 4:33-34. Mark 1:23-24.

35 "Be quiet!" Jesus said sternly. "Come out of him!" Then the evil spirit shook the man violently, threw the man down before them all and came out of him with a shriek without injuring him. Luke 4:35. Mark 1:25-26.

27 The people were all so amazed that they asked each other, "What is this? A new teaching with authority and power! He even gives orders to evil spirits, they obey him and come out!" Mark 1:27. Luke 4:36.

28 News about him spread quickly throughout the surrounding area and over the whole region of Galilee. Mark 1:28. Luke 4:37.

His Simon's Mother-in-Law

29 As soon as they left the synagogue, they went with James and John to the home of Simon and Andrew. 30 Jesus saw Simon's mother-in-law was lying in bed suffering with a high fever, and they told Jesus about her and asked Jesus to help her. Mark 1:29-30. Matthew 8:14. Luke 4:38

31 So he went to her, bent over and rebuked the fever; he touched and took her hand and helped her up. The fever left her and she began to wait on them. Mark 1:31. Luke 4:39. Matthew 8:15.

16 When evening came, many who were demon-possessed were brought to him, and he drove out the spirits with a word and healed all the sick. Matthew 8:16.

32 That evening when the sun was setting, the people brought to Jesus all the sick and demon-possessed. 33 The whole town gathered at the door, 34a and Jesus drove out the spirits with a word and laying his hands on each one, healed them who had various diseases. Mark 1:32-34a. Luke 4:40. Matthew 8:16.

41 Moreover, he drove out many demons out of many people, shouting, "You are the Son of God!" But he rebuked them and would not allow them to speak, because they knew he was the Christ. Luke 4:41. Mark 1:34b.

17 This was to fulfill what was spoken through the prophet Isaiah: "He took up our infirmities and carried our diseases." Matthew 8:17.

His Let's Go

35 Very early in the morning, while it was still dark, Jesus got up, left the house and went off to a solitary place, where he prayed. Mark 1:35. Luke 1:42a.

36 Simon and his companions went to look for him, 37 and when they found him, they exclaimed: "Everyone is looking for you!" When the people came to where he was, they tried to keep him from leaving them. Mark 1:36-37. Luke 4:42b.

38 But Jesus replied, "Let us go somewhere else-to the nearby villages-and towns so I can preach the good news of the kingdom of God there also. That is why I have come." Mark 1:38. Luke 4:43.

23 So Jesus traveled throughout Galilee and Judea, and kept on teaching in their synagogues, preaching the good news of the

kingdom, driving out demons, healing every disease and sickness among the people. Mark 1:39. Matthew 4:23. Luke 4:44.

24 News about him spread all over Syria, and people brought to him all who were ill with various diseases, those suffering severe pain, the demon-possessed, those having seizures, and the paralyzed, and he healed them. 25 Large crowds from Galilee, the Decapolis, Jerusalem, Judea and the region across the Jordan followed him. Matthew 4:24-25.

His Committed Disciples

1 One day as Jesus was standing by the Lake of Gennesaret, with the people crowding around him and listening to the word of God, 2 he saw at the water's edge two boats, left there by the fishermen, who were washing their nets. 3 He got into one of the boats, the one belonging to Simon, and asked him to put out a little from shore. Then he sat down and taught the people from the boat.

4 When he had finished speaking, he said to Simon, "Put out into deep water, and let down the nets for a catch."

5 Simon answered, "Master, we've worked hard all night and haven't caught anything. But because you say so, I will let down the nets." 6 When they had done so, they caught such a large number of fish that their nets began to break. 7 So they signaled their partners in the other boat to come and help them, and they came and filled both boats so full that they began to sink. 8 When Simon Peter saw this, he fell at Jesus' knees and said, "Go away from me, Lord; I am a sinful man!" 9 For he and all his companions were astonished at the catch of fish they had taken, 10 and so were James and John, the sons of Zebedee, Simon's partners.

Then Jesus said to Simon, "Don't be afraid; from now on you will catch men." 11 So they pulled their boats up on shore, left everything and followed him. Luke 5:1-11.

His Touch

1 When he came down from the mountainside, large crowds followed him. Matthew 8:1.

12 While Jesus was in one of the towns, a man came along who was covered with leprosy. When he saw Jesus, knelt before him, fell with his face to the ground and begged him on his knees, "Lord, if you are willing, you can make me clean." Luke 5:12. Mark 1:40. Matthew 8:2.

41 Filled with compassion, Jesus reached out his hand and touched the man. "I am willing," he said. "Be clean!" 42 Immediately the leprosy left him and he was cured. Mark 1:41-42. Luke 5:13. Matthew 8:3.

43 Jesus sent him away at once with a strong warning: 44 "See that you don't tell this to anyone. But go, show yourself to the priest and offer the sacrifices and gift that Moses commanded for your cleansing, as a testimony to them." Mark 1:43-44. Luke 5:14. Matthew 8:4.

45 Instead he went out and began to talk freely, spreading the news about Jesus, so that crowds of people came to hear him and to be healed of their sicknesses. As a result, Jesus could no longer enter a town openly. He often withdrew and stayed outside in lonely places and prayed. Yet the people still came to him from everywhere. Mark 1:45. Luke 5:15-16.

His Teaching

1 Jesus stepped into a boat, crossed over and came to his own town. Matthew 9:1.

1 A few days later, when Jesus again entered Capernaum, the people heard that he had come home. 2 So many gathered that there was no room left, not even outside the door, the Pharisees and teachers of the law, who had come from every village of Galilee and from Judea and Jerusalem, were sitting there. The power of the Lord was present for him to heal the sick. and he preached the word to them. Mark 2:1-2. Luke 5:17.

3 Some men came, bringing to him a paralytic on a mat, carried by four of them, they tried to take him into the house to lay him before Jesus. 4 When they could not find a way to Jesus because of the crowd; they went up on the roof and made an opening in the roof above Jesus. And after digging through it, they lowered the mat the paralyzed man was lying on through the tiles, into the middle of the crowd, right in front of Jesus. Mark 2:3-4. Luke 5:18-19.

2 Some men brought to Jesus the paralytic, lying on a mat. When Jesus saw their faith, he said to the paralytic, "Take heart, son; your sins are forgiven." Matthew 9:2. Mark 2:5. Luke 5:20.

6 At this, some the Pharisees and teachers of the law were sitting there, began thinking to themselves, 7 "Who is this fellow? Why does this fellow talk like that? He's blaspheming! Who can forgive sins but God alone?" Mark 2:6-7. Matthew 9:3. Luke 5:21.

8 Immediately Jesus knew in his spirit that this was what they were thinking in their hearts, and he said to them, "Why are you

entertaining evil thoughts in your hearts? 9 Which is easier: to say to the paralytic, 'Your sins are forgiven,' or to say, 'Get up, take your mat and walk'? 10 But so that you may know that the Son of Man has authority on earth to forgive sins," He said to the paralyzed man, 11 "I tell you, get up, take your mat and go home." Mark 2:8-11. Matthew 9:4-6. Luke 5:22-24.

25 Immediately he stood up in front of them, took what he had been lying on, walked out in full view of them all and went home praising God. Luke 5:25. Mark 2:12a. Matthew 9:7.

8 When the crowd saw this, they were filled with awe; everyone was amazed and gave praise to God saying, "We have never seen anything like this! We have seen remarkable things today" and they praised God, who had given such authority to men. Matthew 9:8. Luke 5:26. Mark 2:12b.

His Mercy

13 Once again Jesus went out beside the lake. A large crowd came to him, and he began to teach them. 14 As he walked along, he saw Levi (known as Matthew) son of Alphaeus, a tax collector sitting at his tax collector's booth. "Follow me," Jesus said to him, and Levi got up, left everything and followed him. Mark 2:13-14. Luke 5:27. Matthew 9:9.

29 Then Levi held a great banquet for Jesus at his house, and a large crowd of tax collectors and "sinners" came and ate with him and his disciples, for there were many who followed him. Luke 5:29. Matthew 9:10. Mark 2:15.

16 But when the Pharisees and teachers of the law who belonged to their sect saw him eating with the "sinners" and tax collectors,

they complained to his disciples: "Why does your teacher eat with tax collectors and 'sinners'?" Mark 2:16. Matthew 9:11. Luke 5:30.

12 On hearing this, Jesus answered and said to them, "It is not the healthy who need a doctor, but the sick. 13 But go and learn what this means: 'I desire mercy, not sacrifice.' For I have not come to call the righteous, but sinners to repentance." Matthew 9:12-13. Mark 2:17. Luke 5: 31-32.

His Wine

18 Now John's disciples and the Pharisees were fasting. John's disciples came and asked him, "How is it that we and the Pharisees often fast and pray, but your disciples go on eating and drinking and do not fast?" Mark 2:18. Matthew 9:14. Luke 5:33.

19 Jesus answered, "How can the guests of the bridegroom mourn and fast while he is with them? They cannot, so long as they have him with them. 20 But the time will come when the bridegroom will be taken from them, and in those days they will fast. Mark 2:19-20. Luke 5:34-35. Matthew 9:15.

36 He told them this parable: "No one tears a patch from a new unshrunk garment and sews it on an old garment. If he does, he will have torn the new garment, and the patch from the new will pull away from the old, making the tear worse and will not match the old. Luke 5:36. Mark 2:21. Matthew 9:16.

17 Neither do men pour new wine into old wineskins. If they do, the skins will burst, the wine will run out and the wineskins will be ruined. No, they must pour new wine into new wineskins, and both are preserved." Matthew 9:17. Mark 2:22. Luke 5:37-38.

39 And no one after drinking old wine wants the new, for he says, 'The old is better.'" Luke 5:39.

His Sabbath

1 Some time later, Jesus went up to Jerusalem for a feast of the Jews. 2 Now there is in Jerusalem near the Sheep Gate a pool, which in Aramaic is called Bethesda and which is surrounded by five covered colonnades. 3 Here a great number of disabled people used to lie-the blind, the lame, the paralyzed.

5 One who was there had been an invalid for thirty-eight years. 6 When Jesus saw him lying there and learned that he had been in this condition for a long time, he asked him, "Do you want to get well?"

7 "Sir," the invalid replied, "I have no one to help me into the pool when the water is stirred. While I am trying to get in, someone else goes down ahead of me."

8 Then Jesus said to him, "Get up! Pick up your mat and walk." 9 At once the man was cured; he picked up his mat and walked.

The day on which this took place was a Sabbath, 10 and so the Jews said to the man who had been healed, "It is the Sabbath; the law forbids you to carry your mat."

11 But he replied, "The man who made me well said to me, 'Pick up your mat and walk.'"

12 So they asked him, "Who is this fellow who told you to pick it up and walk?"

13 The man who was healed had no idea who it was, for Jesus had slipped away into the crowd that was there.

14 Later Jesus found him at the temple and said to him, "See, you are well again. Stop sinning or something worse may happen to you."

15 The man went away and told the Jews that it was Jesus who had made him well. John 5:1-15.

16 So, because Jesus was doing these things on the Sabbath, the Jews persecuted him.

17 Jesus said to them, "My Father is always at his work to this very day, and I, too, am working."

18 For this reason the Jews tried all the harder to kill him; not only was he breaking the Sabbath, but he was even calling God his own Father, making himself equal with God.

19 Jesus gave them this answer: "I tell you the truth, the Son can do nothing by himself; he can do only what he sees his Father doing, because whatever the Father does, the Son also does. 20 For the Father loves the Son and shows him all he does. Yes, to your amazement he will show him even greater things than these. 21 For just as the Father raises the dead and gives them life, even so the Son gives life to whom he is pleased to give it.

22 Moreover, the Father judges no one, but has entrusted all judgment to the Son, 23 that all may honor the Son just as they honor the Father. He who does not honor the Son does not honor the Father, who sent him.

24 "I tell you the truth, whoever hears my word and believes him who sent me has eternal life and will not be condemned; he has crossed over from death to life.

25 I tell you the truth, a time is coming and has now come when the dead will hear the voice of the Son of God and those who hear will live. 26 For as the Father has life in himself, so he has granted the Son to have life in himself. 27 And he has given him authority to judge because he is the Son of Man.

28 "Do not be amazed at this, for a time is coming when all who are in their graves will hear his voice 29 and come out-those who have done good will rise to live, and those who have done evil will rise to be condemned.

30 By myself I can do nothing; I judge only as I hear, and my judgment is just, for I seek not to please myself but him who sent me. John 5:16-30.

His Testimony

31 "If I testify about myself, my testimony is not valid. 32 There is another who testifies in my favor, and I know that his testimony about me is valid. 33 "You have sent to John and he has testified to the truth. 34 Not that I accept human testimony; but I mention it that you may be saved. 35 John was a lamp that burned and gave light, and you chose for a time to enjoy his light.

36 "I have testimony weightier than that of John. For the very work that the Father has given me to finish, and which I am doing, testifies that the Father has sent me. 37 And the Father who sent me has himself testified concerning me. You have never heard his voice nor seen his form, 38 nor does his word dwell in you, for you do not believe the one he sent. 39 You diligently study the Scriptures because you think that by them you possess eternal life. These are the Scriptures that testify about me, 40 yet you refuse to come to me to have life.

41 "I do not accept praise from men, 42 but I know you. I know that you do not have the love of God in your hearts. 43 I have come in my Father's name, and you do not accept me; but if someone else comes in his own name, you will accept him. 44 How can you believe if you accept praise from one another, yet make no effort to obtain the praise that comes from the only God?

45 "But do not think I will accuse you before the Father. Your accuser is Moses, on whom your hopes are set. 46 If you believed Moses, you would believe me, for he wrote about me. 47 But since you do not believe what he wrote, how are you going to believe what I say?" John 5:31-47.

His Lordship

1 One Sabbath Jesus was going through the grain fields, and as his disciples walked along they were hungry and began to pick some heads of grain, rub them in their hands and eat the kernels. Luke 6:1. Matthew 12:1. Mark 2:23.

2 When the Pharisees saw this, some of them said to him, "Look! Why are your disciples doing what is unlawful on the Sabbath." Matthew 12:2. Luke 6:2. Mark 2:24.

3 He answered, "Haven't you read what David did when he and his companions were hungry and in need? 4 In the days of Abiathar the high priest, he entered the house of God and taking the consecrated bread, he and his companions ate the consecrated bread-which was not lawful for them to do, but only for the priests to eat. 5 Or haven't you read in the Law that on the Sabbath the priests in the temple desecrate the day and yet are innocent? 6 I tell you that one greater than the temple is here. 7 If you had known what these words mean, 'I desire mercy, not sacrifice,' you would not have condemned the innocent. 8 For the

Son of Man is Lord of the Sabbath." Matthew 12:3-8. Mark 2:25-26. Luke 6:3-4.

27 Then Jesus said to them, "The Sabbath was made for man, not man for the Sabbath. 28 So the Son of Man is Lord even of the Sabbath." Mark 2:27-28. Luke 6:5.

His Accusers

6 Going on from that place, on another Sabbath, he went into their synagogue and was teaching, and a man was there whose right hand was shriveled. 7 The Pharisees and the teachers of the law were looking for a reason to accuse Jesus, so they watched him closely to see if he would heal on the Sabbath. Luke 6:6-7. Matthew 12:9-10a. Mark 3:1-2.

8 But Jesus knew what they were thinking and said to the man with the shriveled hand, "Get up and stand in front of everyone." So he got up and stood there. Luke 6:8. Mark 3:3.

10b they asked him, "Is it lawful to heal on the Sabbath?" Matthew 12:10b.

11 He said to them, "If any of you has a sheep and it falls into a pit on the Sabbath, will you not take hold of it and lift it out? 12 How much more valuable is a man than a sheep! Therefore it is lawful to do good on the Sabbath." Matthew 12:11-12.

9 Then Jesus said to them, "I ask you, which is lawful on the Sabbath: to do good or to do evil, to save life or to destroy it?" But they remained silent. Luke 6:9. Mark 3:4.

5 He looked around at them all in anger and, deeply distressed at their stubborn hearts, said to the man, "Stretch out your hand."

So he stretched it out, and his hand was completely restored, just as sound as the other. 6 But then the Pharisees were furious. They went out and began to discuss with one another what they might do to Jesus with the Herodians and plot how they might kill Jesus. Mark 3:5-6. Matthew 12:13-14. Luke 6:10-11.

7 Aware of this, Jesus withdrew with his disciples from that place to the lake, and a large crowd from Galilee followed him and he healed all their sick. 8 When they heard all he was doing, many people came to him from Judea, Jerusalem, Idumea, and the regions across the Jordan and around Tyre and Sidon. Mark 3:7-8. Matthew 12:15.

9 Because of the crowd he told his disciples to have a small boat ready for him, to keep the people from crowding him. 10 For he had healed many, so that those with diseases were pushing forward to touch him. 11 Whenever the evil spirits saw him, they fell down before him and cried out, "You are the Son of God." Mark 3:9-11.

12 But he gave them strict orders not to tell who he was. Mark 3:12. Matthew 12:16.

17 This was to fulfill what was spoken through the prophet Isaiah: 18 "Here is my servant whom I have chosen, the one I love, in whom I delight; I will put my Spirit on him, and he will proclaim justice to the nations. 19 He will not quarrel or cry out; no one will hear his voice in the streets. 20 A bruised reed he will not break, and a smoldering wick he will not snuff out, till he leads justice to victory. 21 In his name the nations will put their hope." Matthew 12:17-21.

His Twelve Disciples

12 One of those days Jesus went out to a mountainside to pray, and spent the night praying to God. Luke 6:12.

13 When morning came, Jesus went up on a mountainside and called to him those disciples he wanted, and they came to him. 14 He appointed twelve of them, whom he also designated, apostles: that they might be with him and that he might send them out to preach 15 and to have authority to drive out demons. Mark 3:13-15. Luke 6:13.

14 These are the twelve he appointed: Simon (whom he gave the name Peter), his brother Andrew, James son of Zebedee and his brother John (to them he gave the name Boanerges, which means the Sons of Thunder); Philip, Bartholomew, 15 Matthew, Thomas, James son of Alphaeus, Thaddaeus, Simon who was called the Zealot, 16 Judas son of James, and Judas Iscariot, who became a traitor and betrayed him. Luke 6:14-16. Mark 3:16-19.

His Blessings

1 Now when he saw the crowds, he went up on a mountainside and sat down. His disciples came to him, Matthew 5:1.

17 He went down with them and stood on a level place. A large crowd of his disciples was there and a great number of people from all over Judea, from Jerusalem, and from the coast of Tyre and Sidon, 18 who had come to hear him and to be healed of their

diseases. Those troubled by evil spirits were cured, 19 and the people all tried to touch him, because power was coming from him and healing them all. Luke 6:17-19.

20 Looking at his disciples, he began to teach them, saying: "Blessed are you who are poor in spirit, for yours is heaven, the kingdom of God. Luke 6:20. Matthew 5:2-3.

4 Blessed are those who mourn, for they will be comforted. 5 Blessed are the meek, for they will inherit the earth. Matthew 5:4-5.

6 Blessed are you who hunger now and thirst for righteousness, for you will be satisfied. Matthew 5:6. Luke 6:21a.

7 Blessed are the merciful, for they will be shown mercy.

8 Blessed are the pure in heart, for they will see God.

9 Blessed are the peacemakers, for they will be called sons of God.

10 Blessed are those who are persecuted because of righteousness, for theirs is the kingdom of heaven. Matthew 5:7-10.

11 "Blessed are you when people insult, hate and exclude you; persecute you, reject your name as evil and falsely say all kinds of evil against you because of me, the Son of Man. Matthew 5:11. Luke 6:22.

12 Rejoice and be glad, because great is your reward in heaven, for in the same way they persecuted the prophets who were before you. Matthew 5:12.

21b Blessed are you who weep now, for you will laugh. Luke 6:21b.

23 "Rejoice in that day and leap for joy, because great is your reward in heaven. For that is how their fathers treated the prophets. Luke 6:23.

24 "But woe to you who are rich, for you have already received your comfort. 25 Woe to you who are well fed now, for you will go hungry. Woe to you who laugh now, for you will mourn and weep. 26 Woe to you when all men speak well of you, for that is how their fathers treated the false prophets. Luke 6:24-26.

His Value

13 "You are the salt of the earth. But if the salt loses its saltiness, how can it be made salty again? It is no longer good for anything, except to be thrown out and trampled by men. Matthew 5:13.

14 "You are the light of the world. A city on a hill cannot be hidden. 15 Neither do people light a lamp and puts it in a place where it will be hidden, or under a bowl. Instead they put it on its stand, and it gives light to everyone in the house; and to those who come in may see the light. 16 In the same way, let your light shine before men, that they may see your good deeds and praise your Father in heaven. Matthew 5:14-16. Luke 11:33.

His Law

17 "Do not think that I have come to abolish the Law or the Prophets; I have not come to abolish them but to fulfill them. 18 I tell you the truth, until heaven and earth disappear, not the

smallest letter, not the least stroke of a pen, will by any means disappear from the Law until everything is accomplished.

19 Anyone who breaks one of the least of these commandments and teaches others to do the same will be called least in the kingdom of heaven, but whoever practices and teaches these commands will be called great in the kingdom of heaven. 20 For I tell you that unless your righteousness surpasses that of the Pharisees and the teachers of the law, you will certainly not enter the kingdom of heaven. Matthew 5:17-20.

21 "You have heard that it was said to the people long ago, 'Do not murder, and anyone who murders will be subject to judgment.' 22 But I tell you that anyone who is angry with his brother will be subject to judgment. Again, anyone who says to his brother, 'Raca,' is answerable to the Sanhedrin. But anyone who says, 'You fool!' will be in danger of the fire of hell.

23 "Therefore, if you are offering your gift at the altar and there remember that your brother has something against you, 24 leave your gift there in front of the altar. First go and be reconciled to your brother; then come and offer your gift.

25 "Settle matters quickly with your adversary who is taking you to court. Do it while you are still with him on the way, or he may hand you over to the judge, and the judge may hand you over to the officer, and you may be thrown into prison. 26 I tell you the truth, you will not get out until you have paid the last penny. Matthew 5:21-26.

27 "You have heard that it was said, 'Do not commit adultery.' 28 But I tell you that anyone who looks at a woman lustfully has already committed adultery with her in his heart.

29 If your right eye causes you to sin, gouge it out and throw it away. It is better for you to lose one part of your body than for your whole body to be thrown into hell.

30 And if your right hand causes you to sin, cut it off and throw it away. It is better for you to lose one part of your body than for your whole body to go into hell. Matthew 5:27-30.

31 "It has been said, 'Anyone who divorces his wife must give her a certificate of divorce.' 32 But I tell you that anyone who divorces his wife, except for marital unfaithfulness, causes her to become an adulteress, and anyone who marries the divorced woman commits adultery. Matthew 5:31-32.

33 "Again, you have heard that it was said to the people long ago, 'Do not break your oath, but keep the oaths you have made to the Lord.' 34 But I tell you, Do not swear at all: either by heaven, for it is God's throne; 35 or by the earth, for it is his footstool; or by Jerusalem, for it is the city of the Great King. 36 And do not swear by your head, for you cannot make even one hair white or black. 37 Simply let your 'Yes' be 'Yes,' and your 'No,' 'No'; anything beyond this comes from the evil one. Matthew 5:33-37.

38 "You have heard that it was said, 'Eye for eye, and tooth for tooth.' 39 But I tell you, Do not resist an evil person. If someone strikes you on the right cheek, turn to him the other also. 40 And if someone wants to sue you and take your tunic, let him have your cloak as well.

41 If someone forces you to go one mile, go with him two miles. 42 Give to the one who asks you, and do not turn away from the one who wants to borrow from you. Matthew 5:38-42.

43 "You have heard that it was said, 'Love your neighbor and hate your enemy.' Matthew 5:43.

44 But I tell you who hear me: Love your enemies, do good to those who hate you, bless those who curse you and pray for those who persecute and mistreat you, 45 that you may be sons of your Father in heaven. He causes his sun to rise on the evil and

the good, and sends rain on the righteous and the unrighteous. Matthew 5:44-45. Luke 6:27-28.

32 "If you love those who love you, what credit or reward is that to you? Even 'sinners' love those who love them. 33 And if you do good to those who are good to you, what credit is that to you? Even 'sinners' and the tax collectors do that. Luke 6:32-33. Matthew 5:46.

47 And if you greet only your brothers, what are you doing more than others? Do not even pagans do that? 48 Be perfect, therefore, as your heavenly Father is perfect. Matthew 5:47-48.

29 If someone strikes you on one cheek, turn to him the other also. If someone takes your cloak, do not stop him from taking your tunic. 30 Give to everyone who asks you, and if anyone takes what belongs to you, do not demand it back. 31 Do to others as you would have them do to you. Luke 6:29-31.

34 And if you lend to those from whom you expect repayment, what credit is that to you? Even 'sinners' lend to 'sinners,' expecting to be repaid in full. 35 But love your enemies, do good to them, and lend to them without expecting to get anything back. Then your reward will be great, and you will be sons of the Most High, because he is kind to the ungrateful and wicked. Luke 6:34-35.

36 Be merciful, just as your Father is merciful. Luke 6:36.

1 "Be careful not to do your 'acts of righteousness' before men, to be seen by them. If you do, you will have no reward from your Father in heaven. 2 "So when you give to the needy, do not announce it with trumpets, as the hypocrites do in the synagogues and on the streets, to be honored by men. I tell you the truth, they have received their reward in full. 3 But when you give to the needy, do not let your left hand know what your right hand is doing, 4 so that your giving may be in secret. Then your Father, who sees what is done in secret, will reward you. Matthew 6:1-4.

5 "And when you pray, do not be like the hypocrites, for they love to pray standing in the synagogues and on the street corners to be seen by men. I tell you the truth, they have received their reward in full. 6 But when you pray, go into your room, close the door and pray to your Father, who is unseen. Then your Father, who sees what is done in secret, will reward you.

7 And when you pray, do not keep on babbling like pagans, for they think they will be heard because of their many words. 8 Do not be like them, for your Father knows what you need before you ask him. Matthew 6:5-8.

14 For if you forgive men when they sin against you, your heavenly Father will also forgive you. 15 But if you do not forgive men their sins, your Father will not forgive your sins. Matthew 6:14-15.

16 "When you fast, do not look somber as the hypocrites do, for they disfigure their faces to show men they are fasting. I tell you the truth, they have received their reward in full. 17 But when you fast, put oil on your head and wash your face, 18 so that it will not be obvious to men that you are fasting, but only to your Father, who is unseen; and your Father, who sees what is done in secret, will reward you. Matthew 6:16-18.

32 "Do not be afraid, little flock, for your Father has been pleased to give you the kingdom. 33a Sell your possessions and give to the poor. Luke 12:32-33a.

19 "Do not store up for yourselves treasures on earth, where moth and rust destroy, and where thieves break in and steal. 20 Provide purses for yourselves that will not wear out; but store up for yourselves treasures in heaven that will not be exhausted, where moth and rust do not destroy, and where thieves do not come near to break in and steal. 21 For where your treasure is, there your heart will be also. Matthew 6:19-21. Luke 12:33b-34.

34 Your eye is the lamp of your body. When your eyes are good, your whole body also is full of light. But when your eyes are bad, your whole body also is full of darkness. 35 See to it, then, that the light within you is not darkness. If then the light within you is darkness, how great is that darkness! 36 Therefore, if your whole body is full of light, and no part of it dark, it will be completely lighted, as when the light of a lamp shines on you." Luke 11:34-36. Matthew 6:22-23.

24 "No one can serve two masters. Either he will hate the one and love the other, or he will be devoted to the one and despise the other. You cannot serve both God and Money. Matthew 6:24.

25 Then Jesus said to his disciples: "Therefore I tell you, do not worry about your life, what you will eat or drink; or about your body, what you will wear. Is not life more important than food, and the body more important than clothes? 26 Look at and consider the ravens of the air; they do not sow or reap or store away in storerooms or barns, and yet God, your heavenly Father feeds them. How much more valuable are you? Are you not much more valuable than birds? Matthew 6:25-26. Luke 12:22-24.

25 Who of you by worrying can add a single hour to his life? 26 Since you cannot do this very little thing, why do you worry about the rest? Luke 12:25-26. Matthew 6:27.

28 "And why do you worry about clothes? See and consider how the lilies of the field grow. They do not labor or spin. 29 Yet I tell you that not even Solomon in all his splendor was dressed like one of these. 30 If that is how God clothes the grass of the field, which is here today and tomorrow is thrown into the fire, will he not much more clothe you, O you of little faith? Matthew 6:28-30. Luke 12:27-28.

31 So do not set your heart on worry, saying, 'What shall we eat?' or 'What shall we drink?' or 'What shall we wear? Do not worry about it. 32 For the pagan world runs after all these things, and

your heavenly Father knows that you need them. Matthew 6:31-32. Luke 12:29-30.

33 But seek first his kingdom and his righteousness, and all these things will be given to you as well. Matthew 6:33. Luke 12:31.

34 Therefore do not worry about tomorrow, for tomorrow will worry about itself. Each day has enough trouble of its own. Matthew 6:34.

37 "Do not judge, and you will not be judged. For in the same way you judge others, you will be judged, and with the measure you use, it will be measured to you. Do not condemn, and you will not be condemned. Forgive, and you will be forgiven. Luke 6:37. Matthew 7:1-2.

38 Give, and it will be given to you. A good measure, pressed down, shaken together and running over, will be poured into your lap. For with the measure you use, it will be measured to you." Luke 6:38.

39 He also told them this parable: "Can a blind man lead a blind man? Will they not both fall into a pit? 40 A student is not above his teacher, but everyone who is fully trained will be like his teacher. Luke 6:39-40.

41 "Why do you look at the speck of sawdust in your brother's eye and pay no attention to the plank in your own eye? 42 How can you say to your brother, 'Brother, let me take the speck out of your eye,' when you yourself fail to see all the time there is a plank in your own eye? You hypocrite, first take the plank out of your own eye, and then you will see clearly to remove the speck from your brother's eye. Luke 6:41-42. Matthew 7:3-5.

6 "Do not give dogs what is sacred; do not throw your pearls to pigs. If you do, they may trample them under their feet, and then turn and tear you to pieces. Matthew 7:6.

7 " So I say to you: Ask and it will be given to you; seek and you will find; knock and the door will be opened to you. 8 For everyone who asks receives; he who seeks finds; and to him who knocks, the door will be opened. Matthew 7:7-8. Luke 11:9-10.

9 "Which of you fathers, if his son asks for bread, will give him a stone? 10 Or if he asks for a fish, will give him a snake instead? Or if he asks for an egg, will give him a scorpion? 11 If you, then, though you are evil, know how to give good gifts to your children, how much more will your Father in heaven give good gifts and the Holy Spirit to those who ask him! Matthew 7:9-11. Luke 11:11-13.

5 Then he said to them, "Suppose one of you has a friend, and he goes to him at midnight and says, 'Friend, lend me three loaves of bread, 6 because a friend of mine on a journey has come to me, and I have nothing to set before him.' 7 "Then the one inside answers, 'Don't bother me. The door is already locked, and my children are with me in bed. I can't get up and give you anything.' 8 I tell you, though he will not get up and give him the bread because he is his friend, yet because of the man's boldness he will get up and give him as much as he needs. Luke 11:5-8.

12 So in everything, do to others what you would have them do to you, for this sums up the Law and the Prophets. Matthew 7:12.

His Road

13 "Enter through the narrow gate. For wide is the gate and broad is the road that leads to destruction, and many enter through it. 14 But small is the gate and narrow the road that leads to life, and only a few find it. Matthew 7:13-14.

His Fruit

15 "Watch out for false prophets. They come to you in sheep's clothing, but inwardly they are ferocious wolves. 16a By their fruit you will recognize them. Matthew 7:15-16a.

44a Each tree is recognized by its own fruit. Luke 6:44a.

16b Do people pick grapes or figs from thorn bushes, or figs or grapes from thistles or briers? Matthew 7:16b. Luke 7:44b.

17 Likewise every good tree bears good fruit, but a bad tree bears bad fruit. Matthew 7:17.

18 A good tree cannot bear bad fruit, and a bad tree cannot bear good fruit. Matthew 7:18. Luke 6:43.

19 Every tree that does not bear good fruit is cut down and thrown into the fire. 20 Thus, by their fruit you will recognize them. Matthew 7:19-20.

45 The good man brings good things out of the good stored up in his heart, and the evil man brings evil things out of the evil stored up in his heart. For out of the overflow of his heart his mouth speaks. Luke 6:45.

His Lifestyle

21 "Not everyone who says to me, 'Lord, Lord,' will enter the kingdom of heaven, but only he who does the will of my Father who is in heaven. 22 Many will say to me on that day, 'Lord, Lord, did we not prophesy in your name, and in your name drive out demons and perform many miracles?' 23 Then I will tell them plainly, "Why do you call me, 'Lord, Lord,' and do not do what I say? 'I never knew you, away from me, you evildoers!' Matthew 7:21-23. Luke 6:46.

47 Therefore I will show everyone what he is like who comes to me and hears my words and puts them into practice. 48 He is like a wise man building his house, who dug down deep and laid the foundation on the rock. The rain came down, the streams rose. When a flood came, the torrent struck that house but could not shake it, because it had its foundation on the rock. And the winds blew and beat against that house; yet it did not fall because it was well built. Luke 6:47-48. Matthew 7:24-25.

26 But everyone who hears these words of mine and does not put them into practice is like a foolish man who built his house on sandy ground without a foundation. 27 The moment the torrent rain came down, the streams rose, and the winds blew and struck against that house, it collapsed and fell with a great crash; its destruction was complete." Matthew 7:26-27. Luke 6:49.

28 When Jesus had finished saying these things, the crowds were amazed at his teaching, 29 because he taught as one who had authority, and not as their teachers of the law. Matthew 7:28-29.

His Centurion

1a When Jesus had finished saying all this in the hearing of the people, Luke 7:1a.

5a When Jesus had entered Capernaum, Matthew 8:5a. Luke 7:1b.

2 There a centurion's servant, whom his master valued highly, was sick and about to die. Luke 7:2.

3 The centurion heard of Jesus and sent some elders of the Jews to him, asking him to come for help and heal his servant; that lies at home paralyzed and in terrible suffering. 4 When they came to Jesus, they pleaded earnestly with him, "This man deserves to have you do this, 5 because he loves our nation and has built our synagogue." Luke 7:3-5. Matthew 8:5b-6.

7 Jesus said to him, "I will go and heal him." Matthew 8:7.

6a So Jesus went with them. Luke 7:6a.

6b He was not far from the house when the centurion sent friends to say to him: "Lord, don't trouble yourself, for I do not deserve to have you come under my roof. 7 That is why I did not even consider myself worthy to come to you. But say the word, and my servant will be healed. 8 For I myself am a man under authority, with soldiers under me. I tell this one, 'Go,' and he goes; and that one, 'Come,' and he comes. I say to my servant, 'Do this,' and he does it." Luke 7:6b-8. Matthew 8:8-9.

10 When Jesus heard this, he was astonished and amazed at him and turning to the crowd said to those following him, "I tell you

the truth, I have not found anyone in all of Israel with such great faith. Matthew 8:10. Luke 7:9.

11 I say to you that many will come from the east and the west, and will take their places at the feast with Abraham, Isaac and Jacob in the kingdom of heaven. 12 But the subjects of the kingdom will be thrown outside, into the darkness, where there will be weeping and gnashing of teeth." Matthew 8:11-12.

13 Then Jesus said to the centurion, "Go! It will be done just as you believed it would." And his servant was healed at that very hour. Matthew 8:13.

10 Then the men who had been sent returned to the house and found the servant well. Luke 7:10.

His Heart

11 Soon afterward, Jesus went to a town called Nain, and his disciples and a large crowd went along with him. 12 As he approached the town gate, a dead person was being carried out- the only son of his mother, and she was a widow. And a large crowd from the town was with her.

13 When the Lord saw her, his heart went out to her and he said, "Don't cry." 14 Then he went up and touched the coffin, and those carrying it stood still. He said, "Young man, I say to you, get up!" 15 The dead man sat up and began to talk, and Jesus gave him back to his mother.

16 They were all filled with awe and praised God. "A great prophet has appeared among us," they said. "God has come to help his people." 17 This news about Jesus spread throughout Judea and the surrounding country. Luke 7:11-17.

His Preparer Honored

1 After Jesus had finished instructing his twelve disciples, he went on from there to teach and preach in the towns of Galilee. Matthew 11:1.

18 When John heard in prison from his disciples what Christ was doing, calling two of his disciples, 19 he sent them to the Lord to ask, "Are you the one who was to come, or should we expect someone else?" 20 When the men came to Jesus, they said, "John the Baptist sent us to you to ask, 'Are you the one who was to come, or should we expect someone else?'" Luke 7:18-20. Matthew 11:2-3.

21 At that very time Jesus cured many who had diseases, sicknesses and evil spirits, and gave sight to many who were blind. Luke 7:21.

22 So Jesus replied to the messengers, "Go back and report to John what you have seen and heard: The blind receive sight, the lame walk, those who have leprosy are cured, the deaf hear, the dead are raised, and the good news is preached to the poor. 23 Blessed is the man who does not fall away on account of me." Luke 7:22-23. Matthew 11:4-6.

7 After John's messengers left and as John's disciples were leaving, Jesus began to speak to the crowd about John: "What did you go out into the desert to see? A reed swayed by the wind? 8 If not, what did you go out to see? A man dressed in fine clothes? No, those who wear fine expensive clothes and indulge in luxury are in kings' palaces. 9 Then what did you go out to see? A prophet? Yes, I tell you, and more than a prophet. 10 This is the one about whom it is written: "'I will send my messenger

ahead of you, who will prepare your way before you.' Matthew 11:7-10. Luke 7:24-27.

11 I tell you the truth: Among those born of women there has not risen anyone greater than John the Baptist; yet he who is least in the kingdom of heaven is greater than he. Matthew 11:11. Luke 7:28.

12 From the days of John the Baptist until now, the kingdom of heaven has been forcefully advancing, and forceful men lay hold of it. 13 For all the Prophets and the Law prophesied until John. 14 And if you are willing to accept it, he is the Elijah who was to come. 15 He who has ears, let him hear. Matthew 11:12-15.

29 (All the people, even the tax collectors, when they heard Jesus' words, acknowledged that God's way was right, because they had been baptized by John. 30 But the Pharisees and experts in the law rejected God's purpose for themselves, because they had not been baptized by John.) Luke 7:29-30.

31 "To what, then, can I compare the people of this generation? What are they like? 32 They are like children sitting in the marketplace and calling out to each other: "'We played the flute for you, and you did not dance; we sang a dirge, and you did not cry or mourn.' Luke 7:31-32. Matthew 11:16-17.

33 For John the Baptist came neither eating bread nor drinking wine, and you say, 'He has a demon.' 34 The Son of Man came eating and drinking, and you say, 'Here is a glutton and a drunkard, a friend of tax collectors and "sinners." 35 But wisdom is proved right by all her children's actions." Luke 7:33-35. Matthew 11:18-19.

His Prophecy

20 Then Jesus began to denounce the cities in which most of his miracles had been performed, because they did not repent. 21 "Woe to you, Korazin! Woe to you, Bethsaida! If the miracles that were performed in you had been performed in Tyre and Sidon, they would have repented long ago in sackcloth and ashes. 22 But I tell you, it will be more bearable for Tyre and Sidon on the day of judgment than for you. 23 And you, Capernaum, will you be lifted up to the skies? No, you will go down to the depths. If the miracles that were performed in you had been performed in Sodom, it would have remained to this day. 24 But I tell you that it will be more bearable for Sodom on the day of judgment than for you." Matthew 11:20-24.

His Knowing

25 At that time Jesus said, "I praise you, Father, Lord of heaven and earth, because you have hidden these things from the wise and learned, and revealed them to little children. 26 Yes, Father, for this was your good pleasure. 27 "All things have been committed to me by my Father. No one knows the Son except the Father, and no one knows the Father except the Son and those to whom the Son chooses to reveal him. Matthew 11:25-27.

His Yoke

28 "Come to me, all you who are weary and burdened, and I will give you rest. 29 Take my yoke upon you and learn from me, for I am gentle and humble in heart, and you will find rest for your souls. 30 For my yoke is easy and my burden is light." Matthew 11:28-30.

His Anointing

36 Now one of the Pharisees invited Jesus to have dinner with him, so he went to the Pharisee's house and reclined at the table. 37 When a woman who had lived a sinful life in that town learned that Jesus was eating at the Pharisee's house, she brought an alabaster jar of perfume, 38 and as she stood behind him at his feet weeping, she began to wet his feet with her tears. Then she wiped them with her hair, kissed them and poured perfume on them.

39 When the Pharisee who had invited him saw this, he said to himself, "If this man were a prophet, he would know who is touching him and what kind of woman she is-that she is a sinner."

40 Jesus answered him, "Simon, I have something to tell you." "Tell me, teacher," he said. 41 "Two men owed money to a certain moneylender. One owed him five hundred denarii, and the other fifty. 42 Neither of them had the money to pay him back, so he canceled the debts of both. Now which of them will love him more?"

43 Simon replied, "I suppose the one who had the bigger debt canceled." "You have judged correctly," Jesus said.

44 Then he turned toward the woman and said to Simon, "Do you see this woman? I came into your house. You did not give me any water for my feet, but she wet my feet with her tears and wiped them with her hair. 45 You did not give me a kiss, but this woman, from the time I entered, has not stopped kissing my feet. 46 You did not put oil on my head, but she has poured perfume on my feet. 47 Therefore, I tell you, her many sins have been forgiven-for she loved much. But he who has been forgiven little loves little."

48 Then Jesus said to her, "Your sins are forgiven."

49 The other guests began to say among themselves, "Who is this who even forgives sins?"

50 Jesus said to the woman, "Your faith has saved you; go in peace." Luke 7:36-50.

His Fellowship

1 After this, Jesus traveled about from one town and village to another, proclaiming the good news of the kingdom of God. The Twelve were with him, 2 and also some women who had been cured of evil spirits and diseases: Mary (called Magdalene) from whom seven demons had come out; 3 Joanna the wife of Cuza, the manager of Herod's household; Susanna; and many others. These women were helping to support them out of their own means. Luke 8:1-3.

His Prayer

1 One day Jesus was praying in a certain place. When he finished, one of his disciples said to him, "Lord, teach us to pray, just as John taught his disciples." Luke 11:1.

2 He said to them, "This then, is how you should pray, say: "'Our Father in heaven, hallowed be your name, your kingdom come, your will be done on earth as it is in heaven. 3 Give us each day our daily bread. 4 Forgive us our sins and debts, as we also have forgiven our debtors and everyone who sins against us. And lead us not into temptation, but deliver us from the evil one.'" Luke 11:2-4. Matthew 6:9-13.

His Kingdom

20 Then Jesus entered a house, and again a crowd gathered, so that he and his disciples were not even able to eat. 21 When his family heard about this, they went to take charge of him, for they said, "He is out of his mind." Mark 3:20-21.

22 Then they brought him a demon-possessed man who was blind and mute, and Jesus drove out the demon that was mute. When the demon left, the man who had been mute, spoke and was healed, so that he could both talk and see. 23 All the people were astonished and amazed said, "Could this be the Son of David?" Matthew 12:22-23. Luke 11:14.

22 And when the Pharisees, teachers of the law who came down from Jerusalem heard this, they said, "He is possessed

by Beelzebub! By Beelzebub, the prince of demons this fellow is driving out demons." Others tested him by asking for a sign from heaven. Mark 3:22. Matthew 12:24. Luke 11:15-16.

25 Jesus knew their thoughts and said to them in parables, "Any and every kingdom divided against itself will be ruined, and every city or household divided against itself will fall and not stand. 26 If Satan drives out Satan, he is divided against himself. How then can his kingdom stand? "How can Satan drive out Satan? And if Satan opposes himself and is divided, he cannot stand; how can his kingdom stand? His end has come. I say this because you claim that I drive out demons by Beelzebub. 27 And now if I drive out demons by Beelzebub, by whom do your followers drive them out? So then, they will be your judges. 28 But if I drive out demons by the finger of God, the Spirit of God, then the kingdom of God has come upon you. Matthew 12:25-28. Mark 3:23-26. Luke 11:17-20.

29 "Or again, in fact how can anyone enter a strong man's house and carry off his possessions, when a strong man, fully armed, guards his own house and his possessions are safe? Unless when someone stronger attacks first and overpowers him, takes away the armor in which the man trusted and ties up the strong man. Then he can rob his house and divides up the spoils. Matthew 12:29. Mark 3:27. Luke 11:21-22.

30 "He who is not with me is against me, and he who does not gather with me scatters. Matthew 12:30. Luke 11:23.

31 And so I tell you the truth, every sin and blasphemy of men will be forgiven of them, but whoever blasphemies against the Spirit will never be forgiven. 32 Anyone who speaks a word against the Son of Man will be forgiven, but anyone who speaks against the Holy Spirit will never be forgiven, either in this age or in the age to come; he is guilty of an eternal sin. Matthew 12:31-32. Mark 3:28-29. Luke 12:10.

33 "Make a tree good and its fruit will be good, or make a tree bad and its fruit will be bad, for a tree is recognized by its fruit. 34 You brood of vipers, how can you who are evil say anything good? For out of the overflow of the heart the mouth speaks. 35 The good man brings good things out of the good stored up in him, and the evil man brings evil things out of the evil stored up in him. 36 But I tell you that men will have to give account on the Day of Judgment for every careless word they have spoken. 37 For by your words you will be acquitted, and by your words you will be condemned." Matthew 12:33-37.

30 He said this because they were saying, "He has an evil spirit." Mark 3:30.

His Sign

38 Then some of the Pharisees and teachers of the law said to him, "Teacher, we want to see a miraculous sign from you." Matthew 12:38.

39 As the crowds increased, Jesus answered, "This is a wicked and adulterous generation asks for a miraculous sign! But none will be given it except the sign of the prophet Jonah. 40 For as Jonah was three days and three nights in the belly of a huge fish, so the Son of Man will be three days and three nights in the heart of the earth. 41 For as Jonah was a sign to the Ninevites, so also will the Son of Man be to this generation. The men of Nineveh will stand up at the judgment with this generation and condemn it; for they repented at the preaching of Jonah, and now one greater than Jonah is here. 42 The Queen of the South will rise at the judgment with the men of this generation and condemn them; for she came from the ends of the earth to listen to Solomon's wisdom, and now one greater than Solomon is here. Matthew 12:39-42. Luke 11:29-32.

43 "When an evil spirit comes out of a man, it goes through arid places seeking rest and does not find it. 44 Then it says, 'I will return to the house I left.' When it arrives, it finds the house unoccupied, swept clean and put in order. 45 Then it goes and takes with it seven other spirits more wicked than itself, and they go in and live there. And the final condition of that man is worse than the first. That is how it will be with this wicked generation." Matthew 12:43-45. Luke 11:24-26.

27 As Jesus was saying these things, a woman in the crowd called out, "Blessed is the mother who gave you birth and nursed you." 28 He replied, "Blessed rather are those who hear the word of God and obey it." Luke 11:27-28.

His Family

19 Now then Jesus' mother and brothers arrived and came to see him, but they were not able to get near him because of the crowd. Luke 8:19. Mark 3:31a.

32 A crowd was sitting around him, and they told him, "Your mother and brothers are outside looking for you." Mark 3:32.

46 While Jesus was still talking to the crowd, his mother and brothers stood outside, wanting to speak to him; they sent someone in to call him. Matthew 12:46. Mark 3:31b.

47 Someone told him, "Your mother and brothers are standing outside, wanting to see and speak to you." Matthew 12:47. Luke 8:20.

48 He replied to him, "Who is my mother, and who are my brothers?" Matthew 12:48. Mark 3:33.

21 He replied, "My mother and brothers are those who hear God's word and put it into practice." Luke 8:21.

34 Then he looked at those seated in a circle around him and pointing to his disciples he said, "Here are my mother and my brothers! 35 For whoever does the will of my Father in heaven is my brother and sister and mother." Mark 3:34-35. Matthew 12:49-50.

His Sowing

1 That same day Jesus went out of the house and sat by the lake; he began to teach. 2 Such large crowds gathered around him that he got into a boat and sat in it out on the lake, while all the people stood on the shore at the water's edge. Matthew 13:1-2. Mark 4:1.

4a While a large crowd was gathering and people were coming to Jesus from town after town, Luke 8:4a.

2 He taught them many things by parables, and in his teaching told this parable: he said, 3 "Listen! A farmer went out to sow his seed. 4 As he was scattering the seed, some fell along the path; it was trampled on, and the birds of the air came and ate it up. Mark 4:2-4. Matthew 13:3-4. Luke 8:4b-5.

5 Some fell on rocky places, where it did not have much soil. When it sprang up quickly, because the soil was shallow. 6 But when the sun came up, the plants were scorched, and they withered because they had no moisture and no root. Matthew 13:5-6. Mark 4:5-6. Luke 8:6.

7 Other seed fell among thorns, which grew up with it and choked the plants, so that they did not bear grain. Mark 4:7. Matthew 13:7. Luke 8:7.

8 Still other seed fell on good soil. It came up, grew where it produced and yielded a crop, multiplying thirty, sixty, or even a hundred times more than was sow." Mark 4:8. Matthew 13:8. Luke 8:8a.

9 When Jesus said this, he called out "He who has ears to hear, let him hear." Mark 4:9. Matthew 13:9. Luke 8:8b

His Parables

10 When he was alone, the twelve disciples came to him and asked him what this parable meant, "Why do you speak to the people in parables?" and the others around him asked him about the parables; Mark 4:10. Matthew 13:10. Luke 8:9.

11 He replied, and told them "The knowledge of the secrets of the kingdom of God and heaven has been given to you, but not to those on the outside, everything is said in parables. 12 Whoever has will be given more, and he will have an abundance. Whoever does not have, even what he has will be taken from him. 13 This is why I speak to them in parables so that: "Though they may be ever seeing, they do not see, never perceiving; and though ever hearing, they do not hear or may not understand; but never understanding; otherwise they might turn and be forgiven!'" Matthew 13:11-13. Mark 4:11-12. Luke 8:10.

14 In them is fulfilled the prophecy of Isaiah: "'You will be ever hearing but never understanding; you will be ever seeing but never perceiving. 15 For this people's heart has become calloused; they hardly hear with their ears, and they have closed their eyes. Otherwise they might see with their eyes, hear with their ears, understand with their hearts and turn, and I would heal them.' 16 But blessed are your eyes because they see, and your ears because they hear. 17 For I tell you the truth, many prophets and

righteous men longed to see what you see but did not see it, and to hear what you hear but did not hear it. Matthew 13:14-17.

13 Then Jesus said to them, "Don't you understand this parable? How then will you understand any parable? Mark 4:13.

18 "Listen then to what the meaning of the parable of the sower means: The seed is the word of God. Matthew 13:18. Luke 8:11.

19a When anyone hears the message about the kingdom and does not understand it, the evil one comes and snatches away what was sown in his heart. Matthew 13:19a.

14 The farmer sows the word. Mark 4:14.

19b This is the seed sown along the path. Matthew 13:19b.

15 Some people are like those seed along the path, where the word is sown. As soon as they hear it, Satan the devil comes and takes away the word that was sown in them, from their hearts, so that they may not believe and be saved. Mark 13:15. Luke 8:12.

20 Those other ones, who received the sown seed that fell on rocky places, is the man who hears the word and at once receives it with joy. 21 But since he has no root, his belief lasts only a short time. When trouble or persecution comes, because of the word, in his time of testing he quickly falls away. Matthew 13:20-21. Luke 8:13. Mark 4:16-17.

22 Still the other ones, who received the sown seed that fell among the thorns, stands for those who hear the word, but as they go on their way they choke the word by the worries of this life and the deceitfulness of wealth; riches, pleasures and the desires for other things, making it unfruitful, and they do not mature. Matthew 13:22. Luke 8:14. Mark 4:18-19.

23 But the other ones, who received the sown seed that fell on good soil, stands for those with a noble and good heart who hear the word, accepts it, understands it and retains it. And by persevering they produce a crop, yielding a hundred, sixty or thirty times what was sown." Matthew 13:23. Luke 8:15. Mark 4:20.

21 He said to them, "Do you bring in a lighted lamp to put it under a bowl, hide it in a jar or put it under a bed? Instead, don't you put the lighted lamp on its stand so that those who come in can see the light? Mark 4:21. Luke 8:16.

22 For whatever is hidden is meant to be disclosed, and whatever is concealed is meant to be brought out into the open. Mark 4:22. Luke 8:17.

23 If anyone has ears to hear, let him hear." Mark 4:23.

24 "Therefore consider carefully what you hear and how you listen," he continued. "With the measure you use, it will be measured to you-and even more. 25 Whoever has will be given more; whoever does not have, even what he thinks has will be taken from him." Mark 4:24-25. Luke 8:18.

26 He also said, "This is what the kingdom of God is like. A man scatters seed on the ground. 27 Night and day, whether he sleeps or gets up, the seed sprouts and grows, though he does not know how. 28 All by itself the soil produces grain-first the stalk, then the head, then the full kernel in the head. 29 As soon as the grain is ripe, he puts the sickle to it, because the harvest has come." Mark 4:26-29.

24 Jesus told them another parable: "The kingdom of heaven is like a man who sowed good seed in his field. 25 But while everyone was sleeping, his enemy came and sowed weeds among the wheat, and went away. 26 When the wheat sprouted and formed heads, then the weeds also appeared. 27 "The owner's

servants came to him and said, 'Sir, didn't you sow good seed in your field? Where then did the weeds come from?' 28 "'An enemy did this,' he replied. "The servants asked him, 'Do you want us to go and pull them up?' 29 "'No,' he answered, 'because while you are pulling the weeds, you may root up the wheat with them. 30 Let both grow together until the harvest. At that time I will tell the harvesters: First collect the weeds and tie them in bundles to be burned; then gather the wheat and bring it into my barn.'" Matthew 13:24-30.

30 Again he said, "What shall we say the kingdom of God is like, or what parable shall we use to describe it? Mark 4:30.

31 Then Jesus asked, "What is the kingdom of God like? What shall I compare it to? Then he told them another parable: "The kingdom of heaven is like a mustard seed, which a man took and planted in his garden or field. 32 Though it is the smallest of all your seeds you plant in the ground. Yet when planted, it grows and becomes the largest of all garden plants and becomes a tree with such big branches, so that the birds of the air can come and perch in its branches and shade." Matthew 13:31-32. Mark 4:31-32. Luke 13:18-19.

33 Again he asked, "What shall I compare the kingdom of God to? He told them still another parable: the kingdom of heaven is like yeast that a woman took and mixed into a large amount of flour until it worked all through the dough." Matthew 13:33. Luke 13:20-21.

34 Jesus spoke all these things to the crowd in parables; he did not say anything to them without using a parable. 35 So was fulfilled what was spoken through the prophet: "I will open my mouth in parables, I will utter things hidden since the creation of the world." Matthew 13:34-35.

36 Then he left the crowd and went into the house. His disciples came to him and said, "Explain to us the parable of the weeds in

the field."37 He answered, "The one who sowed the good seed is the Son of Man. 38 The field is the world, and the good seed stands for the sons of the kingdom. The weeds are the sons of the evil one, 39 and the enemy who sows them is the devil. The harvest is the end of the age, and the harvesters are angels. 40 "As the weeds are pulled up and burned in the fire, so it will be at the end of the age. 41 The Son of Man will send out his angels, and they will weed out of his kingdom everything that causes sin and all who do evil. 42 They will throw them into the fiery furnace, where there will be weeping and gnashing of teeth. 43 Then the righteous will shine like the sun in the kingdom of their Father. He who has ears, let him hear. Matthew 13:36-43.

44 "The kingdom of heaven is like treasure hidden in a field. When a man found it, he hid it again, and then in his joy went and sold all he had and bought that field. Matthew 13:44.

45 "Again, the kingdom of heaven is like a merchant looking for fine pearls. 46 When he found one of great value, he went away and sold everything he had and bought it. Matthew 13:45-46.

47 "Once again, the kingdom of heaven is like a net that was let down into the lake and caught all kinds of fish. 48 When it was full, the fishermen pulled it up on the shore. Then they sat down and collected the good fish in baskets, but threw the bad away. 49 This is how it will be at the end of the age. The angels will come and separate the wicked from the righteous 50 and throw them into the fiery furnace, where there will be weeping and gnashing of teeth. Matthew 13:47-50.

33 With many similar parables Jesus spoke the word to them, as much as they could understand. 34 He did not say anything to them without using a parable. But when he was alone with his own disciples, he explained everything. Mark 4:33-34.

51 "Have you understood all these things?" Jesus asked. "Yes," they replied. Matthew 13:51.

52 He said to them, "Therefore every teacher of the law who has been instructed about the kingdom of heaven is like the owner of a house who brings out of his storeroom new treasures as well as old." Matthew 13:52.

His Sleep

35 That day when evening came, Jesus said to his disciples, "Let us go over to the other side of the lake." Then he got into the boat and his disciples follow him and they set out. 36 Leaving the crowd behind, they took him along, just as he was, in the boat. There were also other boats with him. Mark 4:35-36. Luke 8:22. Matthew 8:23.

23 As they sailed, he fell asleep. Without warning, a furious storm came up and a furious squall came down on the lake, that the waves swept over the boat; so that it was nearly swamped, and they were in great danger. But Jesus was sleeping. Luke 8:23. Matthew 8:24a. Mark 4:37.

38 Jesus was in the stern, sleeping on a cushion. The disciples went and woke him and said to him, "Lord, save us! Master, Master , we're going to drown! Teacher, don't you care if we drown?" Mark 4:38. Luke 8:24b. Matthew 8:25.

26 He replied, "You of little faith, why are you so afraid?" Then he got up and rebuked the winds and said to the raging waves, "Quiet! Be still!" Then the wind and waters died down, the storm subsided, and it was all completely calm. Matthew 8:26. Mark 4:39. Luke 8:24.

40 He said to his disciples, "Where is your faith? Why are you so afraid? Do you still have no faith?" Mark 4:40. Luke 8:25a

25b In terrified fear and amazement they asked one another, "Who is this? What kind of man is this? He commands even the winds and the water, and they obey him." Luke 8:25b. Mark 4:41. Matthew 8:27.

His Deliverance

1 They sailed across the lake to the region of the Gerasenes which is across the lake from Galilee. 2 When they arrived at the other side, Jesus got out of the boat and stepped ashore, two men with an evil demon-possessed spirits came from the town tombs to meet him. They were so violent that no one could pass that way. 3 For a long time these men had not worn clothes or lived in a house, but lived in the tombs, and no one could bind them any more, not even with a chain. 4 For many times it had seized them, and though they had often been chained hand and foot and kept under guard; they tore the chains apart, broke the irons on their feet and had been driven by the demons into solitary places. No one was strong enough to subdue them. 5 Night and day among the tombs and in the hills they would cry out and cut themselves with stones. Mark 5:1-5. Luke 8:26-27. Matthew 8:28.

6 When the man saw Jesus from a distance, they ran, cried out and fell on their knees in front of him. 7 They shouted at the top of their voices, "What do you want with us, Jesus, Son of the Most High God? We beg you, Swear to God that you won't torture us!" "Have you come here to torture us before the appointed time?" 8 For Jesus had said to them, "I command you to come out of these men, you evil spirits!" Mark 5:6-8. Luke 8:28. Matthew 8:29.

30 Then Jesus asked him, "What is your name?" "My name is Legion," he replied, "for we are many demons had gone into

them." 31 And they begged Jesus again and again not to order them to go into the Abyss. Luke 8:30-31. Mark 5:9-10.

30 Some distance from them on the nearby hillside, a large herd of pigs was feeding there. 31 The demons begged Jesus, "If you drive us out, send us into the herd of pigs; allow us to go into them." 32 He gave them permission and said, "Go!" When the demons came out of the men, they went into the pigs, and the whole herd, about two thousand in number; rushed down the steep bank into the lake and were drowned in the water. Matthew 8:30-32. Mark 5:11-13. Luke 8:32-33.

34 When those tending the pigs saw what had happened, they ran off and reported all this in the town and countryside, 35 and the people went out to see what had happened. When the whole town went out to meet Jesus, they found and saw the men who had been possessed by the legion demons had gone out, sitting there, at Jesus' feet, dressed and in their right mind; and they were afraid. 36 Those who had seen it told the people what happened to the demon-possessed men had been cured and the pigs as well. Luke 8:34-36. Mark 5:14-16. Matthew 8:33-34a.

37a Then all the people of the region of the Gerasenes began to plead with Jesus to leave their region, because they were overcome with fear. Luke 8:37a. Mark 5:17. Matthew 8:34b.

18 As Jesus was getting into the boat, the man from whom had been demon-possessed begged to go with him. 19 Jesus did not let him, but sent him away saying, "Return home to your family and tell them how much the Lord has done for you, and how God has had mercy on you." Mark 5:18-19. Luke 8:38-39a.

37b So Jesus got into the boat and left. Luke 8:37b.

20 The man went away and told all over the Decapolis, a ten-city Greco-Roman federation, how much Jesus had done for him. And all the people were amazed. Mark 5:20. Luke 8:39b.

His Clothes

21 When Jesus had again crossed over by boat to the other side of the lake, a large crowd welcomed and gathered around him while he was by the lake, for they were all expecting his return Mark 5:21. Luke 8:40.

22 Then one of the synagogue rulers, a man named Jairus, came there. Seeing Jesus, he fell and knelt at his feet 23 and pleaded earnestly with him, "My little daughter is dying. Please come to my house and put your hands on her so that she will be healed and live." She was his only daughter, a girl of about twelve. Mark 5:22-23. Matthew 9:18. Luke 8:41-42a

19 Jesus got up and went with him, and so did his disciples. As Jesus was on his way, the large crowds followed, pressed around him and almost crushed him. Matthew 9:19. Mark 5:24. Luke 8:42b.

25 Just then a woman was there who had been subject to bleeding for twelve years, but no one could heal her. 26 She had suffered a great deal under the care of many doctors and had spent all she had, yet instead of getting better she grew worse. 27 When she heard about Jesus, she came up behind him in the crowd and touched the edge of his cloak, 28 because she thought to herself, "If I just touch his clothes, I will be healed." 29 Immediately her bleeding stopped and she felt in her body that she was freed from her suffering. Mark 5:25-29. Luke 8:43-44. Matthew 9:20-21.

30 At once Jesus realized that power had gone out from him. He turned around in the crowd and asked, "Who touched my clothes?" Mark 5:30. Luke 8:45a.

31 "You see the people crowding against you," his disciples answered, "and yet you can ask, 'Who touched me?'" Mark 5:31.

45b When they all denied it, Peter said, "Master, the people are crowding and pressing against you." Luke 8:45b.

46 But Jesus said, "Someone touched me; I know that power has gone out from me." Luke 8:46.

32 But Jesus kept looking around to see who had done it. Mark 5:32.

47a Then the woman, seeing that she could not go unnoticed and knowing what had happened to her, came and fell at his feet, trembling with fear, Luke 8:47a. Mark 5:33a.

22a Jesus turned and saw her. Matthew 9:22a.

47b In the presence of all the people, she told him the whole truth why she had touched him and how she had been instantly healed. 48 Then he said to her, "Take heart, daughter, your faith has healed you. Go in peace and be freed from your suffering." And the woman was healed from that moment. Luke 8:47b-48. Matthew 9:22b. Mark 5:33b-34.

His Jairus' Daughter

35 While Jesus was still speaking, some men came from the house of Jairus, the synagogue ruler. "Your daughter is dead," they said. "Don't bother the teacher any more?" Mark 5:35. Luke 8:49.

36 Ignoring what they said, Jesus said to Jairus, the synagogue ruler, "Don't be afraid; just believe, and she will be healed." Mark 5:36. Luke 8:50.

37 He did not let anyone follow him except Peter, James and John the brother of James. Mark 5:37.

38 When they arrived at the home of Jairus, the synagogue ruler, Jesus saw a commotion, with people crying, wailing loudly. 39 When Jesus entered the ruler's house and saw the flute players and the noisy crowd and said to them, "Why all this commotion and wailing? The child is not dead but asleep." Mark 5:38-39. Matthew 9:23. Luke 8:51a.

51b he did not let anyone go in with him except Peter, John and James, and the child's father and mother. Luke 8:51b.

52 Meanwhile, all the people were wailing and mourning for her. "Stop wailing," Jesus said. "She is not dead but asleep." Luke 8:52.

53 But they laughed at him, knowing that she was dead. Luke 8:53. Mark 5:40a.

24 he said, "Go away. The girl is not dead but asleep." But they laughed at him. Matthew 9:24.

40b After he put the crowd all outside, he took the child's father and mother and the disciples who were with him, and went in where the child was. Mark 5:40b. Matthew 9:25a.

41 He took her by the hand and said to her, "Talitha koum!" (which means, "Little girl, I say to you, My child, get up!"). 42 Her spirit returned, and immediately the girl stood up and walked around (she was twelve years old). At this her parents were completely astonished. 43 He gave them strict orders not to tell anyone about this or what had happened, and told them to give her something to eat. Mark 5:41-43. Matthew 9:25b. Luke 8:54-56.

26 News of this spread through all that region. Matthew 9:26.

His Blind See

27 As Jesus went on from there, two blind men followed him, calling out, "Have mercy on us, Son of David!" 28 When he had gone indoors, the blind men came to him, and he asked them, "Do you believe that I am able to do this?" "Yes, Lord," they replied. 29 Then he touched their eyes and said, "According to your faith will it be done to you"; 30 and their sight was restored. Jesus warned them sternly, "See that no one knows about this." 31 But they went out and spread the news about him all over that region. Matthew 9:27-31.

His Mute Speak

32 While they were going out, a man who was demon-possessed and could not talk was brought to Jesus. 33 And when the demon was driven out, the man who had been mute spoke. The crowd was amazed and said, "Nothing like this has ever been seen in Israel." 34 But the Pharisees said, "It is by the prince of demons that he drives out demons." Matthew 9:32-34.

His Hometown Honor

53 When Jesus had finished these parables, Jesus left there and went to his hometown, accompanied by his disciples. Matthew 13:53. Mark 6:1.

54 Coming to his hometown, when the Sabbath came, he began teaching the people in their synagogue, and many who heard were amazed. Where did this man get these things?" they asked. "What's this wisdom and where did this man get this wisdom and he even does these miracles with these miraculous powers?" Matthew 13:54. Mark 6:2.

55 "Isn't this the carpenter's son? Isn't his mother's name Mary, and aren't his brothers James, Joseph, Simon and Judas? 56 Aren't all his sisters with us? Where then did this man get all these things?" 57 And they took offense at him. But Jesus said to them, "Only in his hometown and in his own house among his relatives is a prophet without honor." Matthew 13:55-57. Mark 6:3-4.

5 He could not and did not do many miracles there because of their lack of faith, except lay his hands on a few sick people and heal them. 6 And he was amazed at their lack of faith. Then Jesus went around teaching from village to village. Mark 6:5-6. Matthew 13:58.

His Harvest

35 Jesus went through all the towns and villages, teaching in their synagogues, preaching the good news of the kingdom and healing every disease and sickness. 36 When he saw the crowds, he had compassion on them, because they were harassed and helpless, like sheep without a shepherd. 37 Then he said to his disciples, "The harvest is plentiful but the workers are few. 38 Ask the Lord of the harvest, therefore, to send out workers into his harvest field." Matthew 9:35-38.

His Ministry's Fruits

1 When Jesus had called the twelve disciples together to him, he gave them power and authority to drive out all evil demon spirits and to cure every disease, 2 and he sent them out two by two to preach the kingdom of God, to heal every sickness and gave them authority over evil spirits. Luke 9:1-2. Matthew 10:1. Mark 6:7.

2 These are the names of the twelve apostles: first, Simon (who is called Peter) and his brother Andrew; James son of Zebedee, and his brother John; 3 Philip and Bartholomew; Thomas and Matthew the tax collector; James son of Alphaeus, and Thaddaeus; 4 Simon the Zealot and Judas Iscariot, who betrayed him. Matthew 10:2-4.

5 These twelve Jesus sent out and he told them these following instructions: "Do not go among the Gentiles or enter any town of the Samaritans. 6 Go rather to the lost sheep of Israel. 7 As you go, preach this message: 'The kingdom of heaven is near.' 8 Heal the sick, raise the dead, cleanse those who have leprosy, drive out demons. Freely you have received, freely give. Matthew 10:5-8. Mark 6:8a.

8b "Take nothing for the journey except a staff or no staff, no bread, no bag, no gold or silver or copper in your belts. 9 Wear sandals but not an extra tunic, for the worker is worth his keep. Mark 6:8b-9. Luke 9:3. Matthew 10:9-10.

11 "Whatever town or village you enter, search for some worthy person there and whenever you stay at his house, stay there until you leave that town. 12 As you enter the home, give it your greeting. 13 If the home is deserving, let your peace rest on it; if it is not, let your peace return to you. 14 If people or a place will not welcome you or listen to your words, shake the dust off your feet

when you leave their home or town as a testimony against them."
Matthew 10:11-14. Mark 6:10-11. Luke 9:4-5.

15 I tell you the truth, it will be more bearable for Sodom and
Gomorrah on the day of judgment than for that town. Matthew
10:15.

His Insights

16 I am sending you out like sheep among wolves. Therefore be
as shrewd as snakes and as innocent as doves. Matthew 10:16.

17 "Be on your guard against men; they will hand you over to the
local councils and flog you in their synagogues. 18 On my account
you will be brought before governors, kings, synagogues, rulers
and authorities as witnesses to them and to the Gentiles. 19 But
when they arrest you, do not worry about how you will defend
yourselves or what you will say or how to say it. At that time you
will be given what to say, 20 for it will not be you speaking, but
the Holy Spirit of your Father speaking through you; will teach
you at that time what you should say." Matthew 10:17-20. Luke
12:11-12.

21 "Brother will betray brother to death, and a father his child;
children will rebel against their parents and have them put to
death. 22 All men will hate you because of me, but he who stands
firm to the end will be saved. 23 When you are persecuted in one
place, flee to another. I tell you the truth, you will not finish going
through the cities of Israel before the Son of Man comes.

24 "A student is not above his teacher, nor a servant above his
master. 25 It is enough for the student to be like his teacher, and
the servant like his master. If the head of the house has been

called Beelzebub, how much more the members of his household! Matthew 10:21-25.

26 "So do not be afraid of them. There is nothing concealed that will not be disclosed, or hidden that will not be made known. 27 What I tell you in the dark, speak in the daylight, what you have said in the dark will be heard in the daylight; and what is whispered in your ear, proclaim from the roofs, what you have whispered in the ear in the inner rooms will be proclaimed from the roofs.

28 I tell you, my friends, do not be afraid of those who kill the body but cannot kill the soul; and after that can do no more. But rather, I will show you whom you should fear: be afraid of the One who, after the killing of the body, has power to throw you into hell and can destroy both soul and body in hell. Yes, I tell you, fear him. 29 Are not two sparrows sold for a penny and five sparrows sold for two pennies? Yet not one of them will fall to the ground apart from the will of your Father and not one of them is forgotten by God. 30 And indeed, even the very hairs of your head are all numbered. 31 So don't be afraid; you are worth more than many sparrows." Matthew 10:26-31. Luke 12:2-7.

32 " I tell you, whoever acknowledges me before men, I the Son of Man will also acknowledge him before the angels of God and my Father in heaven. 33 But whoever disowns me before men, I will disown him before the angels of God and my Father in heaven. Matthew 10:32-33. Luke 12:8-9.

34 "Do not suppose that I have come to bring peace to the earth. I did not come to bring peace, but a sword. 35 For I have come to turn "'a man against his father, a daughter against her mother, a daughter-in-law against her mother-in-law- 36 a man's enemies will be the members of his own household.'

37 "Anyone who loves his father or mother more than me is not worthy of me; anyone who loves his son or daughter more than

me is not worthy of me; 38 and anyone who does not take his cross and follow me is not worthy of me. 39 Whoever finds his life will lose it, and whoever loses his life for my sake will find it.

40 "He who receives you receives me, and he who receives me receives the one who sent me. 41 Anyone who receives a prophet because he is a prophet will receive a prophet's reward, and anyone who receives a righteous man because he is a righteous man will receive a righteous man's reward.

42 And if anyone gives even a cup of cold water to one of these little ones because he is my disciple, I tell you the truth, he will certainly not lose his reward." Matthew 10:34-42.

12 So they set out and went from village to village, preaching the gospel and that people should repent. 13 They drove out many demons and anointed many sick people with oil and healing people everywhere. Mark 6:12-13. Luke 9:6.

His Mistaken Identity

14 Now at that time, King Herod the tetrarch heard the reports about all that was going on with Jesus, for Jesus' name had become well known. And he was perplexed, because some were saying," John the Baptist has been raised from the dead, and that is why miraculous powers are at work in him." 15 Others said, "He is Elijah." Others that Elijah had appeared. Others, that one of the prophets of long ago had come back to life. And still others claimed, "He is a prophet, like one of the prophets of long ago." 16 But when Herod heard this, he said to his attendants, "John, the man I beheaded, has been raised from the dead! Who, then, is this I hear such things about? And he tried to see him." Mark 6:14-16. Luke 9:7-9. Matthew14:1-2.

His Preparer's Death

17 For now Herod himself had given orders to have John arrested, and he had him bound and put in prison. He did this because of Herodias, his brother Philip's wife, whom he had married. 18 For John had been saying to Herod, "It is not lawful for you to have your brother's wife." 19 So Herod and Herodias nursed a grudge against John and wanted to kill him. But they were not able to, because Herod was afraid of the people, because they considered him a prophet. 20 Herod feared John and protected him, knowing him to be a righteous and holy man. When Herod heard John, he was greatly puzzled; yet he liked to listen to him. Mark 6:17-20. Matthew 14:3-5.

21 Finally the opportune time came. On Herod's birthday Herod gave a banquet for his high officials and military commanders and the leading men of Galilee.

22 When the daughter of Herodias came in and danced for them, she pleased Herod so much and his dinner guests. The king said to the girl, "Ask me for anything you want, and I'll give it to you." 23 And he promised her with an oath, "Whatever you ask I will give you, up to half my kingdom."

24 She went out and said to her mother, "What shall I ask for?" Prompted by her mother, she said, "Give me here on a platter the head of John the Baptist," she answered. 25 At once the girl hurried in to the king with the request: "I want you to give me right now the head of John the Baptist on a platter."

26 The king was greatly distressed, but because of his oaths and his dinner guests, he did not want to refuse her; he ordered that her request be granted.

27 So he immediately sent an executioner with orders to bring John's head. The man went and had beheaded John in the prison, 28 and brought back his head on a platter. He presented and gave it to the girl, and she carried it and gave it to her mother. Mark 6:21-28. Matthew 14:6-11.

29 On hearing of this, John's disciples came and took his body and laid it in a tomb. Then they went and told Jesus. Mark 6:29. Matthew 14:12.

His Pantry

30 When the apostles returned and gathered around Jesus, they reported to Jesus all what they had done and taught. 31 Then when Jesus heard what had happened, because so many people were coming and going that they did not even have a chance to eat, he said to them, "Come with me by yourselves to a quiet place and get some rest." 32 So then he took them with him and they withdrew by themselves in a boat privately to a town called Bethsaida, a solitary place. Mark 6:30-32. Luke 9:10. Matthew 14:13a.

1 Some time after this, Jesus crossed to the far shore of the Sea of Galilee (that is, the Sea of Tiberias), John 6:1.

33 But the crowds: who saw them leaving, learned about it, recognized them and hearing of this; followed him and ran on foot from all the towns and got there ahead of them. 34 When Jesus landed and saw a great crowd of people followed him, because they saw the miraculous signs he had performed on the sick. He welcomed them and he had compassion on them, because they were like sheep without a shepherd. So he began teaching them many things about the kingdom of God, and healed their sick

and those who needed healing. Mark 6:33-34. Luke 9:11. Matthew 14:13b-14. John 6:2.

3 Then Jesus went up on a mountainside and sat down with his disciples. 4 The Jewish Passover Feast was near. 5 When Jesus looked up and saw a great crowd coming toward him, he said to Philip, "Where shall we buy bread for these people to eat?" 6 He asked this only to test him, for he already had in mind what he was going to do. 7 Philip answered him, "Eight months' wages would not buy enough bread for each one to have a bite!" John 6:3-7.

35 By this time it was late in the afternoon as evening approached, so his twelve disciples came to him. "This is a remote place here," they said, "and it's already getting very late. 36 Send the crowds of people away so they can go to the surrounding countryside and villages to find and buy themselves some food to eat and lodging." Mark 6:35-36. Matthew 14:15. Luke 9:12.

37 But Jesus answered, "They do not need to go away. You give them something to eat." They said to him, "That would take eight months of a man's wages! Are we to go and spend that much on bread and give it to them to eat?" 38 "How many loaves do you have?" he asked. "Go and see." When they found out, they answered, "We have only five loaves of bread and two fish-unless we go and buy food for all this crowd." Another of his disciples, Andrew, Simon Peter's brother, spoke up, "Here is a boy with five small barley loaves and two small fish, but how far will they go among so many?" "Bring them here to me," he said. Mark 6:37-38. Matthew 14:16-18. Luke 9:13. John 6:8-9.

39 Then Jesus directed his disciples, "Have all the people sit down in groups of about fifty each on the green grass." The disciples did so, and there was plenty of grass in that place, and everybody sat down, about five thousand of them. 40 So they sat down in groups of hundreds and fifties. 41 Jesus then took the five loaves and the two fish and looking up to heaven, he gave thanks and broke

the loaves. Then he distributed them to his disciples and the disciples set them before the people who were seated as much as they wanted. He also divided the two fish among them all. Mark 6:39-41. Matthew 14:19. Luke 9:14-16. John 6:10-11.

42 When they all had enough to eat and were satisfied, he said to his disciples, "Gather the pieces that are left over. Let nothing be wasted." 43 and so the disciples gathered them and picked up twelve basketfuls of the broken pieces of the five barley loaves of bread and fish that were left over by those who had eaten. 44 The number of those who ate was about five thousand men, besides women and children. Mark 6:42-44. Matthew 14:20-21. Luke 9:17. John 6:12-13.

14 After the people saw the miraculous sign that Jesus did, they began to say, "Surely this is the Prophet who is to come into the world." 15 Jesus, knowing that they intended to come and make him king by force, withdrew again to a mountain by himself. John 6:14-15.

His Walking on Water

45 Immediately Jesus made his disciples get into the boat and go on ahead of him to the other side to Bethsaida, while he dismissed the crowd. Mark 6:45. Matthew 14:22.

16 After he had dismissed and left them, he went up on a mountainside by himself to pray. When evening came, his disciples went down to the lake, 17 where they got into a boat and set off across the lake for Capernaum. By now it was dark, and Jesus was alone on land and had not yet joined them. 18 A strong wind was blowing and the waters grew rough. The boat was in the middle of the lake already a considerable distance from land. He saw the disciples straining at the oars, buffet by the waves

because the wind was against them. John 6:16-18. Matthew 14:23-24. Mark 6:46-48a.

48b About during the fourth watch of the night when they had rowed three or three and a half miles, Jesus went out to them, walking on the water. He was about to pass by them, 49 but when the disciples saw him walking on the lake, they thought he was a ghost. They cried out in fear, 50a because they all saw Jesus approaching the boat and they were terrified. "It's a ghost," they said. Mark 6:48b-50a. Matthew 14:25-26. John 6:19.

27 But Jesus immediately spoke to them and said: "Take courage! It is I. Don't be afraid." Matthew 14:27. Mark 6:50b. John 6:20.

28 "Lord, if it's you," Peter replied, "tell me to come to you on the water." 29 "Come," he said. Then Peter got down out of the boat, walked on the water and came toward Jesus. 30 But when he saw the wind, he was afraid and, beginning to sink, cried out, "Lord, save me!" 31 Immediately Jesus reached out his hand and caught him. "You of little faith," he said, "why did you doubt?" Matthew 14:28-31.

32 Then they were willing to take them into the boat. When they climbed into the boat with them, the wind died down. 33 They were completely amazed, for they had not understood about the loaves; their hearts were hardened. Then those who were in the boat worshiped him, saying, "Truly you are the Son of God." Matthew 14:32-33. Mark 6:51-52. John 6:21a.

21b and immediately the boat reached the shore where they were heading. John 6:21b.

His Fame

53 When they had crossed over, they landed at Gennesaret and anchored there. Mark 6:53. Matthew 14:34.

54 As soon as they got out of the boat, the people of that place recognized Jesus. Mark 6:54. Matthew 14:35a.

55 They ran throughout that whole region and sent word to all the surrounding country. People brought all their sick to him and carried the sick on mats to wherever they heard he was. Mark 6:55. Matthew 14:35b.

56 And wherever he went-into villages, towns or countryside-they placed the sick in the marketplaces. They begged him to let the sick just touch even the edge of his cloak, and all who touched him were healed. Mark 6:56. Matthew 14:36.

His Bread

22 The next day the crowd that had stayed on the opposite shore of the lake realized that only one boat had been there, and that Jesus had not entered it with his disciples, but that they had gone away alone. 23 Then some boats from Tiberias landed near the place where the people had eaten the bread after the Lord had given thanks. 24 Once the crowd realized that neither Jesus nor his disciples were there, they got into the boats and went to Capernaum in search of Jesus.

25 When they found him on the other side of the lake, they asked him, "Rabbi, when did you get here?" 26 Jesus answered, "I tell you the truth, you are looking for me, not because you saw miraculous signs but because you ate the loaves and had your fill. 27 Do not work for food that spoils, but for food that endures to eternal life, which the Son of Man will give you. On him God the Father has placed his seal of approval."

28 Then they asked him, "What must we do to do the works God requires?"29 Jesus answered, "The work of God is this: to believe in the one he has sent."

30 So they asked him, "What miraculous sign then will you give that we may see it and believe you? What will you do? 31 Our forefathers ate the manna in the desert; as it is written: 'He gave them bread from heaven to eat.'" 32 Jesus said to them, "I tell you the truth, it is not Moses who has given you the bread from heaven, but it is my Father who gives you the true bread from heaven. 33 For the bread of God is he who comes down from heaven and gives life to the world." 34 "Sir," they said, "from now on give us this bread."

35 Then Jesus declared, "I am the bread of life. He who comes to me will never go hungry, and he who believes in me will never be thirsty. 36 But as I told you, you have seen me and still you do not believe.

37 All that the Father gives me will come to me, and whoever comes to me I will never drive away. 38 For I have come down from heaven not to do my will but to do the will of him who sent me. 39 And this is the will of him who sent me, that I shall lose none of all that he has given me, but raise them up at the last day. 40 For my Father's will is that everyone who looks to the Son and believes in him shall have eternal life, and I will raise him up at the last day." John 6:22-40.

41 At this the Jews began to grumble about him because he said, "I am the bread that came down from heaven." 42 They said, "Is this not Jesus, the son of Joseph, whose father and mother we know? How can he now say, 'I came down from heaven'?"

43 "Stop grumbling among yourselves," Jesus answered. 44 "No one can come to me unless the Father who sent me draws him, and I will raise him up at the last day. 45 It is written in the Prophets: 'They will all be taught by God.' Everyone who listens to the Father and learns from him comes to me. 46 No one has seen the Father except the one who is from God; only he has seen the Father.

47 I tell you the truth, he who believes has everlasting life. 48 I am the bread of life. 49 Your forefathers ate the manna in the desert, yet they died. 50 But here is the bread that comes down from heaven, which a man may eat and not die. 51 I am the living bread that came down from heaven. If anyone eats of this bread, he will live forever. This bread is my flesh, which I will give for the life of the world."

52 Then the Jews began to argue sharply among themselves, "How can this man give us his flesh to eat?"

53 Jesus said to them, "I tell you the truth, unless you eat the flesh of the Son of Man and drink his blood; you have no life in you. 54 Whoever eats my flesh and drinks my blood has eternal life, and I will raise him up at the last day. 55 For my flesh is real food and my blood is real drink. 56 Whoever eats my flesh and drinks my blood remains in me, and I in him. 57 Just as the living Father sent me and I live because of the Father, so the one who feeds on me will live because of me. 58 This is the bread that came down from heaven. Your forefathers ate manna and died, but he who feeds on this bread will live forever." 59 He said this while teaching in the synagogue in Capernaum. John 6:41-59.

60 On hearing it, many of his disciples said, "This is a hard teaching. Who can accept it?"

61 Aware that his disciples were grumbling about this, Jesus said to them, "Does this offend you? 62 What if you see the Son of Man ascend to where he was before! 63 The Spirit gives life; the flesh counts for nothing. The words I have spoken to you are spirit and they are life. 64 Yet there are some of you who do not believe." For Jesus had known from the beginning which of them did not believe and who would betray him.

65 He went on to say, "This is why I told you that no one can come to me unless the Father has enabled him."

66 From this time many of his disciples turned back and no longer followed him. 67 "You do not want to leave too, do you?" Jesus asked the Twelve. 68 Simon Peter answered him, "Lord, to whom shall we go? You have the words of eternal life. 69 We believe and know that you are the Holy One of God." 70 Then Jesus replied, "Have I not chosen you, the Twelve? Yet one of you is a devil!" 71 (He meant Judas, the son of Simon Iscariot, who, though one of the Twelve, was later to betray him.) John 6:60-71.

His Cleanliness

1 The Pharisees and some of the teachers of the law who had come from Jerusalem gathered around Jesus and 2 saw some of his disciples eating food with hands that were "unclean," that is, unwashed. 3 (The Pharisees and all the Jews do not eat unless they give their hands a ceremonial washing, holding to the tradition of the elders. 4 When they come from the marketplace they do not eat unless they wash. And they observe many other traditions, such as the washing of cups, pitchers and kettles.) Mark 7:1-4.

1 So then some Pharisees and teachers of the law came to Jesus from Jerusalem and asked, 2 "Why do your disciples break the tradition instead of living according to the tradition of the elders? They don't wash their 'unclean' hands before they eat their food!" Matthew 15:1-2. Mark 7:5.

3 Jesus replied, "And why do you break the command of God for the sake of your tradition?" Matthew 15:3.

8 "You have let go of the commands of God and are holding on to the traditions of men." 9 And he said to them: "You have a fine way of setting aside the commands of God in order to observe your own traditions! Mark 7:8-9.

10 "For God and Moses said, 'Honor your father and your mother,' and, 'Anyone who curses his father or mother must be put to death.' 11 But you say that if a man says to his father or mother: 'Whatever help you might otherwise have received from me is Corban' (that is, a gift devoted to God), 12 then you no longer let him do anything for his father or mother. 13 Thus you nullify the word of God for the sake of your tradition that you have handed down. And you do many things like that." Mark 7:10-13. Matthew 15:4-6.

7 "You hypocrites!" He replied, "Isaiah was right when he prophesied about you; as it is written: 8 "'These people honor me with their lips, but their hearts are far from me. 9 They worship me in vain; their teachings are but rules taught by men.'" Matthew 15:7-9. Mark 7:6-7

14 Again Jesus called the crowd to him and said, "Listen to me, everyone, and understand this. 15 Nothing outside a man can make him 'unclean' by going into him. What goes into a man's mouth does not make him 'unclean,' But rather, it is what comes out of a man's mouth, that is what makes him 'unclean.'" Mark 7:14-15. Matthew 15:10-11.

12 Then the disciples came to him and asked, "Do you know that the Pharisees were offended when they heard this?" 13 He replied, "Every plant that my heavenly Father has not planted will be pulled up by the roots. 14 Leave them; they are blind guides. If a blind man leads a blind man, both will fall into a pit." Matthew 15:12-14.

17 After he had left the crowd and entered the house, his disciples asked him about this parable. Peter said, "Explain the parable to us." 18 "Are you still so dull?" Jesus asked them. "Don't you see that nothing that enters a man from the outside can make him 'unclean'? 19 For whatever enters the mouth, it doesn't go into the heart but goes into the stomach and then out of his body? (In saying this, Jesus declared all foods "clean.") 20 He went on: "But what things that come out of a man's mouth is what makes him 'unclean.' 21 For from within, out of men's hearts, come evil thoughts, sexual immorality, theft, murder, adultery, 22 greed, malice, deceit, lewdness, envy, false testimony, slander, arrogance and folly. 23 All these evils come from inside and are what make a man 'unclean; but eating with unwashed hands does not make him 'unclean.'" Mark 7:17-23. Matthew 15:15-20.

His Greek Woman

24 Jesus left that place and withdrew to the region in the vicinity of Tyre and Sidon. He entered a house and did not want anyone to know it; yet he could not keep his presence secret. Mark 7:24. Matthew 15:21.

25 In fact, as soon as she heard about him; a Canaanite woman from that vicinity whose little daughter was possessed by an evil spirit came to him and fell at his feet, crying out, "Lord, Son of David, have mercy on me! My daughter is suffering terribly from demon-possession." 26 The woman was a Greek, born in

Syrian Phoenicia. She begged Jesus to drive the demon out of her daughter. Mark 7:25-26. Matthew 15:22.

23 Jesus did not answer a word. So his disciples came to him and urged him, "Send her away, for she keeps crying out after us." 24 He answered, "I was sent only to the lost sheep of Israel." Matthew 15:23-24.

25 The woman came and knelt before him. "Lord, help me!" she said. Matthew 15:25.

27 He replied, "First let the children eat all they want," he told her, "for it is not right to take the children's bread and toss it to their dogs." 28 "Yes, Lord," she replied, "but even the dogs under the table eat the children's crumbs that fall from their masters' table." Mark 7:27-28. Matthew 15:26-27.

28 Then Jesus answered, "Woman, you have great faith! Your request is granted." Then he told her, "For such a reply, you may go; the demon has left your daughter." And her daughter was healed from that very hour. Matthew 15:28. Mark 7:29.

30 She went home and found her child lying on the bed, and the demon gone. Mark 7:30.

His Ephphatha

31 Then Jesus left the vicinity of Tyre and went through Sidon, down to along the Sea of Galilee and into the region of the Decapolis (ten city Greco-Roman Federation). Then he went up on a mountainside and sat down. 32 There some people brought to him a man who was deaf and could hardly talk, and they begged him to place his hand on the man. 33 After he took him aside, away from the crowd, Jesus put his fingers into the man's ears.

Then he spit and touched the man's tongue. 34 He looked up to heaven and with a deep sigh said to him, "Ephphatha!" (which means, "Be opened!"). 35 At this, the man's ears were opened, his tongue was loosened and he began to speak plainly. Great crowds came to him, bringing the lame, the blind, the crippled, the mute and many others, and laid them at his feet; and he healed them. 36 Jesus commanded them not to tell anyone. But the more he did so, the more they kept talking about it. Mark 7:31-36. Matthew 15:29-30.

31 The people were overwhelmed with amazement when they saw the mute speaking; the crippled made well, the lame walking and the blind seeing. And they praised the God of Israel, "He has done everything well," they said. "He even makes the deaf hear and the mute speak." Matthew 15:31. Mark 7:37.

His Luncheon

1 During those days another large crowd gathered. Since they had nothing to eat, Jesus called his disciples to him and said, 2 "I have compassion for these people; they have already been with me three days and have nothing to eat. 3 I do not want to send them away hungry; if I send them home hungry, they will collapse on the way, because some of them have come a long distance." Mark 8:1-3. Matthew 15:32.

4 His disciples answered, "But where could we get enough bread in this remote place to feed such a crowd? Can anyone get enough bread to feed them?" 5 "How many loaves do you have?" Jesus asked. "Seven," they replied, "and a few small fish." Mark 8:4-5. Matthew 15:33-34.

6 He told the crowd to sit down on the ground. Then when he had taken the seven loaves and he had given thanks, he broke them

and gave them to his disciples to set before the people, and they in turn did so to the people. 7 They had a few small fish as well; he gave thanks for them also and told the disciples to distribute them. Mark 8:6-7. Matthew 15:35-36.

37 The people all ate and were satisfied. Afterward the disciples picked up seven basketfuls of broken pieces that were left over. 38 The number of those who were present was about four thousand men who ate, besides women and children. 39 After Jesus had sent the crowd away, he got into the boat with his disciples and went to the region of Dalmanutha, the vicinity of Magadan. Matthew 15:37-39. Mark 8:8-10.

His Intrepret

1 The Pharisees and Sadducees came and began to question Jesus, and tested him by asking him to show them a sign from heaven. Matthew 16:1. Mark 8:11.

2 He replied and said to the crowd, "When evening comes, you say, 'It will be fair weather, for the sky is red,' 3 and in the morning, 'Today it will be stormy, for the sky is red and overcast.' When you see a cloud rising in the west, immediately you say, 'It's going to rain,' and it does. And when the south wind blows, you say, 'It's going to be hot,' and it is. Hypocrites! You know how to interpret the appearance of the earth and the sky, but how is it you don't know how and cannot interpret the signs of the present times?" Matthew 16:2-3. Luke 12:54-56.

57 "Why don't you judge for yourselves what is right? 58 As you are going with your adversary to the magistrate, try hard to be reconciled to him on the way, or he may drag you off to the judge, and the judge turn you over to the officer, and the officer throw

you into prison. 59 I tell you, you will not get out until you have paid the last penny." Luke 12:57-59.

4 He sighed deeply and said, "Why does this wicked and adulterous generation ask and looks for a miraculous sign? I tell you the truth, but no sign will be given to it except the sign of Jonah." Jesus then left them and went away. Matthew 16:4. Mark 8:12.

His Yeast

1 Meanwhile, when a crowd of many thousands had gathered, so that they were trampling on one another, Jesus began to speak first to his disciples, saying: "Be on your guard against the yeast of the Pharisees, which is hypocrisy. Luke 12:1.

13 Then he left them, got back into the boat and when they went across the lake, to the other side. 14 The disciples had forgotten to bring bread, except for one loaf they had with them in the boat. 15 "Be careful," Jesus warned them. "Watch out for and be on your guard against the yeast of the Pharisees, Sadducees and that of Herod." Mark 8:13-15. Matthew 16:5-6.

7 They discussed this with one another and among themselves and said, "It is because we didn't bring or have any bread." Matthew 16:7. Mark 8:16.

17 Aware of their discussion, Jesus asked them: "You of little faith, why are you talking among yourselves about having no bread? Do you still not see or understand? Are your hearts hardened? 18 Do you have eyes but fail to see, and ears but fail to hear? And don't you remember? 19 When I broke the five loaves for the five thousand, and how many basketfuls of pieces did you gather and pick up?" "Twelve," they replied. 20 "Or and when I broke the

seven loaves for the four thousand, and how many basketfuls of pieces did you gather and pick up?" They answered, "Seven." 21 He said to them, "Do you still not understand?" Mark 8:17-21. Matthew 16:8-10.

11 How is it you don't understand that I was not talking to you about bread? But be on your guard against the yeast of the Pharisees and Sadducees." 12 Then they understood that he was not telling them to guard against the yeast used in bread, but against the teaching of the Pharisees and Sadducees. Matthew 16:11-12.

His Hands

22 They came to Bethsaida, and some people brought a blind man and begged Jesus to touch him. 23 He took the blind man by the hand and led him outside the village. When he had spit on the man's eyes and put his hands on him, Jesus asked, "Do you see anything?" 24 He looked up and said, "I see people; they look like trees walking around." 25 Once more Jesus put his hands on the man's eyes. Then his eyes were opened, his sight was restored, and he saw everything clearly. 26 Jesus sent him home, saying, "Don't go into the village." Mark 8:22-26.

His Ministry Strengthening

27 Jesus and his disciples went on to the villages in the region around Caesarea Philippi. On the way he asked his disciples, "Who do people say the Son of Man is? When Jesus was praying in private and his disciples were with him, he asked them, "Who do the crowds say I am?" Mark 8:27. Matthew 16:13. Luke 9:18.

19 They replied, "Some say John the Baptist; others say Elijah; and still others, that Jeremiah or one of the prophets of long ago has come back to life." Luke 9:19. Matthew 16:14. Mark 8:28.

15 "But what about you?" he asked. "Who do you say I am?" 16 Simon Peter answered, "You are the Christ, the Son of the living God, the Christ of God." Matthew 16:15-16. Mark 8:29. Luke 9:20.

17 Jesus replied, "Blessed are you, Simon son of Jonah, for this was not revealed to you by man, but by my Father in heaven. 18 And I tell you that you are Peter, and on this rock I will build my church, and the gates of Hades will not overcome it. 19 I will give you the keys of the kingdom of heaven; whatever you bind on earth will be bound in heaven, and whatever you loose on earth will be loosed in heaven." Matthew 16:17-19.

20 Then Jesus warned his disciples not to tell anyone that he was the Christ. Matthew16:20. Mark 8:30.

His Rejection

31 From that time on Jesus then began to explain and teach his disciples. Jesus strictly warned them not to tell this to anyone. And he said, "the Son of Man, must go to Jerusalem and suffer many things and be rejected by the hands of the elders, chief priests and teachers of the law," and that he must be killed and after three days, on the third day rise again to life. Mark 8:31. Luke 9:21-22. Matthew 16:21.

32 He spoke plainly about this, and Peter took him aside and began to rebuke him. "Never, Lord!" he said. "This shall never happen to you!" 33 But when Jesus turned and looked at his disciples, he rebuked Peter, "Get behind me, Satan! You are a stumbling block

to me" And he said, "You do not have in mind the things of God, but the things of men." Mark 8:32-33. Matthew 16:22-23.

34 Then he called the crowd to him along with his disciples and said to them all: "If anyone would come after me, he must deny himself and take up his cross daily and follow me. 35 For whoever wants to save his life will lose it, but whoever loses his life for me and for the gospel will find it and save it. 36 What good is it for a man if he gains the whole world, yet lose or forfeit his very self and soul? 37 Or what can a man give in exchange for his soul?

38 If anyone is ashamed of me and my words in this adulterous and sinful generation, the Son of Man will be ashamed of him. For when he, the Son of Man, is going to come in his glory and in the glory of his Father's glory with his holy angels; and then he will reward each person according to what he has done." Mark 8:34-38. Matthew16:24-27. Luke 9:23-26.

1 And he said to them, "I tell you the truth, some who are standing here will not taste death before they see the Son of Man coming in his kingdom with the power of God" Mark 9:1. Matthew16:28. Luke 9:27.

His Transfiguration

1 About six to eight days after Jesus said this; he took with him Peter, James and John the brother of James with him, and led them up onto a high mountain to pray by themselves, where they were all alone. 2 As he was praying there, he was transfigured before them. The appearance of his face changed and shone like the sun, and his clothes became dazzling bright white light as a flash of lightning; whiter than anyone in the world could bleach them. Matthew 17:1-2. Mark 9:2-3. Luke 9:28-29.

30 Just then there appeared before them two men, Moses and Elijah, 31 appeared in glorious splendor, who were talking with Jesus. They spoke about his departure, which he was about to bring to fulfillment at Jerusalem. Luke 9:30-31. Matthew 17:3. Mark 9:4.

32 Peter and his companions were very sleepy, but when they became fully awake, they saw his glory and the two men standing with him. 33a As the men were leaving Jesus, Luke 9:32-33a

33b Peter said to Jesus, "Rabbi, Master, Lord, it is good for us to be here. If you wish, let us put up three shelters-one for you, one for Moses and one for Elijah." (He did not know what he was saying, they were so frightened.) Luke 9:33b. Matthew 17:4. Mark 9:5-6.

5 Then while he was still speaking, a bright cloud appeared and enveloped them, and they were afraid as they entered the cloud. A voice from the cloud said, "This is my Son, whom I have chosen and love; with him I am well pleased. Listen to him!" 6 Suddenly when the disciples heard the voice had spoken, they fell facedown to the ground, terrified. 7 But Jesus came and touched them. "Get up," he said. "Don't be afraid." 8 When they looked up and around, they no longer saw anyone, except Jesus was alone. Matthew 7:5-8. Mark 9:7-8. Luke 9:34-36a

9 As they were coming down the mountain, Jesus gave them instructed orders, "Don't tell anyone what you have seen, until the Son of Man has been raised from the dead." 10 The disciples kept this matter to themselves and told no one at that time what they had seen, discussing what "rising from the dead" meant. Mark 9:9-10. Matthew 17:9. Luke 9:36b.

10 And the disciples asked him, "Why then do the teachers of the law say that Elijah must come first?" 11 Jesus replied, "To be sure, Elijah does comes and will restore all things. Why then is it written that the Son of Man must suffer much and be rejected? 12

But I tell you, Elijah has already come, and they did not recognize him, but have done to him everything they wished, just as it is written about him. In the same way the Son of Man is going to suffer at their hands." 13 Then the disciples understood that he was talking to them about John the Baptist. Matthew 17:10-13. Mark 9:11-13.

His Possible

14 The next day, when they came down from the mountain, to the crowd and other disciples, they saw a large crowd around them and the teachers of the law arguing with them. 15 As soon as the large crowd saw Jesus, they were overwhelmed with wonder and ran to met and greet him. 16 "What are you arguing with them about?" he asked. 17 A man in the crowd approached Jesus and knelt before him; called out and answered, "Lord, have mercy on my son," he said. "Teacher, I brought you my son; I beg you to look at my son, for he is my only child who is possessed by a spirit that has robbed him of speech. He has seizures and is suffering greatly. He often falls into the fire or into the water. 18a Whenever a spirit seizes him, he suddenly screams; it throws him to the ground and into convulsions so that he foams at the mouth. He foams at the mouth, gnashes his teeth and becomes rigid. It scarcely ever leaves him and is destroying him. Mark 9:14-18a. Luke 9:37-39. Matthew 17:14-15.

16 I brought him to your disciples, I asked and begged your disciples to drive out the spirit but they could not heal him." Matthew 17:16. Mark 9:18b. Luke 9:40.

19 "O unbelieving and perverse generation," Jesus replied, "how long shall I stay with you? How long shall I put up with you? Bring the boy, your son here to me." 20 So they brought him. Even while boy was coming, the spirit saw Jesus, the demon immediately

threw the boy into a convulsion. He fell to the ground and rolled around, foaming at the mouth. 21 Jesus asked the boy's father, "How long has he been like this?" "From childhood," he answered. 22 "It has often thrown him into fire or water to kill him. But if you can do anything, take pity on us and help us." 23 "'If you can'?" said Jesus. "Everything is possible for him who believes." 24 Immediately the boy's father exclaimed, "I do believe; help me overcome my unbelief!" 25 When Jesus saw that a crowd was running to the scene, he rebuked the evil demon spirit. "You deaf and mute spirit," he said, "I command you, come out of him and never enter him again." 26 The spirit shrieked, convulsed him violently and came out of the boy. The boy looked so much like a corpse that many said, "He's dead." 27 But Jesus healed the boy from that moment; took him by the hand and lifted him to his feet, and he stood up and gave him back to his father. Mark 9:19-27. Luke 9:41-42. Matthew 17:17-18.

43a And they were all amazed at the greatness of God. While everyone was marveling at all that Jesus did, Luke 9:43a.

19 After Jesus had gone indoors the disciples came to Jesus in private and they asked him privately, "Why couldn't we drive it out?" 20 He replied, "Because you have so little faith. This kind can come out only by prayer. I tell you the truth, if you have faith as small as a mustard seed, you can say to this mountain, 'Move from here to there' and it will move. Nothing will be impossible for you." Matthew 17:19-20. Mark 9:28-29.

5 The apostles said to the Lord, "Increase our faith!" 6 He replied, "If you have faith as small as a mustard seed, you can say to this mulberry tree, 'Be uprooted and planted in the sea,' and it will obey you. Luke 17:5-6.

His Betrayal Warning

30 They left that place and they passed through and came together in Galilee. Jesus did not want anyone to know where they were, 31 because he was teaching his disciples. He said to them, "Listen carefully to what I am about to tell you: The Son of Man is going to be betrayed into the hands of men. They will kill him, and after three days, on the third day, he will be raised to life." Mark 9:30-31. Matthew 17:22-23a. Luke 9:43b-44.

45 But they did not understand what this meant. It was hidden from them, so that they did not grasp it, and they were afraid to ask him about it. And the disciples were filled with grief. Luke 9:45. Mark 9:32. Matthew 17:23b.

His Taxes

24 After Jesus and his disciples arrived in Capernaum, the collectors of the two-drachma tax came to Peter and asked, "Doesn't your teacher pay the temple tax?" 25 "Yes, he does," he replied.

When Peter came into the house, Jesus was the first to speak. "What do you think, Simon?" he asked. "From whom do the kings of the earth collect duty and taxes-from their own sons or from others?" 26 "From others," Peter answered. "Then the sons are exempt," Jesus said to him.

27 "But so that we may not offend them, go to the lake and throw out your line. Take the first fish you catch; open its mouth and

you will find a four-drachma coin. Take it and give it to them for my tax and yours." Matthew 17:24-27.

His Greatest

33 They came to Capernaum. An argument started among the disciples as to which of them would be the greatest. When he was in the house, he asked them, "What were you arguing about on the road?" 34 But they kept quiet because on the way they had argued about who was the greatest. Mark 9:33-34. Luke 9:46.

1 At that time the disciples came to Jesus and asked, "Who is the greatest in the kingdom of heaven?" Matthew 18:1.

35 Sitting down, Jesus called the Twelve and said, "If anyone wants to be first, he must be the very last, and the servant of all." Mark 9:35.

47 Jesus, knowing their thoughts, he called and took a little child and had him stand among them and beside him. Taking him in his arms, he said to them, Luke 9:47. Matthew 18:2. Mark 9:36.

3 And he said: "I tell you the truth, unless you change and become like little children, you will never enter the kingdom of heaven. 4 Therefore, whoever humbles himself like this child is the greatest in the kingdom of heaven. Matthew 18:3-4.

5 Then he said to them, "And whoever welcomes one of these little children like this in my name welcomes me; and whoever welcomes me does not welcome me but the one who sent me. For he who is least among you all-he is the greatest." Matthew 18:5. Mark 9:37. Luke 9:48.

6 But if anyone causes one of these little ones who believe in me to sin, it would be better for him to have a large millstone hung around his neck and to be drowned in the depths of the sea. Matthew 18:6.

His Different Followers

38 "Master and Teacher," said John, "we saw a man driving out demons in your name and we tried and told him to stop, because he was not one of us." Mark 9:38. Luke 9:49.

39 "Do not stop him," Jesus said. "No one who does a miracle in my name can in the next moment say anything bad about me, 40 for whoever is not against us is for us. Mark 9:39-40. Luke 9:50.

41 I tell you the truth; anyone who gives you a cup of water in my name because you belong to Christ will certainly not lose his reward. Mark 9:41.

1 Jesus said to his disciples: "Things that cause people to sin are bound to come, but woe to that person through whom they come. Luke 17:1.

42 "And if anyone causes one of these little ones who believe in me to sin, it would be better for him to be thrown into the sea with a large millstone tied around his neck than for him to cause one of these little ones to sin. So watch yourselves." Mark 9:42. Luke 17:2-3a.

His Focus

7 "Woe to the world because of the things that cause people to sin! Such things must come, but woe to the man through whom they come! Matthew 18:7

8 If your hand or your foot causes you to sin, cut it off and throw it away. It is better for you to enter life maimed or crippled than to have two hands or two feet to go into hell and be thrown into eternal fire, where the fire never goes out. Matthew 18:8. Mark 9:43-46.

47 And if your eye causes you to sin, gouge and pluck it out, and throw it away. It is better for you to enter life, the kingdom of God, with one eye than to have two eyes and be thrown into the fire of hell, Mark 9:47. Matthew 18:9.

48 where "'their worm does not die, and the fire is not quenched.' 49 Everyone will be salted with fire. Mark 9:48-49.

50 "Salt is good, but if it loses its saltiness, how can you make it salty again? It is fit neither for the soil nor for the manure pile; it is thrown out. "He who has ears to hear, let him hear. Have salt in yourselves, and be at peace with each other." Mark 9:50. Luke 14:34-35.

His Lost Sheep

1 Now the tax collectors and "sinners" were all gathering around to hear him. 2 But the Pharisees and the teachers of the law muttered, "This man welcomes sinners and eats with them." Luke 15:1-2.

10 "See that you do not look down on one of these little ones. For I tell you that their angels in heaven always see the face of my Father in heaven. Matthew 18:10.

3 Then Jesus told them this parable: 4 "What do you think? Suppose if one of you owns a hundred sheep, one wanders away and loses one of them. Does he not leave the ninety-nine on the hills in the open country and go to look after the lost sheep that wandered off, until he finds it? 5 If and when he finds it, I tell you the truth, he is happier about the one sheep than about the ninety-nine that didn't wander off; he joyfully puts it on his shoulders 6 and goes home. Then he calls his friends and neighbors together and says, 'Rejoice with me; I have found my lost sheep.' In the same way your Father in heaven is not willing that any of these little ones should be lost. 7 I tell you that in the same way there will be more rejoicing in heaven over one sinner who repents than over ninety-nine righteous persons who do not need to repent. Luke 15:3-7. Matthew 18:12-14.

His Reconciliation

15 "If your brother sins against you, go and show him his fault; just between the two of you, rebuke him and if he listens to you and repents, you have won your brother over, forgive him. If he sins against you seven times in a day, and seven times comes back to you and says, 'I repent,' forgive him.

16 But if he will not listen, take one or two others along, so that 'every matter may be established by the testimony of two or three witnesses.' 17 If he refuses to listen to them, tell it to the church; and if he refuses to listen even to the church, treat him as you would a pagan or a tax collector. Matthew 18:15-17. Luke 17:3b-4.

His Bind on Earth

18 "I tell you the truth, whatever you bind on earth will be bound in heaven, and whatever you loose on earth will be loosed in heaven. Matthew 18:18.

His Presence

19 "Again, I tell you that if two of you on earth agree about anything you ask for, it will be done for you by my Father in heaven. 20 For where two or three come together in my name, there am I with them." Matthew 18:19-20.

His Settlement

21 Then Peter came to Jesus and asked, "Lord, how many times shall I forgive my brother when he sins against me? Up to seven times?" 22 Jesus answered, "I tell you, not seven times, but seventy-seven times.

23 "Therefore, the kingdom of heaven is like a king who wanted to settle accounts with his servants. 24 As he began the settlement, a man who owed him ten thousand talents was brought to him. 25 Since he was not able to pay, the master ordered that he and his wife and his children and all that he had be sold to repay the debt. 26 "The servant fell on his knees before him. 'Be patient with me,' he begged, 'and I will pay back everything.' 27 The servant's master took pity on him, canceled the debt and let him go.

28 "But when that servant went out, he found one of his fellow servants who owed him a hundred denarii. He grabbed him and began to choke him. 'Pay back what you owe me!' he demanded. 29 "His fellow servant fell to his knees and begged him, 'Be patient with me, and I will pay you back.' 30 "But he refused. Instead, he went off and had the man thrown into prison until he could pay the debt.

31 When the other servants saw what had happened, they were greatly distressed and went and told their master everything that had happened. 32 "Then the master called the servant in. 'You wicked servant,' he said, 'I canceled all that debt of yours because you begged me to. 33 Shouldn't you have had mercy on your fellow servant just as I had on you?' 34 In anger his master turned him over to the jailers to be tortured, until he should pay back all he owed.

35 "This is how my heavenly Father will treat each of you unless you forgive your brother from your heart." Matthew 18:21-35.

His Right Time

1 After this, Jesus went around in Galilee, purposely staying away from Judea because the Jews there were waiting to take his life.

2 But when the Jewish Feast of Tabernacles was near, 3 Jesus' brothers said to him, "You ought to leave here and go to Judea, so that your disciples may see the miracles you do. 4 No one who wants to become a public figure acts in secret. Since you are doing these things, show yourself to the world." 5 For even his own brothers did not believe in him.

6 Therefore Jesus told them, "The right time for me has not yet come; for you any time is right.

7 The world cannot hate you, but it hates me because I testify that what it does is evil. 8 You go to the Feast. I am not yet going up to this Feast, because for me the right time has not yet come." 9 Having said this, he stayed in Galilee. John 7:1-9.

His Ministry's Commitment

18 When Jesus saw the crowd around him, he gave orders to cross to the other side of the lake. Matthew 8:18.

19 Then as they were along the road, a teacher of the law came to him and said, "Teacher, I will follow you wherever you go." 20 Jesus replied, "Foxes have holes and birds of the air have nests,

but the Son of Man has no place to lay his head." Matthew 8:19-20. Luke 9:57-58.

59 Jesus said to another man, "Follow me." But the disciple replied, "Lord, first let me go and bury my father." 60 Jesus said to him, "Let the dead bury their own dead, but you go and proclaim the kingdom of God." Luke 9:59-60. Matthew 8:21-22.

61 Still another said, "I will follow you, Lord; but first let me go back and say good-by to my family." 62 Jesus replied, "No one who puts his hand to the plow and looks back is fit for service in the kingdom of God." Luke 9:61-62.

His Preparation

51 As the time approached for him to be taken up to heaven, Jesus resolutely set out for Jerusalem. 52 And he sent messengers on ahead, who went into a Samaritan village to get things ready for him; 53 but the people there did not welcome him, because he was heading for Jerusalem.

54 When the disciples James and John saw this, they asked, "Lord, do you want us to call fire down from heaven to destroy them?" 55 But Jesus turned and rebuked them, 56 and they went to another village. Luke 9:51-56.

His Knowledge

10 However, after his brothers had left for the Feast, he went also, not publicly, but in secret. 11 Now at the Feast the Jews were watching for him and asking, "Where is that man?" 12 Among the

crowds there was widespread whispering about him. Some said, "He is a good man." Others replied, "No, he deceives the people." 13 But no one would say anything publicly about him for fear of the Jews.

14 Not until halfway through the Feast did Jesus go up to the temple courts and begin to teach. 15 The Jews were amazed and asked, "How did this man get such learning without having studied?"

16 Jesus answered, "My teaching is not my own. It comes from him who sent me. 17 If anyone chooses to do God's will, he will find out whether my teaching comes from God or whether I speak on my own. 18 He who speaks on his own does so to gain honor for himself, but he who works for the honor of the one who sent him is a man of truth; there is nothing false about him. 19 Has not Moses given you the law? Yet not one of you keeps the law. Why are you trying to kill me?"

20 "You are demon-possessed," the crowd answered. "Who is trying to kill you?"

21 Jesus said to them, "I did one miracle, and you are all astonished. 22 Yet, because Moses gave you circumcision (though actually it did not come from Moses, but from the patriarchs), you circumcise a child on the Sabbath. 23 Now if a child can be circumcised on the Sabbath so that the law of Moses may not be broken, why are you angry with me for healing the whole man on the Sabbath? 24 Stop judging by mere appearances, and make a right judgment."

25 At that point some of the people of Jerusalem began to ask, "Isn't this the man they are trying to kill? 26 Here he is, speaking publicly, and they are not saying a word to him. Have the authorities really concluded that he is the Christ? 27 But we know where this man is from; when the Christ comes, no one will know where he is from."

28 Then Jesus, still teaching in the temple courts, cried out, "Yes, you know me, and you know where I am from. I am not here on my own, but he who sent me is true. You do not know him, 29 but I know him because I am from him and he sent me."

30 At this they tried to seize him, but no one laid a hand on him, because his time had not yet come. 31 Still, many in the crowd put their faith in him. They said, "When the Christ comes, will he do more miraculous signs than this man?" John 7:10-31.

32 The Pharisees heard the crowd whispering such things about him. Then the chief priests and the Pharisees sent temple guards to arrest him.

33 Jesus said, "I am with you for only a short time, and then I go to the one who sent me. 34 You will look for me, but you will not find me; and where I am, you cannot come."

35 The Jews said to one another, "Where does this man intend to go that we cannot find him? Will he go where our people live scattered among the Greeks, and teach the Greeks? 36 What did he mean when he said, 'You will look for me, but you will not find me,' and 'Where I am, you cannot come'?" John 7:32-36.

37 On the last and greatest day of the Feast, Jesus stood and said in a loud voice, "If anyone is thirsty, let him come to me and drink. 38 Whoever believes in me, as the Scripture has said, streams of living water will flow from within him." 39 By this he meant the Spirit, whom those who believed in him were later to receive. Up to that time the Spirit had not been given, since Jesus had not yet been glorified. 40 On hearing his words, some of the people said, "Surely this man is the Prophet." 41 Others said, "He is the Christ." Still others asked, "How can the Christ come from Galilee? 42 Does not the Scripture say that the Christ will come from David's family and from Bethlehem, the town where David lived?" 43 Thus the people were divided because of Jesus. 44 Some wanted to seize him, but no one laid a hand on him.

45 Finally the temple guards went back to the chief priests and Pharisees, who asked them, "Why didn't you bring him in?" 46 "No one ever spoke the way this man does," the guards declared. 47 "You mean he has deceived you also?" the Pharisees retorted. 48 "Has any of the rulers or of the Pharisees believed in him? 49 No! But this mob that knows nothing of the law-there is a curse on them."

50 Nicodemus, who had gone to Jesus earlier and who was one of their own number, asked, 51 "Does our law condemn anyone without first hearing him to find out what he is doing?"

52 They replied, "Are you from Galilee, too? Look into it, and you will find that a prophet does not come out of Galilee." 53 [The earliest and most reliable manuscripts and other ancient witnesses do not have John 7:53-8:11.] Then each went to his own home. John 7:37-53.

His Protection

1 But Jesus went to the Mount of Olives.

2 At dawn he appeared again in the temple courts, where all the people gathered around him, and he sat down to teach them.

3 The teachers of the law and the Pharisees brought in a woman caught in adultery. They made her stand before the group 4 and said to Jesus, "Teacher, this woman was caught in the act of adultery. 5 In the Law Moses commanded us to stone such women. Now what do you say?" 6a They were using this question as a trap, in order to have a basis for accusing him.

6b But Jesus bent down and started to write on the ground with his finger. 7 When they kept on questioning him, he straightened up and said to them, "If any one of you is without sin, let him be the first to throw a stone at her." 8 Again he stooped down and wrote on the ground.

9 At this, those who heard began to go away one at a time, the older ones first, until only Jesus was left, with the woman still standing there.

10 Jesus straightened up and asked her, "Woman, where are they? Has no one condemned you?" 11 "No one, sir," she said. "Then neither do I condemn you," Jesus declared. "Go now and leave your life of sin." John 8:1-11.

His Father

12 When Jesus spoke again to the people, he said, "I am the light of the world. Whoever follows me will never walk in darkness, but will have the light of life."

13 The Pharisees challenged him, "Here you are, appearing as your own witness; your testimony is not valid."

14 Jesus answered, "Even if I testify on my own behalf, my testimony is valid, for I know where I came from and where I am going. But you have no idea where I come from or where I am going. 15 You judge by human standards; I pass judgment on no one. 16 But if I do judge, my decisions are right, because I am not alone. I stand with the Father, who sent me. 17 In your own Law it is written that the testimony of two men is valid. 18 I am one who testifies for myself; my other witness is the Father, who sent me."

19a Then they asked him, "Where is your father?"

19b "You do not know me or my Father," Jesus replied. "If you knew me, you would know my Father also." 20 He spoke these words while teaching in the temple area near the place where the offerings were put. Yet no one seized him, because his time had not yet come. John 8:12-20.

21 Once more Jesus said to them, "I am going away, and you will look for me, and you will die in your sin. Where I go, you cannot come."

22 This made the Jews ask, "Will he kill himself? Is that why he says, 'Where I go, you cannot come'?"

23 But he continued, "You are from below; I am from above. You are of this world; I am not of this world. 24 I told you that you would die in your sins; if you do not believe that I am [the one I claim to be], you will indeed die in your sins."

25a "Who are you?" they asked.

25b "Just what I have been claiming all along," Jesus replied. 26 "I have much to say in judgment of you. But he who sent me is reliable, and what I have heard from him I tell the world."

27 They did not understand that he was telling them about his Father. 28 So Jesus said, "When you have lifted up the Son of Man, then you will know that I am [the one I claim to be] and that I do nothing on my own but speak just what the Father has taught me. 29 The one who sent me is with me; he has not left me alone, for I always do what pleases him." John 8:21-29.

30 Even as he spoke, many put their faith in him. 31 To the Jews who had believed him, Jesus said, "If you hold to my teaching, you are really my disciples. 32 Then you will know the truth, and the truth will set you free."

33 They answered him, "We are Abraham's descendants and have never been slaves of anyone. How can you say that we shall be set free?"

34 Jesus replied, "I tell you the truth, everyone who sins is a slave to sin. 35 Now a slave has no permanent place in the family, but a son belongs to it forever. 36 So if the Son sets you free, you will be free indeed. 37 I know you are Abraham's descendants. Yet you are ready to kill me, because you have no room for my word. 38 I am telling you what I have seen in the Father's presence, and you do what you have heard from your father."

39a "Abraham is our father," they answered.

39b"If you were Abraham's children," said Jesus, "then you would do the things Abraham did. 40 As it is, you are determined to kill me, a man who has told you the truth that I heard from God. Abraham did not do such things. 41a You are doing the things your own father does."

41b "We are not illegitimate children," they protested. "The only Father we have is God himself."

42 Jesus said to them, "If God were your Father, you would love me, for I came from God and now am here. I have not come on my own; but he sent me. 43 Why is my language not clear to you? Because you are unable to hear what I say. 44 You belong to your father, the devil, and you want to carry out your father's desire. He was a murderer from the beginning, not holding to the truth, for there is no truth in him. When he lies, he speaks his native language, for he is a liar and the father of lies. 45 Yet because I tell the truth, you do not believe me! 46 Can any of you prove me guilty of sin? If I am telling the truth, why don't you believe me? 47 He who belongs to God hears what God says. The reason you do not hear is that you do not belong to God." John 8:30-47.

48 The Jews answered him, "Aren't we right in saying that you are a Samaritan and demon-possessed?"

49 "I am not possessed by a demon," said Jesus, "but I honor my Father and you dishonor me. 50 I am not seeking glory for myself; but there is one who seeks it, and he is the judge. 51 I tell you the truth, if anyone keeps my word, he will never see death."

52 At this the Jews exclaimed, "Now we know that you are demon-possessed! Abraham died and so did the prophets, yet you say that if anyone keeps your word, he will never taste death. 53 Are you greater than our father Abraham? He died, and so did the prophets. Who do you think you are?"

54 Jesus replied, "If I glorify myself, my glory means nothing. My Father, whom you claim as your God, is the one who glorifies me. 55 Though you do not know him, I know him. If I said I did not, I would be a liar like you, but I do know him and keep his word. 56 Your father Abraham rejoiced at the thought of seeing my day; he saw it and was glad."

57 "You are not yet fifty years old," the Jews said to him, "and you have seen Abraham!"

58 "I tell you the truth," Jesus answered, "before Abraham was born, I am!" 59 At this, they picked up stones to stone him, but Jesus hid himself, slipping away from the temple grounds John 8:48-59.

His Seventy Two

1 After this the Lord appointed seventy-two others and sent them two by two ahead of him to every town and place where he was about to go.

2 He told them, "The harvest is plentiful, but the workers are few. Ask the Lord of the harvest, therefore, to send out workers into his harvest field. 3 Go! I am sending you out like lambs among wolves. 4 Do not take a purse or bag or sandals; and do not greet anyone on the road. 5 "When you enter a house, first say, 'Peace to this house.' 6 If a man of peace is there, your peace will rest on him; if not, it will return to you. 7 Stay in that house, eating and drinking whatever they give you, for the worker deserves his wages. Do not move around from house to house.

8 "When you enter a town and are welcomed, eat what is set before you. 9 Heal the sick who are there and tell them, 'The kingdom of God is near you.'

10 But when you enter a town and are not welcomed, go into its streets and say, 11' Even the dust of your town that sticks to our feet we wipe off against you. Yet be sure of this: The kingdom of God is near.' 12 I tell you, it will be more bearable on that day for Sodom than for that town.

13 "Woe to you, Korazin! Woe to you, Bethsaida! For if the miracles that were performed in you had been performed in Tyre and Sidon, they would have repented long ago, sitting in sackcloth and ashes. 14 But it will be more bearable for Tyre and Sidon at the judgment than for you.

15 And you, Capernaum, will you be lifted up to the skies? No, you will go down to the depths. 16 "He who listens to you listens to me; he who rejects you rejects me; but he who rejects me rejects him who sent me." Luke 10:1-16.

17 The seventy-two returned with joy and said, "Lord, even the demons submit to us in your name."

18 He replied, "I saw Satan fall like lightning from heaven. 19 I have given you authority to trample on snakes and scorpions and to overcome all the power of the enemy; nothing will harm

you. 20 However, do not rejoice that the spirits submit to you, but rejoice that your names are written in heaven."

21 At that time Jesus, full of joy through the Holy Spirit, said, "I praise you, Father, Lord of heaven and earth, because you have hidden these things from the wise and learned, and revealed them to little children. Yes, Father, for this was your good pleasure.

22 "All things have been committed to me by my Father. No one knows who the Son is except the Father, and no one knows who the Father is except the Son and those to whom the Son chooses to reveal him."

23 Then he turned to his disciples and said privately, "Blessed are the eyes that see what you see. 24 For I tell you that many prophets and kings wanted to see what you see but did not see it, and to hear what you hear but did not hear it." Luke 10:17-24.

His Samaritan

25 On one occasion an expert in the law stood up to test Jesus. "Teacher," he asked, "what must I do to inherit eternal life?"

26 "What is written in the Law?" he replied. "How do you read it?"

27 He answered: "'Love the Lord your God with all your heart and with all your soul and with all your strength and with all your mind'; and, 'Love your neighbor as yourself.'"

28 "You have answered correctly," Jesus replied. "Do this and you will live."

29 But he wanted to justify himself, so he asked Jesus, "And who is my neighbor?" 30 In reply Jesus said: "A man was going down from Jerusalem to Jericho, when he fell into the hands of robbers. They stripped him of his clothes, beat him and went away, leaving him half dead.

31 A priest happened to be going down the same road, and when he saw the man, he passed by on the other side. 32 So too, a Levite, when he came to the place and saw him, passed by on the other side.

33 But a Samaritan, as he traveled, came where the man was; and when he saw him, he took pity on him. 34 He went to him and bandaged his wounds, pouring on oil and wine. Then he put the man on his own donkey, took him to an inn and took care of him.

35 The next day he took out two silver coins and gave them to the innkeeper. 'Look after him,' he said, 'and when I return, I will reimburse you for any extra expense you may have.'

36 "Which of these three do you think was a neighbor to the man who fell into the hands of robbers?"

37 The expert in the law replied, "The one who had mercy on him."
Jesus told him, "Go and do likewise." Luke 10:25-37.

His Priorities

38 As Jesus and his disciples were on their way, he came to a village where a woman named Martha opened her home to him. 39 She had a sister called Mary, who sat at the Lord's feet listening to what he said.

40 But Martha was distracted by all the preparations that had to be made. She came to him and asked, "Lord, don't you care that my sister has left me to do the work by myself? Tell her to help me!"

41 "Martha, Martha," the Lord answered, "you are worried and upset about many things, 42 but only one thing is needed. Mary has chosen what is better, and it will not be taken away from her." Luke 10:38-42.

His Rich

13 Someone in the crowd said to him, "Teacher, tell my brother to divide the inheritance with me." 14 Jesus replied, "Man, who appointed me a judge or an arbiter between you?"

15 Then he said to them, "Watch out! Be on your guard against all kinds of greed; a man's life does not consist in the abundance of his possessions." 16 And he told them this parable: "The ground of a certain rich man produced a good crop. 17 He thought to himself, 'What shall I do? I have no place to store my crops.' 18 "Then he said, 'This is what I'll do. I will tear down my barns and build bigger ones, and there I will store all my grain and my goods. 19 And I'll say to myself, "You have plenty of good things laid up for many years. Take life easy; eat, drink and be merry." 20 "But God said to him, 'You fool! This very night your life will be demanded from you. Then who will get what you have prepared for yourself?' 21 "This is how it will be with anyone who stores up things for himself but is not rich toward God." Luke 12:13-21.

His Fire

49 "I have come to bring fire on the earth, and how I wish it were already kindled!

50 But I have a baptism to undergo, and how distressed I am until it is completed! 51 Do you think I came to bring peace on earth? No, I tell you, but division. 52 From now on there will be five in one family divided against each other, three against two and two against three. 53 They will be divided, father against son and son against father, mother against daughter and daughter against mother, mother-in-law against daughter-in-law and daughter-in-law against mother-in-law." Luke 12:49-53.

His Galileans

1 Now there were some present at that time who told Jesus about the Galileans whose blood Pilate had mixed with their sacrifices.

2 Jesus answered, "Do you think that these Galileans were worse sinners than all the other Galileans because they suffered this way? 3 I tell you, no! But unless you repent, you too will all perish. 4 Or those eighteen who died when the tower in Siloam fell on them-do you think they were more guilty than all the others living in Jerusalem? 5 I tell you, no! But unless you repent, you too will all perish." Luke 13:1-5.

His Fruitless Tree

6 Then he told this parable: "A man had a fig tree, planted in his vineyard, and he went to look for fruit on it, but did not find any. 7 So he said to the man who took care of the vineyard, 'For three years now I've been coming to look for fruit on this fig tree and haven't found any. Cut it down! Why should it use up the soil?'

8 "'Sir,' the man replied, 'leave it alone for one more year, and I'll dig around it and fertilize it. 9 If it bears fruit next year, fine! If not, then cut it down.'" Luke 13:6-9.

His Cripple Woman

10 On a Sabbath Jesus was teaching in one of the synagogues, 11 and a woman was there who had been crippled by a spirit for eighteen years. She was bent over and could not straighten up at all.

12 When Jesus saw her, he called her forward and said to her, "Woman, you are set free from your infirmity." 13 Then he put his hands on her, and immediately she straightened up and praised God.

14 Indignant because Jesus had healed on the Sabbath, the synagogue ruler said to the people, "There are six days for work. So come and be healed on those days, not on the Sabbath."

15 The Lord answered him, "You hypocrites! Doesn't each of you on the Sabbath untie his ox or donkey from the stall and lead it

out to give it water? 16 Then should not this woman, a daughter of Abraham, whom Satan has kept bound for eighteen long years, be set free on the Sabbath day from what bound her?"

17 When he said this, all his opponents were humiliated, but the people were delighted with all the wonderful things he was doing. Luke 13:10-17.

His Ministry's Test

1 As he went along, he saw a man blind from birth. 2 His disciples asked him, "Rabbi, who sinned, this man or his parents, that he was born blind?"

3 "Neither this man nor his parents sinned," said Jesus, "but this happened so that the work of God might be displayed in his life. 4 As long as it is day, we must do the work of him who sent me. Night is coming, when no one can work. 5 While I am in the world, I am the light of the world." 6 Having said this, he spit on the ground, made some mud with the saliva, and put it on the man's eyes. 7 "Go," he told him, "wash in the Pool of Siloam" (this word means Sent). So the man went and washed, and came home seeing.

8 His neighbors and those who had formerly seen him begging asked, "Isn't this the same man who used to sit and beg?" 9 Some claimed that he was. Others said, "No, he only looks like him." But he himself insisted, "I am the man." 10 "How then were your eyes opened?" they demanded. 11 He replied, "The man they call Jesus made some mud and put it on my eyes. He told me to go to Siloam and wash. So I went and washed, and then I could see." 12 "Where is this man?" they asked him. "I don't know," he said. John 9:1-12.

13 They brought to the Pharisees the man who had been blind. 14 Now the day on which Jesus had made the mud and opened the man's eyes was a Sabbath. 15 Therefore the Pharisees also asked him how he had received his sight. "He put mud on my eyes," the man replied, "and I washed, and now I see."

16 Some of the Pharisees said, "This man is not from God, for he does not keep the Sabbath." But others asked, "How can a sinner do such miraculous signs?" So they were divided. 17 Finally they turned again to the blind man, "What have you to say about him? It was your eyes he opened." The man replied, "He is a prophet."

18 The Jews still did not believe that he had been blind and had received his sight until they sent for the man's parents. 19 "Is this your son?" they asked. "Is this the one you say was born blind? How is it that now he can see?"

20 "We know he is our son," the parents answered, "and we know he was born blind. 21 But how he can see now, or who opened his eyes, we don't know. Ask him. He is of age; he will speak for himself." 22 His parents said this because they were afraid of the Jews, for already the Jews had decided that anyone who acknowledged that Jesus was the Christ would be put out of the synagogue. 23 That was why his parents said, "He is of age; ask him."

24 A second time they summoned the man who had been blind. "Give glory to God," they said. "We know this man is a sinner." 25 He replied, "Whether he is a sinner or not, I don't know. One thing I do know. I was blind but now I see!"

26 Then they asked him, "What did he do to you? How did he open your eyes?"

27 He answered, "I have told you already and you did not listen. Why do you want to hear it again? Do you want to become his disciples, too?"

28 Then they hurled insults at him and said, "You are this fellow's disciple! We are disciples of Moses! 29 We know that God spoke to Moses, but as for this fellow, we don't even know where he comes from."

30 The man answered, "Now that is remarkable! You don't know where he comes from, yet he opened my eyes. 31 We know that God does not listen to sinners. He listens to the godly man who does his will. 32 Nobody has ever heard of opening the eyes of a man born blind. 33 If this man were not from God, he could do nothing."

34 To this they replied, "You were steeped in sin at birth; how dare you lecture us!" And they threw him out. John 9:13-34.

35 Jesus heard that they had thrown him out, and when he found him, he said, "Do you believe in the Son of Man?"

36 "Who is he, sir?" the man asked. "Tell me so that I may believe in him."

37 Jesus said, "You have now seen him; in fact, he is the one speaking with you." 38 Then the man said, "Lord, I believe," and he worshiped him. 39 Jesus said, "For judgment I have come into this world, so that the blind will see and those who see will become blind."

40 Some Pharisees who were with him heard him say this and asked, "What? Are we blind too?" 41 Jesus said, "If you were blind, you would not be guilty of sin; but now that you claim you can see, your guilt remains. John 9:35-41.

His Sheep

1 "I tell you the truth, the man who does not enter the sheep pen by the gate, but climbs in by some other way, is a thief and a robber. 2 The man who enters by the gate is the shepherd of his sheep. 3 The watchman opens the gate for him, and the sheep listen to his voice. He calls his own sheep by name and leads them out. 4 When he has brought out all his own, he goes on ahead of them, and his sheep follow him because they know his voice. 5 But they will never follow a stranger; in fact, they will run away from him because they do not recognize a stranger's voice."

6 Jesus used this figure of speech, but they did not understand what he was telling them.

7 Therefore Jesus said again, "I tell you the truth, I am the gate for the sheep. 8 All who ever came before me were thieves and robbers, but the sheep did not listen to them. 9 I am the gate; whoever enters through me will be saved. He will come in and go out, and find pasture. 10 The thief comes only to steal and kill and destroy; I have come that they may have life, and have it to the full.

11 "I am the good shepherd. The good shepherd lays down his life for the sheep. 12 The hired hand is not the shepherd who owns the sheep. So when he sees the wolf coming, he abandons the sheep and runs away. Then the wolf attacks the flock and scatters it. 13 The man runs away because he is a hired hand and cares nothing for the sheep.

14 "I am the good shepherd; I know my sheep and my sheep know me- 15 just as the Father knows me and I know the Father- and I lay down my life for the sheep.

16 I have other sheep that are not of this sheep pen. I must bring them also. They too will listen to my voice, and there shall be one flock and one shepherd.

17 The reason my Father loves me is that I lay down my life-only to take it up again. 18 No one takes it from me, but I lay it down of my own accord. I have authority to lay it down and authority to take it up again. This command I received from my Father."

19 At these words the Jews were again divided. 20 Many of them said, "He is demon-possessed and raving mad. Why listen to him?"

21 But others said, "These are not the sayings of a man possessed by a demon. Can a demon open the eyes of the blind?" John 10:1- 21.

His Solomon's Colonnade

22 Then came the Feast of Dedication at Jerusalem. It was winter, 23 and Jesus was in the temple area walking in Solomon's Colonnade. 24 The Jews gathered around him, saying, "How long will you keep us in suspense? If you are the Christ, tell us plainly."

25 Jesus answered, "I did tell you, but you do not believe. The miracles I do in my Father's name speak for me, 26 but you do not believe because you are not my sheep. 27 My sheep listen to my voice; I know them, and they follow me. 28 I give them eternal life, and they shall never perish; no one can snatch them out of

my hand. 29 My Father, who has given them to me, is greater than all; no one can snatch them out of my Father's hand. 30 I and the Father are one."

31 Again the Jews picked up stones to stone him, 32 but Jesus said to them, "I have shown you many great miracles from the Father. For which of these do you stone me?"

33 "We are not stoning you for any of these," replied the Jews, "but for blasphemy, because you, a mere man, claim to be God."

34 Jesus answered them, "Is it not written in your Law, 'I have said you are gods'? 35 If he called them 'gods,' to whom the word of God came-and the Scripture cannot be broken- 36 what about the one whom the Father set apart as his very own and sent into the world? Why then do you accuse me of blasphemy because I said, 'I am God's Son'? 37 Do not believe me unless I do what my Father does. 38 But if I do it, even though you do not believe me, believe the miracles, that you may know and understand that the Father is in me, and I in the Father."

39 Again they tried to seize him, but he escaped their grasp.

40 Then Jesus went back across the Jordan to the place where John had been baptizing in the early days. Here he stayed 41 and many people came to him. They said, "Though John never performed a miraculous sign, all that John said about this man was true." 42 And in that place many believed in Jesus. John 10:22-42.

His Last

22 Then Jesus went through the towns and villages, teaching as he made his way to Jerusalem.

23 Someone asked him, "Lord, are only a few people going to be saved?" He said to them, 24 "Make every effort to enter through the narrow door, because many, I tell you, will try to enter and will not be able to.

25 Once the owner of the house gets up and closes the door, you will stand outside knocking and pleading, 'Sir, open the door for us.' "But he will answer, 'I don't know you or where you come from.'

26 "Then you will say, 'We ate and drank with you, and you taught in our streets.'

27 "But he will reply, 'I don't know you or where you come from. Away from me, all you evildoers!'

28 "There will be weeping there, and gnashing of teeth, when you see Abraham, Isaac and Jacob and all the prophets in the kingdom of God, but you yourselves thrown out.

29 People will come from east and west and north and south, and will take their places at the feast in the kingdom of God. 30 Indeed there are those who are last who will be first, and first who will be last." Luke 13:22-30.

His Ox that Falls

1 One Sabbath, when Jesus went to eat in the house of a prominent Pharisee, he was being carefully watched. 2 There in front of him was a man suffering from dropsy. 3 Jesus asked the Pharisees and experts in the law, "Is it lawful to heal on the Sabbath or not?" 4 But they remained silent. So taking hold of the man, he healed him and sent him away.

5 Then he asked them, "If one of you has a son or an ox that falls into a well on the Sabbath day, will you not immediately pull him out?" 6 And they had nothing to say. Luke 14:1-6.

His Lowest Place

7 When he noticed how the guests picked the places of honor at the table, he told them this parable:

8 "When someone invites you to a wedding feast, do not take the place of honor, for a person more distinguished than you may have been invited. 9 If so, the host who invited both of you will come and say to you, 'Give this man your seat.' Then, humiliated, you will have to take the least important place. 10 But when you are invited, take the lowest place, so that when your host comes, he will say to you, 'Friend, move up to a better place.' Then you will be honored in the presence of all your fellow guests. 11 For everyone who exalts himself will be humbled, and he who humbles himself will be exalted." Luke 14:7-11.

His Host

12 Then Jesus said to his host, "When you give a luncheon or dinner, do not invite your friends, your brothers or relatives, or your rich neighbors; if you do, they may invite you back and so you will be repaid.

13 But when you give a banquet, invite the poor, the crippled, the lame, the blind, 14 and you will be blessed. Although they cannot repay you, you will be repaid at the resurrection of the righteous." Luke 14:12-14.

His Great Banquet

15 When one of those at the table with him heard this, he said to Jesus, "Blessed is the man who will eat at the feast in the kingdom of God."

16 Jesus replied: "A certain man was preparing a great banquet and invited many guests. 17 At the time of the banquet he sent his servant to tell those who had been invited, 'Come, for everything is now ready.'

18 "But they all alike began to make excuses. The first said, 'I have just bought a field, and I must go and see it. Please excuse me.' 19 "Another said, 'I have just bought five yoke of oxen, and I'm on my way to try them out. Please excuse me.' 20 "Still another said, 'I just got married, so I can't come.'

21 "The servant came back and reported this to his master. Then the owner of the house became angry and ordered his servant, 'Go out quickly into the streets and alleys of the town and bring in the poor, the crippled, the blind and the lame.' 22 "'Sir,' the servant said, 'what you ordered has been done, but there is still room.'

23 "Then the master told his servant, 'Go out to the roads and country lanes and make them come in, so that my house will be full. 24 I tell you, not one of those men who were invited will get a taste of my banquet.'" Luke 14:15-24.

His Cross

25 Large crowds were traveling with Jesus, and turning to them he said: 26 "If anyone comes to me and does not hate his father and mother, his wife and children, his brothers and sisters-yes, even his own life-he cannot be my disciple. 27 And anyone who does not carry his cross and follow me cannot be my disciple. Luke 14:25-27.

His Cost

28 "Suppose one of you wants to build a tower. Will he not first sit down and estimate the cost to see if he has enough money to complete it? 29 For if he lays the foundation and is not able to finish it, everyone who sees it will ridicule him, 30 saying, 'This fellow began to build and was not able to finish.'

31 "Or suppose a king is about to go to war against another king. Will he not first sit down and consider whether he is able with ten thousand men to oppose the one coming against him with twenty thousand? 32 If he is not able, he will send a delegation while the other is still a long way off and will ask for terms of peace. 33 In the same way, any of you who does not give up everything he has cannot be my disciple. Luke 14:28-33.

His Lost Coin

8 "Or suppose a woman has ten silver coins and loses one. Does she not light a lamp, sweep the house and search carefully until she finds it? 9 And when she finds it, she calls her friends and neighbors together and says, 'Rejoice with me; I have found my lost coin.' 10 In the same way, I tell you, there is rejoicing in the presence of the angels of God over one sinner who repents." Luke 15:8-10.

His Lost Son

11 Jesus continued: "There was a man who had two sons.

12 The younger one said to his father, 'Father, give me my share of the estate.' So he divided his property between them.

13 "Not long after that, the younger son got together all he had, set off for a distant country and there squandered his wealth in wild living. 14 After he had spent everything, there was a severe famine in that whole country, and he began to be in need. 15 So he went and hired himself out to a citizen of that country, who sent him to his fields to feed pigs.

16 He longed to fill his stomach with the pods that the pigs were eating, but no one gave him anything.

17 "When he came to his senses, he said, 'How many of my father's hired men have food to spare, and here I am starving to death! 18 I will set out and go back to my father and say to him:

Father, I have sinned against heaven and against you. 19 I am no longer worthy to be called your son; make me like one of your hired men.' 20a So he got up and went to his father.

20b "But while he was still a long way off, his father saw him and was filled with compassion for him; he ran to his son, threw his arms around him and kissed him.

21 "The son said to him, 'Father, I have sinned against heaven and against you. I am no longer worthy to be called your son.'

22 "But the father said to his servants, 'Quick! Bring the best robe and put it on him. Put a ring on his finger and sandals on his feet. 23 Bring the fattened calf and kill it. Let's have a feast and celebrate. 24 For this son of mine was dead and is alive again; he was lost and is found.' So they began to celebrate.

25 "Meanwhile, the older son was in the field. When he came near the house, he heard music and dancing. 26 So he called one of the servants and asked him what was going on. 27 'Your brother has come,' he replied, 'and your father has killed the fattened calf because he has him back safe and sound.'

28 "The older brother became angry and refused to go in. So his father went out and pleaded with him. 29 But he answered his father, 'Look! All these years I've been slaving for you and never disobeyed your orders. Yet you never gave me even a young goat so I could celebrate with my friends. 30 But when this son of yours who has squandered your property with prostitutes comes home, you kill the fattened calf for him!'

31 "'My son,' the father said, 'you are always with me, and everything I have is yours. 32 But we had to celebrate and be glad, because this brother of yours was dead and is alive again; he was lost and is found.'" Luke 15:11-32.

His Shrewd

1 Jesus told his disciples: "There was a rich man whose manager was accused of wasting his possessions. 2 So he called him in and asked him, 'What is this I hear about you? Give an account of your management, because you cannot be manager any longer.'

3 "The manager said to himself, 'What shall I do now? My master is taking away my job. I'm not strong enough to dig, and I'm ashamed to beg- 4 I know what I'll do so that, when I lose my job here, people will welcome me into their houses.'

5 "So he called in each one of his master's debtors. He asked the first, 'How much do you owe my master?' 6 "'Eight hundred gallons of olive oil,' he replied. "The manager told him, 'Take your bill, sit down quickly, and make it four hundred.' 7 "Then he asked the second, 'And how much do you owe?' "'A thousand bushels of wheat,' he replied. "He told him, 'Take your bill and make it eight hundred.'

8a "The master commended the dishonest manager because he had acted shrewdly.

8b For the people of this world are more shrewd in dealing with their own kind than are the people of the light. 9 I tell you, use worldly wealth to gain friends for yourselves, so that when it is gone, you will be welcomed into eternal dwellings. Luke 16:1-9.

His Trust

10 "Whoever can be trusted with very little can also be trusted with much, and whoever is dishonest with very little will also be dishonest with much. 11 So if you have not been trustworthy in handling worldly wealth, who will trust you with true riches? 12 And if you have not been trustworthy with someone else's property, who will give you property of your own?

13 "No servant can serve two masters. Either he will hate the one and love the other, or he will be devoted to the one and despise the other. You cannot serve both God and Money."

14 The Pharisees, who loved money, heard all this and were sneering at Jesus. 15 He said to them, "You are the ones who justify yourselves in the eyes of men, but God knows your hearts. What is highly valued among men is detestable in God's sight.

16 "The Law and the Prophets were proclaimed until John. Since that time, the good news of the kingdom of God is being preached, and everyone is forcing his way into it. 17 It is easier for heaven and earth to disappear than for the least stroke of a pen to drop out of the Law. Luke 16:10-17.

His Beggar

19 "There was a rich man who was dressed in purple and fine linen and lived in luxury every day.

20 At his gate was laid a beggar named Lazarus, covered with sores 21 and longing to eat what fell from the rich man's table. Even the dogs came and licked his sores.

22 "The time came when the beggar died and the angels carried him to Abraham's side. The rich man also died and was buried.

23 In hell, where he was in torment, he looked up and saw Abraham far away, with Lazarus by his side. 24 So he called to him, 'Father Abraham, have pity on me and send Lazarus to dip the tip of his finger in water and cool my tongue, because I am in agony in this fire.'

25 "But Abraham replied, 'Son, remember that in your lifetime you received your good things, while Lazarus received bad things, but now he is comforted here and you are in agony. 26 And besides all this, between us and you a great chasm has been fixed, so that those who want to go from here to you cannot, nor can anyone cross over from there to us.'

27 "He answered, 'Then I beg you, father, send Lazarus to my father's house, 28 for I have five brothers. Let him warn them, so that they will not also come to this place of torment.'

29 "Abraham replied, 'They have Moses and the Prophets; let them listen to them.' 30 "'No, father Abraham,' he said, 'but if someone from the dead goes to them, they will repent.'

31 "He said to him, 'If they do not listen to Moses and the Prophets, they will not be convinced even if someone rises from the dead.'" Luke 16:19-31.

His Duty

7 "Suppose one of you had a servant plowing or looking after the sheep. Would he say to the servant when he comes in from the field, 'Come along now and sit down to eat'? 8 Would he not rather say, 'Prepare my supper, get yourself ready and wait on me while I eat and drink; after that you may eat and drink'? 9 Would he thank the servant because he did what he was told to do? 10 So you also, when you have done everything you were told to do, should say, 'We are unworthy servants; we have only done our duty.'" Luke 17:7-10.

His Lazarus

1 Now a man named Lazarus was sick. He was from Bethany, the village of Mary and her sister Martha.

2 This Mary, whose brother Lazarus now lay sick, was the same one who poured perfume on the Lord and wiped his feet with her hair. 3 So the sisters sent word to Jesus, "Lord, the one you love is sick."

4 When he heard this, Jesus said, "This sickness will not end in death. No, it is for God's glory so that God's Son may be glorified through it." 5 Jesus loved Martha and her sister and Lazarus. 6 Yet when he heard that Lazarus was sick, he stayed where he was two more days.

7 Then he said to his disciples, "Let us go back to Judea."

8 "But Rabbi," they said, "a short while ago the Jews tried to stone you, and yet you are going back there?"

9 Jesus answered, "Are there not twelve hours of daylight? A man who walks by day will not stumble, for he sees by this world's light. 10 It is when he walks by night that he stumbles, for he has no light." 11 After he had said this, he went on to tell them, "Our friend Lazarus has fallen asleep; but I am going there to wake him up." 12 His disciples replied, "Lord, if he sleeps, he will get better." 13 Jesus had been speaking of his death, but his disciples thought he meant natural sleep.

14 So then he told them plainly, "Lazarus is dead, 15 and for your sake I am glad I was not there, so that you may believe. But let us go to him."

16 Then Thomas (called Didymus) said to the rest of the disciples, "Let us also go, that we may die with him." John 11:1-16.

17 On his arrival, Jesus found that Lazarus had already been in the tomb for four days.

18 Bethany was less than two miles from Jerusalem, 19 and many Jews had come to Martha and Mary to comfort them in the loss of their brother. 20 When Martha heard that Jesus was coming, she went out to meet him, but Mary stayed at home. 21 "Lord," Martha said to Jesus, "if you had been here, my brother would not have died. 22 But I know that even now God will give you whatever you ask."

23 Jesus said to her, "Your brother will rise again."

24 Martha answered, "I know he will rise again in the resurrection at the last day."

25 Jesus said to her, "I am the resurrection and the life. He who believes in me will live, even though he dies; 26 and whoever lives and believes in me will never die. Do you believe this?"

27 "Yes, Lord," she told him, "I believe that you are the Christ, the Son of God, who was to come into the world."

28 And after she had said this, she went back and called her sister Mary aside. "The Teacher is here," she said, "and is asking for you."

29 When Mary heard this, she got up quickly and went to him. 30 Now Jesus had not yet entered the village, but was still at the place where Martha had met him.

31 When the Jews who had been with Mary in the house, comforting her, noticed how quickly she got up and went out, they followed her, supposing she was going to the tomb to mourn there.

32 When Mary reached the place where Jesus was and saw him, she fell at his feet and said, "Lord, if you had been here, my brother would not have died."

33 When Jesus saw her weeping, and the Jews who had come along with her also weeping, he was deeply moved in spirit and troubled. 34 "Where have you laid him?" he asked. "Come and see, Lord," they replied. 35 Jesus wept.

36 Then the Jews said, "See how he loved him!" John 11:17-36.

37 But some of them said, "Could not he who opened the eyes of the blind man have kept this man from dying?"

38a Jesus, once more deeply moved, came to the tomb. It was a cave with a stone laid across the entrance. 39 "Take away the stone," he said.

38b "But, Lord," said Martha, the sister of the dead man, "by this time there is a bad odor, for he has been there four days."

40 Then Jesus said, "Did I not tell you that if you believed, you would see the glory of God?" 41 So they took away the stone. Then Jesus looked up and said, "Father, I thank you that you have heard me. 42 I knew that you always hear me, but I said this for the benefit of the people standing here, that they may believe that you sent me." 43 When he had said this, Jesus called in a loud voice, "Lazarus, come out!" 44 The dead man came out, his hands and feet wrapped with strips of linen, and a cloth around his face. Jesus said to them, "Take off the grave clothes and let him go." John 11:37-44.

45 Therefore many of the Jews who had come to visit Mary, and had seen what Jesus did put their faith in him. John 11:45.

His Plotters

46 But some of them went to the Pharisees and told them what Jesus had done. 47 Then the chief priests and the Pharisees called a meeting of the Sanhedrin. "What are we accomplishing?" they asked. "Here is this man performing many miraculous signs. 48 If we let him go on like this, everyone will believe in him, and then the Romans will come and take away both our place and our nation." 49 Then one of them, named Caiaphas, who was high priest that year, spoke up, "You know nothing at all! 50 You do not realize that it is better for you that one man die for the people than that the whole nation perish." 51 He did not say this on his own, but as high priest that year he prophesied that Jesus would die for the Jewish nation, 52 and not only for that nation but also for the scattered children of God, to bring them together and make them one. 53 So from that day on they plotted to take his life.

54 Therefore Jesus no longer moved about publicly among the Jews. Instead he withdrew to a region near the desert, to a village called Ephraim, where he stayed with his disciples.

55 When it was almost time for the Jewish Passover, many went up from the country to Jerusalem for their ceremonial cleansing before the Passover. 56 They kept looking for Jesus, and as they stood in the temple area they asked one another, "What do you think? Isn't he coming to the Feast at all?"

57 But the chief priests and Pharisees had given orders that if anyone found out where Jesus was, he should report it so that they might arrest him. John 11:46-57.

His Leopard

11 Now on his way to Jerusalem, Jesus traveled along the border between Samaria and Galilee. 12 As he was going into a village, ten men who had leprosy met him. They stood at a distance 13 and called out in a loud voice, "Jesus, Master, have pity on us!" 14 When he saw them, he said, "Go, show yourselves to the priests." And as they went, they were cleansed.

15 One of them, when he saw he was healed, came back, praising God in a loud voice. 16 He threw himself at Jesus' feet and thanked him-and he was a Samaritan.

17 Jesus asked, "Were not all ten cleansed? Where are the other nine? 18 Was no one found to return and give praise to God except this foreigner?" 19 Then he said to him, "Rise and go; your faith has made you well." Luke 17:11-19.

His Kingdom of God

20 Once, having been asked by the Pharisees when the kingdom of God would come, Jesus replied, "The kingdom of God does not come with your careful observation, 21 nor will people say, 'Here it is,' or 'There it is,' because the kingdom of God is within you."

22 Then he said to his disciples, "The time is coming when you will long to see one of the days of the Son of Man, but you will not see it. 23 Men will tell you, 'There he is!' or 'Here he is!' Do not go running off after them. 24 For the Son of Man in his day will be like the lightning, which flashes and lights up the sky from one end to the other. 25 But first he must suffer many things and be rejected by this generation. Luke 17:20-25.

His Widow

1 Then Jesus told his disciples a parable to show them that they should always pray and not give up. 2 He said: "In a certain town there was a judge who neither feared God nor cared about men. 3 And there was a widow in that town who kept coming to him with the plea, 'Grant me justice against my adversary.'

4 "For some time he refused. But finally he said to himself, 'Even though I don't fear God or care about men, 5 yet because this widow keeps bothering me, I will see that she gets justice, so that she won't eventually wear me out with her coming!'"

6 And the Lord said, "Listen to what the unjust judge says. 7 And will not God bring about justice for his chosen ones, who cry out

to him day and night? Will he keep putting them off? 8a I tell you, he will see that they get justice, and quickly.

8b However, when the Son of Man comes, will he find faith on the earth?" Luke 18:1-8.

His Humbled

9 To some who were confident of their own righteousness and looked down on everybody else, Jesus told this parable:

10 "Two men went up to the temple to pray, one a Pharisee and the other a tax collector.

11 The Pharisee stood up and prayed about himself: 'God, I thank you that I am not like other men-robbers, evildoers, adulterers-or even like this tax collector. 12 I fast twice a week and give a tenth of all I get.'

13 "But the tax collector stood at a distance. He would not even look up to heaven, but beat his breast and said, 'God, have mercy on me, a sinner.'

14 "I tell you that this man, rather than the other, went home justified before God. For everyone who exalts himself will be humbled, and he who humbles himself will be exalted." Luke 18:9-14.

His Marriage

1 When Jesus had finished saying these things, he then left Galilee and went into the region of Judea to across the other side of the Jordan. 2 Again large crowds of people came and followed him there, and as his custom, he healed and taught them. Matthew 19:1-2. Mark 10:1.

3 Some Pharisees came to him to test him. They asked, "Is it lawful for a man to divorce his wife for any and every reason?" Matthew 19:3. Mark 10:2.

3 "What did Moses command you?" he replied. Mark 10:3.

4 "Haven't you read," he replied, "that at the beginning the Creator 'made them male and female,' 5 and said, 'For this reason a man will leave his father and mother and be united to his wife, and the two will become one flesh'? 6 So they are no longer two, but one. Therefore what God has joined together, let man not separate." Matthew 19:4-6.

7 "Why then," they asked, "did Moses' command permitted a man to write and give his wife a certificate of divorce and send her away?" Matthew 19:7. Mark 10:4.

5 "It was because your hearts were hard that Moses wrote you this law to permit you to divorce your wives," Jesus replied. 6 "But it was not this way from the beginning of creation, God 'made them male and female.' Mark 10:5-6 Matthew 19:8.

7 'For this reason a man will leave his father and mother and be united to his wife, 8 and the two will become one flesh.' So

they are no longer two, but one. 9 Therefore what God has joined together, let man not separate." Mark 10:7-9.

9 I tell you that anyone who divorces his wife, except for marital unfaithfulness, and marries another woman commits adultery." Matthew 19:9.

10 When they were in the house again, the disciples asked Jesus about this. 11 He answered, "Anyone who divorces his wife and marries another woman commits adultery against her, and the man who marries a divorced woman commits adultery. 12 And if she divorces her husband and marries another man, she commits adultery." Mark 10:10-12. Luke 16:18.

10 The disciples said to him, "If this is the situation between a husband and wife, it is better not to marry." Matthew 19:10.

11 Jesus replied, "Not everyone can accept this word, but only those to whom it has been given. 12 For some are eunuchs because they were born that way; others were made that way by men; and others have renounced marriage because of the kingdom of heaven. The one who can accept this should accept it." Matthew 19:11-12.

His Children

13 Then people were bringing little children and babies to Jesus for him to place his hands on them to touch and pray for them. But when the disciples saw this, they rebuked those who brought them. Matthew 19:13. Mark 10:13. Luke 18:15.

14 When Jesus saw this, he was indignant. He called the children to him and said to them, "Let the little children come to me, and do not hinder them, for the kingdom of God and heaven belongs

to such as these. 15 I tell you the truth, anyone who will not receive the kingdom of God like a little child will never enter it." Mark 10:14-15. Matthew 19:14. Luke 18:16-17.

16 And he took the children in his arms, he had placed his hands on them and blessed them; he went from there. Mark 10:16. Matthew 19:15.

His Needle's Eye

17 As Jesus started on his way, a certain ruler ran and came up to him and fell on his knees before him. "Good teacher," he asked, "what good thing must I do to inherit eternal life?" Mark 10:17. Luke 18:18. Matthew 19:16.

18 "Why do you call me good? Why do you ask me about what is good?" Jesus answered. "No one is good-except there is only God alone, who is good. If you want to enter life, obey the commandments." "Which ones?" the man inquired. Jesus replied, 19 "You know the commandments: 'Do not murder, do not commit adultery, do not steal, do not give false testimony, do not defraud, honor your father and mother,' and 'love your neighbor as yourself." Mark 10:18-19. Luke 18:19-20. Matthew 19:17-19.

20 "Teacher," he declared, "all these I have kept since I was a boy," the young man said. "What do I still lack?" Mark 10:20. Matthew 19:20. Luke 18:21.

21 When Jesus heard this, looked at him and loved him. He answered, "If you want to be perfect, you still lack one thing," he said. "Go, sell your possessions and everything you have and give to the poor; and you will have treasure in heaven. Then come, follow me." Mark 10:21. Matthew 19:21. Luke 18:22.

22 When the young man heard this, the man's face fell. He went away sad, because he was a man of great wealth. Matthew 19:22. Mark 10:22. Luke 18:23.

23 Jesus looked around at him and said to his disciples, "I tell you the truth, it is hard for the rich to enter the kingdom of God and heaven!" 24 The disciples were amazed at his words. But Jesus said again, "I tell you children, how hard it is to enter the kingdom of God! 25 Indeed, it is easier for a camel to go through the eye of a needle than for a rich man to enter the kingdom of God." Mark 10:23-25. Matthew 19:23-24. Luke 18:24-25.

25 When the disciples heard this, they were even more greatly astonished and amazed, and said to each other, "Who then can be saved?" 26 Jesus looked at them and replied, "With man this is impossible, but not with God; all things are possible with God." 27 Peter answered and said to him, "We have left everything to follow you! What then will there be for us?" 28 Jesus said to them, "I tell you the truth, at the renewal of all things, when the Son of Man sits on his glorious throne, you who have followed me will also sit on twelve thrones, judging the twelve tribes of Israel. 29 And everyone who has left houses or brothers or sisters or father or mother or children or fields or wife for my sake, the sake of the kingdom of God and the gospel, will receive a hundred many times as much in this present age (homes, brothers, sisters, mothers, children, fields and wife - and with them, persecutions) and in the age to come will inherit eternal life. 30 But many who are first will be last, and many who are last will be first." Matthew 19:25-30. Mark 10:26-31. Luke 18:26-30.

His Landowner

1 "For the kingdom of heaven is like a landowner who went out early in the morning to hire men to work in his vineyard. 2 He

agreed to pay them a denarius for the day and sent them into his vineyard.

3 "About the third hour he went out and saw others standing in the marketplace doing nothing. 4 He told them, 'You also go and work in my vineyard, and I will pay you whatever is right.'

5 So they went. "He went out again about the sixth hour and the ninth hour and did the same thing.

6 About the eleventh hour he went out and found still others standing around. He asked them, 'Why have you been standing here all day long doing nothing?' 7 "'Because no one has hired us,' they answered. "He said to them, 'You also go and work in my vineyard.'

8 "When evening came, the owner of the vineyard said to his foreman, 'Call the workers and pay them their wages, beginning with the last ones hired and going on to the first.'

9 "The workers who were hired about the eleventh hour came and each received a denarius. 10 So when those came who were hired first, they expected to receive more. But each one of them also received a denarius. 11 When they received it, they began to grumble against the landowner. 12'These men who were hired last worked only one hour,' they said, 'and you have made them equal to us who have borne the burden of the work and the heat of the day.'

13 "But he answered one of them, 'Friend, I am not being unfair to you. Didn't you agree to work for a denarius? 14 Take your pay and go. I want to give the man who was hired last the same as I gave you. 15 Don't I have the right to do what I want with my own money? Or are you envious because I am generous?' 16 "So the last will be first, and the first will be last." Matthew 20:1-16.

Chapter Four

His Coming Death

17 Now they were on their way up to Jerusalem, with Jesus leading the way, and the disciples were astonished, while those who followed were afraid. Again he took the twelve disciples aside and said to them what was going to happen to him. 18 "We are going up to Jerusalem," he said, "and everything that is written by the prophets about the Son of Man will be fulfilled; the Son of Man will be betrayed to the chief priests and the teachers of the law. They will condemn him to death 19 and he will be handed over to the Gentiles who will mock him, insult him, spit on him and flog him and crucify him and kill him. Three days later, on the third day he will be raised to life again!" Matthew 20:17-19. Mark 10:32:34. Luke 18:31-33.

34 The disciples did not understand any of this. Its meaning was hidden from them, and they did not know what he was talking about. Luke 18:34.

His Ransom

20 Then the mother of Zebedee's sons, James and John, came to Jesus with her sons and, kneeling down, asked a favor of him. "Teacher," they said, "we want you to do for us whatever we ask." Matthew 20:20. Mark 10:35.

21 "What is it you want me to do for you?" he asked. She said, "Grant that one of these two sons of mine may sit at your right and the other at your left in your kingdom." The sons replied, "Let one of us sit at your right and the other at your left in your glory. Mark 10:36-37. Matthew 20:21.

38 "You don't know what you are asking," Jesus said to them. "Can you drink the cup I am going to drink or be baptized with the baptism I am baptized with?" 39a "We can," they answered. Mark 10:38-39a. Matthew 20:22.

39b Jesus said to them, "You will indeed drink from the cup I drink and be baptized with the baptism I am baptized with, 40 but to sit at my right or left is not for me to grant. These places belong to those for whom they have been prepared by my Father." Mark 10:39b-40. Matthew 20:23.

41 When the ten heard about this, they became indignant with the two brothers, James and John. Mark 10:41. Matthew 20:24.

42 Jesus called them together and said, "You know that those who are regarded as rulers of the Gentiles lord it over them, and their high officials exercise authority over them. 43 Not so with you. Instead, whoever wants to become great among you must be your servant, 44 and whoever wants to be first must be slave of all. 45 For even just as the Son of Man did not come to be served, but to serve, and to give his life as a ransom for many." Mark 10:42-45. Matthew 20:25-28.

His Bartimaeus

46 Then they came to Jericho. As Jesus and his disciples, together with a large crowd followed him, were leaving the city Jericho, two blind men, one named, Bartimaeus (that is, the Son of

Timaeus), were sitting by the roadside begging. 47 He asked what was happening. They told him, "Jesus of Nazareth is passing by." And when he heard that it was the crowd and Jesus of Nazareth going by, he and they began to call and shout out, "Jesus, Lord, Son of David, have mercy on me and us!" Mark 10:46-47. Matthew 20:29-30. Luke 18:35-38.

39 Many who led the way of the crowd rebuked him and told them to be quiet, but they shouted all the more louder, "Lord, Son of David, have mercy on me and us!" Luke 18:39. Mark 10:48. Matthew 20:31.

49 Jesus stopped and ordered the man to be brought to him, "Call him." So they called to the blind man, "Cheer up! On your feet! He's calling you." 50 Throwing his cloak aside, he jumped to his feet and came to Jesus. When he came near, Jesus asked him, 51 "What do you want me to do for you?" "Lord," they replied. The blind man answered, "Rabbi, we want our sight." Mark 10:49-51. Matthew 20:32-33. Luke 18:40-41.

34 Jesus had compassion on them and touched their eyes. Jesus said to them, "Receive your sight; go, your faith has healed you." Immediately they received their sight and followed Jesus along the road, praising God. When all the people saw it, they also praised God. Matthew 20:34. Luke 18:42-43. Mark 10:51.

His Zacchaeus

1 Jesus entered Jericho and was passing through. 2 A man was there by the name of Zacchaeus; he was a chief tax collector and was wealthy.

3 He wanted to see who Jesus was, but being a short man he could not, because of the crowd. 4 So he ran ahead and climbed a sycamore-fig tree to see him, since Jesus was coming that way.

5 When Jesus reached the spot, he looked up and said to him, "Zacchaeus, come down immediately. I must stay at your house today."

6 So he came down at once and welcomed him gladly. 7 All the people saw this and began to mutter, "He has gone to be the guest of a 'sinner.'"

8 But Zacchaeus stood up and said to the Lord, "Look, Lord! Here and now I give half of my possessions to the poor, and if I have cheated anybody out of anything, I will pay back four times the amount."

9 Jesus said to him, "Today salvation has come to this house, because this man, too, is a son of Abraham.

10 For the Son of Man came to seek and to save what was lost." Luke 19:1-10.

His Mina

11 While they were listening to this, he went on to tell them a parable, because he was near Jerusalem and the people thought that the kingdom of God was going to appear at once.

12 He said: "A man of noble birth went to a distant country to have himself appointed king and then to return. 13 So he called ten of his servants and gave them ten minas. 'Put this money to work,' he said, 'until I come back.'

14 "But his subjects hated him and sent a delegation after him to say, 'We don't want this man to be our king.'

15 "He was made king, however, and returned home. Then he sent for the servants to whom he had given the money, in order to find out what they had gained with it.

16 "The first one came and said, 'Sir, your mina has earned ten more.'

17 "'Well done, my good servant!' his master replied. 'Because you have been trustworthy in a very small matter, take charge of ten cities.'

18 "The second came and said, 'Sir, your mina has earned five more.'

19 "His master answered, 'You take charge of five cities.'

20 "Then another servant came and said, 'Sir, here is your mina; I have kept it laid away in a piece of cloth. 21 I was afraid of you, because you are a hard man. You take out what you did not put in and reap what you did not sow.'

22 "His master replied, 'I will judge you by your own words, you wicked servant! You knew, did you, that I am a hard man, taking out what I did not put in, and reaping what I did not sow? 23 Why then didn't you put my money on deposit, so that when I came back, I could have collected it with interest?'

24 "Then he said to those standing by, 'Take his mina away from him and give it to the one who has ten minas.'

25 "'Sir,' they said, 'he already has ten!'

26 "He replied, 'I tell you that to everyone who has, more will be given, but as for the one who has nothing, even what he has will be taken away.

27 But those enemies of mine who did not want me to be king over them-bring them here and kill them in front of me.'" Luke 19:11-27.

His Perfume

1 Six days before the Passover, Jesus arrived at Bethany. While Jesus was in Bethany, reclining at the table in the home of a man known as Simon the Leper, where Lazarus lived, whom Jesus had raised from the dead. 2 Here a dinner was given in Jesus' honor. Martha served, while Lazarus was among those reclining at the table with him. John 12:1-2. Matthew 26:6. Mark 14:3a.

7 a woman came to him with an alabaster jar of very expensive perfume, made of pure nard. She broke the jar and she poured the perfume on his head as he was reclining at the table. Matthew 26:7. Mark 14:3b.

3 Then Mary took about a pint of pure nard, an expensive perfume; she poured it on Jesus' feet and wiped his feet with her hair. And the house was filled with the fragrance of the perfume. John 12:3.

4 When some of the disciples present saw this, they were saying indignantly to one another, "Why this waste of perfume? It could have been sold at a high price, for more than a year's wages and the money given to the poor." But one of his disciples, Judas Iscariot, who was later to betray him, objected, 5 "Why wasn't this perfume sold and the money given to the poor? It was worth a year's wages." 6 He did not say this because he cared about the

poor but because he was a thief; as keeper of the money bag, he used to help himself to what was put into it. Any they rebuked her harshly. John 12:4-6. Matthew 26:8-9. Mark 14:4-5.

7 Aware of this, Jesus said to them, "Leave her alone!" Jesus replied, "Why are you bothering her? She has done a beautiful thing to me. [It was intended] that she should save this perfume for the day of my burial. She did what she could when she poured this perfume on my body; she did it beforehand to prepare me for my burial. 8 You will always have the poor among and with you; you can help them any time you want, but you will not always have me." John 12:7-8. Matthew 26:10-12. Mark 14:6-8.

13 I tell you the truth, wherever this gospel is preached throughout the world, what she has done will also be told, in memory of her." Matthew 26:13. Mark 14:9.

9 Meanwhile a large crowd of Jews found out that Jesus was there and came, not only because of him but also to see Lazarus, whom he had raised from the dead. 10 So the chief priests made plans to kill Lazarus as well, 11 for on account of him many of the Jews were going over to Jesus and putting their faith in him. John 12:9-11.

His Precession

28 After Jesus had said this, he went on ahead, going up to Jerusalem. 29 As they approached Jerusalem and came to Bethphage and Bethany at the hill called the Mount of Olives, Jesus sent two of his disciples, saying to them, 30 "Go to the village ahead of you, and at once just as you enter it, you will find a donkey tied there, with her colt by her, which no one has ever ridden. Untie them and bring them here to me. 31 If anyone says anything to you or asks you, 'Why are you untying them?'

tell him, 'The Lord needs them, and he will send them back here right away." Luke 19:28-31. Matthew 21:1-3. Mark 11:1-3.

4 This took place to fulfill what was spoken and written through the prophet: 5 "Say to the Daughter of Zion, Do not be afraid, O Daughter of Zion; 'See, your king comes to you, gentle seated and riding on a donkey, on a colt, the foal of a donkey.'" Matthew 21:4-5. John 12:14b-15.

6 The disciples went and did as Jesus had instructed them. Matthew 21:6.

32 Those who were sent ahead, went and they found a colt outside in the street, tied at a doorway, just as he had told them. 33 As they were untying the colt, some people standing there - its owners asked them, "Why are you doing, untying that colt?" 34 They replied, "The Lord needs it;" as Jesus had told them to and the people let them go. Luke 19:32-34. Mark 11:4-6.

12 The next day the great crowd that had come for the Feast heard that Jesus was on his way to Jerusalem. John 12:12.

7 When they brought the donkey and the colt to Jesus; they threw and placed their cloaks on them, and Jesus sat upon them. 8 As he went along, a very large crowd of people spread their cloaks on the road, while others cut and took palm branches from the trees in the fields; went out to meet him and spread them on the road, shouting, "Hosanna!" "Blessed is the he who comes in the name of the Lord!" "Blessed is the King of Israel!" Matthew 21:7-8. Mark 11:7-8. Luke 19:35-36. John 12:13-14a.

37 When he came near the place where the road goes down the Mount of Olives, the whole crowd of disciples who went ahead and those that followed began joyfully to praise God in loud voices for all the miracles they had seen: 38 "Blessed is the King who comes in the name of the Lord!" "Hosanna to the Son of David!" "Hosanna!" "Peace in heaven and glory in the highest!" "Blessed

is the he who comes in the name of the Lord!" "Hosanna in the highest!" "Blessed is the coming kingdom of our father David!" 39 Some of the Pharisees in the crowd said to Jesus, "Teacher, rebuke your disciples!" 40 "I tell you," he replied, "if they keep quiet, the stones will cry out." Luke 19:37-40. Matthew 21:9. Mark 11:9-10.

16 At first his disciples did not understand all this. Only after Jesus was glorified did they realize that these things had been written about him and that they had done these things to him. John 12:16.

41 As he approached Jerusalem and saw the city, he wept over it 42 and said, "If you, even you, had only known on this day what would bring you peace-but now it is hidden from your eyes. 43 The days will come upon you when your enemies will build an embankment against you and encircle you and hem you in on every side. 44 They will dash you to the ground, you and the children within your walls. They will not leave one stone on another, because you did not recognize the time of God's coming to you." Luke 19:41-44.

17 Now the crowd that was with him when he called Lazarus from the tomb and raised him from the dead continued to spread the word. 18 Many people, because they had heard that he had given this miraculous sign, went out to meet him. 19 So the Pharisees said to one another, "See, this is getting us nowhere. Look how the whole world has gone after him!" John 12:17-19.

10 When Jesus entered Jerusalem, the whole city was stirred and asked, "Who is this?" 11 The crowds answered, "This is Jesus, the prophet from Nazareth in Galilee." He went to the temple. He looked around at everything, but since it was already late, he went out to Bethany with the Twelve. Matthew 21:10-11. Mark 11:11.

His House of Prayer

12 The next day as they were leaving Bethany, Jesus was hungry. 13 Seeing in the distance a fig tree in leaf, he went to find out if it had any fruit. When he reached it, he found nothing but leaves, because it was not the season for figs. 14 Then he said to the tree, "May no one ever eat fruit from you again." And his disciples heard him say it. Mark 11:12-14.

15 On reaching Jerusalem, Jesus entered the temple area and began driving out all those who were buying and selling there. He overturned the tables of the money changers and the benches of those selling doves, 16 and would not allow anyone to carry merchandise through the temple courts. Mark 11:15-16. Matthew 21:12. Luke 19:45.

17 And as he taught them, he said to them, "Is it not written: "'My house will be called a house of prayer for all nations'? But you have made it 'a den of robbers.'" Mark 11:17. Matthew 21:13. Luke 19:46.

47 Every day he was teaching at the temple. But the chief priests, the teachers of the law and the leaders among the people heard this and began trying to look for a way to kill him; for they feared him. 48 Yet they could not find any way to do it, because the whole crowd of people was amazed at his teaching and hung on his words. Luke 19:47-48. Mark 11:18.

14 The blind and the lame came to him at the temple, and he healed them. 15 But when the chief priests and the teachers of the law saw the wonderful things he did and the children shouting in the temple area, "Hosanna to the Son of David," they were indignant. 16 "Do you hear what these children are saying?" they

asked him. "Yes," replied Jesus, "have you never read, "'From the lips of children and infants you have ordained praise'?" Matthew 21:14-16.

17 When evening came, he and the disciples left them and went out of the city to Bethany, where they spent the night. Matthew 21:17. Mark 11:19.

His Hour

20 Now there were some Greeks among those who went up to worship at the Feast. 21 They came to Philip, who was from Bethsaida in Galilee, with a request. "Sir," they said, "we would like to see Jesus." 22 Philip went to tell Andrew; Andrew and Philip in turn told Jesus.

23 Jesus replied, "The hour has come for the Son of Man to be glorified. 24 I tell you the truth, unless a kernel of wheat falls to the ground and dies, it remains only a single seed. But if it dies, it produces many seeds. 25 The man who loves his life will lose it, while the man who hates his life in this world will keep it for eternal life. 26 Whoever serves me must follow me; and where I am, my servant also will be. My Father will honor the one who serves me.

27 "Now my heart is troubled, and what shall I say? 'Father, save me from this hour'? No, it was for this very reason I came to this hour.

28 Father, glorify your name!" Then a voice came from heaven, "I have glorified it, and will glorify it again."

29 The crowd that was there and heard it said it had thundered; others said an angel had spoken to him.

30 Jesus said, "This voice was for your benefit, not mine.

31 Now is the time for judgment on this world; now the prince of this world will be driven out.

32 But I, when I am lifted up from the earth, will draw all men to myself." 33 He said this to show the kind of death he was going to die.

34 The crowd spoke up, "We have heard from the Law that the Christ will remain forever, so how can you say, 'The Son of Man must be lifted up'? Who is this 'Son of Man'?"

35 Then Jesus told them, "You are going to have the light just a little while longer. Walk while you have the light, before darkness overtakes you. The man who walks in the dark does not know where he is going. 36a Put your trust in the light while you have it, so that you may become sons of light."

36b When he had finished speaking, Jesus left and hid himself from them. John 12:20-36.

37 Even after Jesus had done all these miraculous signs in their presence, they still would not believe in him. 38 This was to fulfill the word of Isaiah the prophet: "Lord, who has believed our message and to whom has the arm of the Lord been revealed?"

39 For this reason they could not believe, because, as Isaiah says elsewhere: 40 "He has blinded their eyes and deadened their hearts, so they can neither see with their eyes, nor understand with their hearts, nor turn-and I would heal them."

41 Isaiah said this because he saw Jesus' glory and spoke about him.

42 Yet at the same time, many even among the leaders believed in him. But because of the Pharisees they would not confess their

faith for fear they would be put out of the synagogue; 43 for they loved praise from men more than praise from God. John 12:37-43.

44 Then Jesus cried out, "When a man believes in me, he does not believe in me only, but in the one who sent me. 45 When he looks at me, he sees the one who sent me. 46 I have come into the world as a light, so that no one who believes in me should stay in darkness.

47 "As for the person who hears my words but does not keep them, I do not judge him. For I did not come to judge the world, but to save it.

48 There is a judge for the one who rejects me and does not accept my words; that very word which I spoke will condemn him at the last day.

49 For I did not speak of my own accord, but the Father who sent me commanded me what to say and how to say it. 50 I know that his command leads to eternal life. So whatever I say is just what the Father has told me to say." John 12:44-50.

His Fig Tree

18 Early in the morning, as they went along on their way back to the city, he was hungry. 19 Seeing a fig tree by the road, he went up to it but found nothing on it except leaves. Then he said to it, "May you never bear fruit again!" Immediately the tree withered. 20 When the disciples saw the fig tree withered from the roots, they were amazed. Peter said to Jesus, "Rabbi, look! The fig tree you cursed has withered!" "How did the fig tree wither so quickly?" they asked. Matthew 21:18-20. Mark 11:20-21.

22 "Have faith in God," Jesus answered. Mark 11:22.

21 Jesus replied, "I tell you the truth, if you have faith and do not doubt, not only can you do what was done to the fig tree, but also if anyone can say to this mountain, 'Go, throw yourself into the sea,' and does not doubt in his heart but believes that what he says will be done for him. 22 Therefore I tell you, if you believe that you have received it, you will receive whatever you ask for in prayer; it will be yours." Matthew 21:21-22. Mark 11:23-24.

25 And when you stand praying, if you hold anything against anyone, forgive him, so that your Father in heaven may forgive you your sins." Mark 11:25.

His Question

26 They arrived again in Jerusalem, one day Jesus entered the temple courts, and, while he was walking; teaching and preaching the gospel with the people in the temple courts, the chief priests, the teachers of the law and together with the elders came to him. 28 "Tells us by what authority are you doing these things?" they asked. "And who gave you authority to do this?" Mark 11:26-28. Luke 20:1-2. Matthew 21:23.

24 Jesus replied, "I will also ask you one question. If you answer me, I will tell you by what authority I am doing these things. 25a John's baptism-where did it come from? Was it from heaven, or from men? Tell me!" Matthew 21:24-25a. Mark 11:29-30. Luke 20:3-4.

25b They discussed it among themselves and said, "If we say, 'From heaven,' he will ask, 'Then why didn't you believe him?' 26 But if we say, 'From men'-we are afraid all of the people will stone us, because they all hold and are persuaded that John really was a prophet." Matthew 21:25b-26. Mark 11:31-32. Luke 20:5-6.

27 So they answered Jesus, "We don't know where it was from." Then Jesus said, "Neither will I tell you by what authority I am doing these things. Matthew 21:27. Mark 11:33. Luke 20:7-8.

His Mind

28 "What do you think? There was a man who had two sons. He went to the first and said, 'Son, go and work today in the vineyard.' 29 "'I will not,' he answered, but later he changed his mind and went.

30 "Then the father went to the other son and said the same thing. He answered, 'I will, sir,' but he did not go.

31a "Which of the two did what his father wanted?" "The first," they answered.

31b Jesus said to them, "I tell you the truth, the tax collectors and the prostitutes are entering the kingdom of God ahead of you. 32 For John came to you to show you the way of righteousness, and you did not believe him, but the tax collectors and the prostitutes did. And even after you saw this, you did not repent and believe him. Matthew 21:28-32.

His Planted Vineyard

33 He began to speak in parables and went on to tell the people this parable: "Listen to another parable: There was a landowner

who planted a vineyard. He put a wall around it, dug a pit for the winepress in it and built a watchtower. Then he rented the vineyard to some farmers and went away on a journey for a long time. Matthew 21:33. Luke 20:9. Mark 12:1.

10 When the harvest time approached to collect his fruit, he sent his servants to the tenants so they would give him some of the fruit of the vineyard. But the tenants seized his servants; they killed one, stoned another and beat a third and sent him away empty-handed. 11 Then he sent other servants to them, more than the first time and the tenants treated them the same way; they struck one man on his head, beat others and treated shamefully and sent them away empty-handed. 12 He sent a third attempt, and they wounded him and threw him out. He sent many others; some of them they beat, others they killed. 13 "Then last of all, the owner of the vineyard had one left to send to them, his son whom he loved; saying, 'What shall I do? I will send my son, whom I love; perhaps they will respect my son.' 14 "But when the tenants saw the son, they talked the matter over to each other. 'This is the heir,' they said. 'Come, let's kill him, and his inheritance will be ours.'" 15a So they took him and threw him out of the vineyard and killed him. Luke 20:10-15a. Matthew 21:34-39. Mark 12:2-8.

40 "Therefore, when the owner of the vineyard comes, what then will he do to those tenants?" 41 "He will come and kill and bring those wretched tenants to a wretched end," they replied, "and he will rent and give the vineyard to other tenants, who will give him his share of the crop at harvest time." When the people heard this, they said, "May this never be!" Matthew 21:40-41. Mark 12:9. Luke 20:15b-16.

His Capstone

42 Jesus said to them, "Have you never read in the Scriptures: "'The stone the builders rejected has become the capstone; the Lord has done this, and it is marvelous in our eyes'? Jesus looked directly at them and asked, "Then what is the meaning of that which is written? 43 Therefore I tell you that the kingdom of God will be taken away from you and given to a people who will produce its fruit. 44 Everyone who falls on this stone will be broken to pieces, but he on whom it falls will be crushed." Matthew 21:42-44. Luke 20:17-18. Mark 12:10-11.

45 When the chief priests and the Pharisees heard Jesus' parables, they knew he was talking about them. Matthew 21:45.

19 Then the teachers of the law and the chief priests looked for a way to arrest him immediately, because they knew he had spoken this parable against them. But they were afraid of the crowd because the people held that he was a prophet; so they left him and went away. Luke 20:19. Matthew 21:46. Mark 12:12.

His Son's Wedding Banquet

1 Jesus spoke to them again in parables, saying: 2 "The kingdom of heaven is like a king who prepared a wedding banquet for his son. 3 He sent his servants to those who had been invited to the banquet to tell them to come, but they refused to come.

4 "Then he sent some more servants and said, 'Tell those who have been invited that I have prepared my dinner: My oxen and

fattened cattle have been butchered, and everything is ready. Come to the wedding banquet.'

5 "But they paid no attention and went off-one to his field, another to his business. 6 The rest seized his servants, mistreated them and killed them. 7 The king was enraged. He sent his army and destroyed those murderers and burned their city.

8 "Then he said to his servants, 'The wedding banquet is ready, but those I invited did not deserve to come. 9 Go to the street corners and invite to the banquet anyone you find.' 10 So the servants went out into the streets and gathered all the people they could find, both good and bad, and the wedding hall was filled with guests.

11 "But when the king came in to see the guests, he noticed a man there who was not wearing wedding clothes. 12'Friend,' he asked, 'how did you get in here without wedding clothes?' The man was speechless.

13 "Then the king told the attendants, 'Tie him hand and foot, and throw him outside, into the darkness, where there will be weeping and gnashing of teeth.'

14 "For many are invited, but few are chosen." Matthew 22:1-14.

His Tribute

20 Then later, the Pharisees keeping a close watch on him, they sent some of their Pharisee and Herodian disciples and spies to Jesus, who pretended to be honest. They went out and laid plans to trap him in his words, and hoped to catch Jesus in his words so that they might hand him over to the power and authority of the governor. Luke 20:20. Matthew 22:15-16a. Mark 12:13.

21 So the spies came to him and questioned him: "Teacher," they said, "we know that you are a man of integrity and that you aren't swayed by men, because you pay no attention to who they are. You speak and teach what is right, and that you do not show partiality; but you teach the way of God in accordance with the truth. 22 Tell us then, what is your opinion? Is it right for us to pay taxes to Caesar or not? Should we pay or shouldn't we?" Luke 20:21-22. Matthew 22:16-17. Mark 12:14-15a.

18 But Jesus, knowing their evil intent saw through their duplicity and hypocrisy, said to them, "You hypocrites, why are you trying to trap me?" he asked. 19 "Bring me a denarius and show me the coin used for paying the tax." They brought him a denarius coin, 20 and he asked them, "Whose portrait is this? And whose inscription is on it?" Matthew 22:18-20. Mark 12:15b-16a. Luke 20:23-24.

25 "Caesar's," they replied. Then Jesus said to them, "Then give to Caesar what is Caesar's, and to God what is God's." 26 They were unable to trap him in what he had said there in public. When they heard this, they were astonished and amazed by his answer, they became silent. So they left him and went away. Luke 20:25-26. Mark 12:16b-17. Matthew 22:21-22.

His Living

27 Then that same day, some of the Sadducees, who say there is no resurrection, came to Jesus with a question. Luke 20:27. Matthew 22:23. Mark 12:18.

24 "Teacher," they said, "Moses told and wrote for us that if a man dies and leaves a wife without having children, his brother must marry the widow and have children for the man. 25 Now there were seven brothers among us. The first one married a woman

and died, and since he had no children, he left his wife to his brother. 26 The same thing happened to the second and third brother, right on down to the seventh died. In fact, none of the seven left any children. 27 Last of all, the woman died too. 28 Now then, at the resurrection, whose wife will she be of the seven, since all of them were married to her?" Matthew 22:24-28. Luke 20:28-33. Mark 12:19-23.

34 Jesus replied, "The people of this age marry and are given in marriage. Are you not in error because you do not know the Scriptures or the power of God? 35 But when those who are considered worthy of taking part in that age and in the resurrection from the dead, will neither marry nor be given in marriage, 36 and they can no longer die; for they will be like the angels in heaven. They are God's children, since they are children of the resurrection. Luke 20:34-36. Matthew 22:29-30. Mark 12:24-25.

31 Now about the resurrection of the dead-have you not read in the book of Moses, in the account of the bush even Moses showed that the dead rise, for he calls the Lord 'the God of Abraham, and the God of Isaac, and the God of Isaac, and the God of Jacob.' And God said to him, 32 'I am the God of Abraham, the God of Isaac, and the God of Jacob'? He is not the God of the dead but of the living, for to him all are alive. You are badly mistaken!" 33 When the crowds heard this, they were astonished at his teaching. Matthew 22:31-33. Mark 12:26-27. Luke 20:37-38.

39 Some of the teachers of the law responded, "Well said, teacher!" 40 And no one dared to ask him any more questions. Luke 20:39-40.

His Greatest Commandment

34 Hearing that Jesus had silenced the Sadducees, the Pharisees got together. Matthew 22:34.

28 One of the teachers an expert of the law came and heard them debating. Noticing that Jesus had given them a good answer, he tested him with this question:, "Teacher, of all the commandments, which is the most important and greatest commandment in the Law?" Mark 12:28. Matthew 22:35-36.

29 "The most important one," answered Jesus, "is this: 'Hear, O Israel, the Lord our God, the Lord is one. 30 Love the Lord your God with all your heart and with all your soul and with all your mind and with all your strength.' This is the first and greatest commandment. 31 And the second is like it: 'Love your neighbor as yourself.' There is no commandment greater than these." All the Law and the Prophets hang on these two commandments." Mark 12:29-31. Matthew 22:37-40.

32 "Well said, teacher," the man replied. "You are right in saying that God is one and there is no other but him. 33 To love him with all your heart, with all your understanding and with all your strength, and to love your neighbor as yourself is more important than all burnt offerings and sacrifices." 34 When Jesus saw that he had answered wisely, he said to him, "You are not far from the kingdom of God." And from then on no one dared ask him any more questions. Mark 12:32-34.

His Lord

41 While the Pharisees were gathered together and Jesus was teaching in the temple courts, Jesus asked them, 42 "What do you think about the Christ? Whose son is he?" "The son of David," they replied. He asked, "How is it that the teachers of the law say that the Christ is the son of David? Matthew 22:41-42. Mark 12:35. Luke 20:41.

43 Then Jesus said to them, "How is it then that David himself declares in the Book of Psalms, speaking by the Holy Spirit, calls him 'Lord'? For he says, 44 "'The Lord said to my Lord: "Sit at my right hand until I make and put your enemies a footstool for under your feet." '45 If then David himself calls him 'Lord,' how can he be his son?" 46 The large crowd listened to him with delight. No one could say a word in reply, and from that day on no one dared to ask him any more questions. Matthew 22:43-46. Mark 12:36-37. Luke 20:42-44.

His Accountability

1 Then Jesus said to the crowds and to his disciples: 2 "The teachers of the law and the Pharisees sit in Moses' seat. 3 So you must obey them and do everything they tell you. But do not do what they do, for they do not practice what they preach. 4 They tie up heavy loads and put them on men's shoulders, but they themselves are not willing to lift a finger to move them. Matthew 23:1-4.

45 While all the people were listening, Jesus taught and said to his disciples, Luke 20:45. Mark 12:38a.

5 "Beware and watch out for the teachers of the law. Everything they do is done for men to see: They make their phylacteries wide and the tassels on their garments long; 6 they love the places of honor at banquets and the most important seats in the synagogues; 7 they like to walk around in flowing robes and love to be greeted in the marketplaces and to have men call them 'Rabbi.' Matthew 23:5-7. Mark 12:38b-39. Luke 20:46.

47 They devour widows' houses and for a show make lengthy prayers. Such men will be punished most severely." Mark 12:40. Luke 20:47.

8 "But you are not to be called 'Rabbi,' for you have only one Master and you are all brothers. 9 And do not call anyone on earth 'father,' for you have one Father, and he is in heaven. 10 Nor are you to be called 'teacher,' for you have one Teacher, the Christ. 11 The greatest among you will be your servant. 12 For whoever exalts himself will be humbled, and whoever humbles himself will be exalted. Matthew 23:8-12.

His Woes

37 When Jesus had finished speaking, a Pharisee invited him to eat with him; so he went in and reclined at the table. 38 But the Pharisee, noticing that Jesus did not first wash before the meal, was surprised. Luke 11:37-38.

13 "Woe to you, teachers of the law and Pharisees, you hypocrites! You shut the kingdom of heaven in men's faces. You yourselves do not enter, nor will you let those enter who are trying to.

15 "Woe to you, teachers of the law and Pharisees, you hypocrites! You travel over land and sea to win a single convert, and when he becomes one, you make him twice as much a son of hell as you are.

16 "Woe to you, blind guides! You say, 'If anyone swears by the temple, it means nothing; but if anyone swears by the gold of the temple, he is bound by his oath.'

17 You blind fools! Which is greater: the gold, or the temple that makes the gold sacred?

18 You also say, 'If anyone swears by the altar, it means nothing; but if anyone swears by the gift on it, he is bound by his oath.'

19 You blind men! Which is greater: the gift, or the altar that makes the gift sacred?

20 Therefore, he who swears by the altar swears by it and by everything on it. 21 And he who swears by the temple swears by it and by the one who dwells in it. 22 And he who swears by heaven swears by God's throne and by the one who sits on it. Matthew 23:13-22.

23 "Woe to you, teachers of the law and Pharisees, you hypocrites! You give God a tenth of your spices-mint, dill, cummin, rue and all other kinds of garden herbs, but you have neglected the more important matters of the law: justice, mercy, faithfulness; the love of God. You should have practiced the latter, without neglecting and leaving the former undone. Matthew 23:23. Luke 11:42.

24 You blind guides! You strain out a gnat but swallow a camel. Matthew 23:24.

25 "Woe to you, teachers of the law and Pharisees, you hypocrites! Then the Lord said to him, "Now then, you Pharisees clean the outside of the cup and dish, but inside you are full of greed, self-

indulgence and wickedness. 26 Blind Pharisee! First clean the inside of the cup and dish, and then the outside also will be clean. Matthew 23:25-26. Luke 11:39.

40 You foolish people! Did not the one who made the outside make the inside also? 41 But give what is inside [the dish] to the poor, and everything will be clean for you. Luke 11:40-41.

27 "Woe to you, teachers of the law and Pharisees, you hypocrites! You are like whitewashed tombs, which look beautiful on the outside but on the inside are full of dead men's bones and everything unclean. 28 In the same way, on the outside you appear to people as righteous but on the inside you are full of hypocrisy and wickedness. Matthew 23:27-28.

43 "Woe to you Pharisees, because you love the most important seats in the synagogues and greetings in the marketplaces. Luke 11:43.

44 "Woe to you, because you are like unmarked graves, which men walk over without knowing it." 45 One of the experts in the law answered him, "Teacher, when you say these things, you insult us also." Luke 11:44-45.

46 Jesus replied, "And you experts in the law, woe to you, because you load people down with burdens they can hardly carry, and you yourselves will not lift one finger to help them. Luke 11:46.

29 "Woe to you, teachers of the law and Pharisees, you hypocrites! Because you build tombs for the prophets and decorate the graves of the righteous. 30 And you say, 'If we had lived in the days of our forefathers who killed them; we would not have taken part with them in shedding the blood of the prophets.' 31 So you testify against yourselves that you are the descendants of those who murdered the prophets and approved of what your forefathers did; they killed the prophets and you build their tombs. 32 Fill up,

then, the measure of the sin of your forefathers! Matthew 23:29-32. Luke 11:47-48.

33 "You snakes! You brood of vipers! How will you escape being condemned to hell? 34 Therefore because of this, God in his wisdom said, I am sending you; prophets and apostles and wise men and teachers. Some of them you will kill, others will persecute and crucify; others you will flog in your synagogues and pursue from town to town. 35 And so upon you will come all the righteous blood that has been shed on earth, from the blood of righteous Abel to the blood of Zechariah son of Berekiah, whom you murdered between the temple and the altar. Matthew 23:33-35. Luke 11:49.

36 I tell you the truth, all this will come upon this generation. Matthew 23:36.

50 Therefore this generation will be held responsible for the blood of all the prophets that has been shed since the beginning of the world, 51 from the blood of Abel to the blood of Zechariah, who was killed between the altar and the sanctuary. Yes, I tell you, this generation will be held responsible for it all. Luke 11:50-51.

52 "Woe to you experts in the law, because you have taken away the key to knowledge. You yourselves have not entered, and you have hindered those who were entering." Luke 11:52.

53 When Jesus left there, the Pharisees and the teachers of the law began to oppose him fiercely and to besiege him with questions, 54 waiting to catch him in something he might say. Luke 11:53-54.

His Longing to Gather

31 At that time some Pharisees came to Jesus and said to him, "Leave this place and go somewhere else. Herod wants to kill you."

32 He replied, "Go tell that fox, 'I will drive out demons and heal people today and tomorrow, and on the third day I will reach my goal.' 33 In any case, I must keep going today and tomorrow and the next day-for surely no prophet can die outside Jerusalem! Luke 13:31-33.

34 "O Jerusalem, Jerusalem, you who kill the prophets and stone those sent to you, how often I have longed to gather your children together, as a hen gathers her chicks under her wings, but you were not willing! 35 Look, your house is left to you desolate. For I tell you, you will not see me again until you say, 'Blessed is he who comes in the name of the Lord.'" Luke 13:34-35. Matthew 23:37-39.

His Offerings

41 Jesus sat down opposite the place where the offerings were put and watched the crowd putting their money into the temple treasury. As he looked up, Jesus saw many of the rich people throw in large amounts and putting their gifts into the temple treasury. 42 He also saw a poor widow came and put in two very small copper coins, worth only a fraction of a penny. 43 Calling his disciples to him, Jesus said, "I tell you the truth," he said, "this poor widow has put more into the treasury than all the others. 44

All these people gave their gifts out of their wealth; but she, out of her poverty, put in everything-all she had to live on." Mark 12:41-44. Luke 21:1-4.

His Coming

1 As Jesus was leaving the temple and was walking away when some of his disciples came up to him to call his attention to its buildings and remarking about how the temple was adorned with beautiful stones and with gifts dedicated to God, one of his disciples said to him, "Look, Teacher! What massive stones! What magnificent buildings!" 2 "Do you see all these great buildings?" replied Jesus. "I tell you the truth, as for what you see here, the time will come when not one stone here will be left on another; every one will be thrown down." Mark 13:1-2. Matthew 24:1-2. Luke 21:5-6.

3 As Jesus was sitting on the Mount of Olives opposite the temple, the disciples; Peter, James, John and Andrew came to him and asked him privately, 4 "Teacher," they said, "Tell us," they asked, "when will these things happen? And what will be the sign that they are all about to take place and be fulfilled in your coming and of the end of the age?" Mark 13:3-4. Matthew 24:3. Luke 21:7.

4 Jesus answered to them: "Watch out that no one deceives you. 5 For many will come in my name, claiming, 'I am the Christ,' and, 'The time is near,' deceiving many. Do not follow them. 6 When you will hear of wars, rumors of wars and revolutions, but see to it that you are not alarmed and frightened. Such things must happen first, but the end still to come will not come right away." 7 Then he said to them: "Nation will rise against nation, and kingdom against kingdom. There will be great famines, earthquakes, pestilences in various places and fearful events and

great signs from heaven. 8 All these are the beginning of birth pains. Matthew 24:4-8. Mark 13:5-8. Luke 21:8-11.

9 "But before all of this, you must be on your guard. They will lay hands on you and persecute you and put to death. You will be delivered and handed over to the local councils, prisons and flogged in the synagogues. On account of me, you will be hated by all nations; you will stand before governors and kings all on the result of my name and your being witnesses to them. 10 And the gospel must first be preached to all nations. 11 Whenever you are arrested and brought to trial, make up your mind not to worry beforehand about what to say and how you will defend yourselves. Just say whatever is given you at the time, for it is not you speaking, but the Holy Spirit. For I will give you words and wisdom that none of your adversaries will be able to resist or contradict. Mark 13:9-11. Luke 21:12-15. Matthew 24:9.

10 At that time many will turn away from the faith and will betray and hate each other, 11 and many false prophets will appear and deceive many people. 12 Because of the increase of wickedness, the love of most will grow cold, 13 but he who stands firm to the end will be saved. 14 And this gospel of the kingdom will be preached in the whole world as a testimony to all nations, and then the end will come. Matthew 24:10-14.

16 "You will be betrayed even by parents, brothers, relatives and friends, and they will put some of you to death. Brother will betray brother to death, and a father his child. Children will rebel against their parents and have them put to death. 17 All men will hate you because of me. 18 But not a hair of your head will perish. 19 But you who by standing firm to the end, you will gain life." Luke 21:16-19. Mark 13:12-13.

20 "When you see Jerusalem being surrounded by armies, you will know that its desolation is near. When you see standing in the holy place 'the abomination that causes desolation' where it does not belong, spoken of through the prophet Daniel-let the

reader understand. 21 Then let those who are in Judea flee to the mountains, let those in the city get out, and let those in the country not enter the city. Luke 21:20-21. Mark 13:14. Matthew 24:15-16.

30 "It will be just like this on the day the Son of Man is revealed. 31 On that day let no one who is on the roof of his house, with his goods inside, should go down to get anything out of the house. Likewise, let no one in the field should go back to get his cloak or anything. Luke 17:30-31. Matthew 24:17-18. Mark 13:15-16.

32 Remember Lot's wife! 33 Whoever tries to keep his life will lose it, and whoever loses his life will preserve it. 34 I tell you, on that night two people will be in one bed; one will be taken and the other left. 35 Two women will be grinding grain together; one will be taken and the other left." Luke 17:32-35.

22 For this is the time of punishment in fulfillment of all that has been written. Luke 21:22.

17 How dreadful it will be in those days for pregnant women and nursing mothers! 18 Pray that your flight will not take place in winter or on the Sabbath, 19 because those will be days of great distress in the land and wrath against this people unequaled from the beginning, when God created the world, until now-and never to be equaled again. They will fall by the sword and will be taken as prisoners to all the nations. Jerusalem will be trampled on by the Gentiles until the times of the Gentiles are fulfilled. 20 If the Lord had not cut short those days, no one would survive. But for the sake of the elect, whom he has chosen, he has shortened them. Mark 13:17-20. Matthew 24:19-22. Luke 21:23-24.

23 At that time if anyone says to you, 'Look, here is the Christ!' or, 'Look, there he is!' do not believe it. 24 For false Christs and false prophets will appear and perform great signs and miracles to deceive even the elect-if that were possible. 25 See and be on

your guard, I have told you everything ahead of time. Matthew 24:23-25. Mark 13:21-23.

20 Once, having been asked by the Pharisees when the kingdom of God would come, Jesus replied, "The kingdom of God does not come with your careful observation, 21 nor will people say, 'Here it is,' or 'There it is,' because the kingdom of God is within you." Luke 17:20-21.

22 Then he said to his disciples, "The time is coming when you will long to see one of the days of the Son of Man, but you will not see it. Luke 17:22.

26 "So if men or anyone tells you, 'There he is, out in the desert,' do not go running off out after them; or, 'Here he is, in the inner rooms,' do not believe it. 27 For like as the lightning, which flashes and lights up the sky from one end to other, comes from the east is visible even in the west, so will be the coming of the Son of Man in his day. But first he must suffer many things and be rejected by this generation. Matthew 24:26-27. Luke 17:23-25.

37 "Where, Lord?" they asked. He replied, "Where there is a dead carcass, there the vultures will gather." Luke 17:37. Matthew 24:28.

29 "But in those days, following immediately after the distress of those days there will be signs in the sun, moon and stars. The sun will be darkened, and the moon will not give its light; the stars will fall from the sky, and the heavenly bodies will be shaken.' On the earth, nations will be in anguish and perplexity at the roaring and tossing of the sea. Men will faint from terror, apprehensive of what is coming on the world. 30 "At that time the sign of the Son of Man will appear in the sky, and all the nations of the earth will mourn. At that time men will see the Son of Man coming on the clouds of the sky, with great power and great glory. Matthew 24:29-30. Mark 13:24-26. Luke 21:25-27.

31 When these things begin to take place, stand up and lift up your heads, because your redemption is drawing near. And he will send his angels with a loud trumpet call, and they will gather his elect from the four winds, from one end of the heavens to the ends of the earth. 32 He told them this parable: "Now look and learn this lesson from the fig tree and all the trees: As soon as its twigs get tender and when its leaves sprout out, you can see and know that summer is near. 33 Even so, when you see all these things happening, you know that the kingdom of God is near, right at the door. Matthew 24:31-33. Mark 13:27-29. Luke 21:28-31.

34 I tell you the truth, this generation will certainly not pass away until all these things have happened. 35 Heaven and earth will pass away, but my words will never pass away. Matthew 24:34-35. Mark 13:30-31. Luke 21:32-33.

36 "No one knows about that day or hour, not even the angels in heaven, nor the Son, but only the Father. 37 Just as it was in the days of Noah, so it will be in the days at the coming of the Son of Man. 38 For in the days before the flood, people were eating and drinking, marrying and being given in marriage, up to the day Noah entered the ark; 39 and they knew nothing about what would happen until the flood came and took them all away. Then the flood came and destroyed them all. That is how it will be at the coming of the Son of Man. Matthew 24:36-39. Luke 17:26-27.

28 "It was the same in the days of Lot. People were eating and drinking, buying and selling, planting and building. 29 But the day Lot left Sodom, fire and sulfur rained down from heaven and destroyed them all. Luke 17:28-29.

40 Two men will be in the field; one will be taken and the other left. 41 Two women will be grinding with a hand mill; one will be taken and the other left. 42 "Therefore keep watch, because you do not know on what day your Lord will come. Matthew 24:40-42.

35 "Be dressed ready for service and keep your lamps burning, 36 like men waiting for their master to return from a wedding banquet, so that when he comes and knocks they can immediately open the door for him. 37 It will be good for those servants whose master finds them watching when he comes. I tell you the truth, he will dress himself to serve, will have them recline at the table and will come and wait on them. 38 It will be good for those servants whose master finds them ready, even if he comes in the second or third watch of the night. Luke 12:35-38.

43 But understand this: If the owner of the house had known at what hour or time of night the thief was coming, he would have kept watch and would not have let his house be broken into. 44 So you also must be ready, because the Son of Man will come at an hour when you do not expect him. Peter asked, "Lord, are you telling this parable to us, or to everyone?" Matthew 24:43-44. Luke 12:39-41.

42 The Lord answered, "Who then is the faithful, servant and wise manager, whom the master has put in charge of his servants in his household to give them their food allowance at the proper time? 43 It will be good for that servant whom the master finds doing so when he returns. 44 I tell you the truth; he will put him in charge of all his possessions. Luke 12:42-44. Matthew 24:45-47.

48 But suppose that servant is wicked and says to himself, 'My master is staying away and taking a long time in coming,' 49 and he then begins to beat his fellow men and maid servants and to eat and drink and get drunk with drunkards. 50 The master of that servant will come on a day when he does not expect him and at an hour he is not aware of. 51 He will cut him to pieces and assign him a place with the unbelievers and hypocrites, where there will be weeping and gnashing of teeth. Matthew 24:48-51. Luke 12:45-46.

47 "That servant who knows his master's will and does not get ready or does not do what his master wants will be beaten with

many blows. 48 But the one who does not know and does things deserving punishment will be beaten with few blows. From everyone who has been given much, much will be demanded; and from the one who has been entrusted with much, much more will be asked. Luke 12:47-48.

32 "No one knows about that day or hour, not even the angels in heaven, nor the Son, but only the Father. 33 Be on guard! Be alert! You do not know when that time will come. 34 It's like a man going away: He leaves his house and puts his servants in charge, each with his assigned task, and tells the one at the door to keep watch. 35 "Therefore keep watch because you do not know when the owner of the house will come back-whether in the evening, or at midnight, or when the rooster crows, or at dawn. 36 If he comes suddenly, do not let him find you sleeping. 37 What I say to you, I say to everyone: 'Watch!'" Mark 13:32-37.

34 "Be careful, or your hearts will be weighed down with dissipation, drunkenness and the anxieties of life, and that day will close on you unexpectedly like a trap. 35 For it will come upon all those who live on the face of the whole earth. 36 Be always on the watch, and pray that you may be able to escape all that is about to happen, and that you may be able to stand before the Son of Man." Luke 21:34-36.

37 Each day Jesus was teaching at the temple, and each evening he went out to spend the night on the hill called the Mount of Olives, 38 and all the people came early in the morning to hear him at the temple. Luke 21:37-38.

His Virgins

1 "At that time the kingdom of heaven will be like ten virgins who took their lamps and went out to meet the bridegroom. 2

Five of them were foolish and five were wise. 3 The foolish ones took their lamps but did not take any oil with them. 4 The wise, however, took oil in jars along with their lamps. 5 The bridegroom was a long time in coming, and they all became drowsy and fell asleep.

6 "At midnight the cry rang out: 'Here's the bridegroom! Come out to meet him!'

7 "Then all the virgins woke up and trimmed their lamps. 8 The foolish ones said to the wise, 'Give us some of your oil; our lamps are going out.'

9 "'No,' they replied, 'there may not be enough for both us and you. Instead, go to those who sell oil and buy some for yourselves.' 10 "But while they were on their way to buy the oil, the bridegroom arrived. The virgins who were ready went in with him to the wedding banquet. And the door was shut.

11 "Later the others also came. 'Sir! Sir!' they said. 'Open the door for us!'

12 "But he replied, 'I tell you the truth, I don't know you.'

13 "Therefore keep watch, because you do not know the day or the hour. Matthew 25:1-13.

His Property

14 "Again, it will be like a man going on a journey, who called his servants and entrusted his property to them. 15 To one he gave five talents of money, to another two talents, and to another one talent, each according to his ability. Then he went on his journey. 16 The man who had received the five talents went at once and

put his money to work and gained five more. 17 So also, the one with the two talents gained two more. 18 But the man who had received the one talent went off, dug a hole in the ground and hid his master's money.

19 "After a long time the master of those servants returned and settled accounts with them. 20 The man who had received the five talents brought the other five. 'Master,' he said, 'you entrusted me with five talents. See, I have gained five more.'

21 "His master replied, 'Well done, good and faithful servant! You have been faithful with a few things; I will put you in charge of many things. Come and share your master's happiness!'

22 "The man with the two talents also came. 'Master,' he said, 'you entrusted me with two talents; see, I have gained two more.'

23 "His master replied, 'Well done, good and faithful servant! You have been faithful with a few things; I will put you in charge of many things. Come and share your master's happiness!'

24 "Then the man who had received the one talent came. 'Master,' he said, 'I knew that you are a hard man, harvesting where you have not sown and gathering where you have not scattered seed. 25 So I was afraid and went out and hid your talent in the ground. See, here is what belongs to you.'

26 "His master replied, 'You wicked, lazy servant! So you knew that I harvest where I have not sown and gather where I have not scattered seed? 27 Well then, you should have put my money on deposit with the bankers, so that when I returned I would have received it back with interest.

28 "'Take the talent from him and give it to the one who has the ten talents.

29 For everyone who has will be given more, and he will have an abundance. Whoever does not have, even what he has will be taken from him.

30 And throw that worthless servant outside, into the darkness, where there will be weeping and gnashing of teeth.' Matthew 25:14-30.

His Hunger

31 "When the Son of Man comes in his glory, and all the angels with him, he will sit on his throne in heavenly glory.

32 All the nations will be gathered before him, and he will separate the people one from another as a shepherd separates the sheep from the goats. 33 He will put the sheep on his right and the goats on his left.

34 "Then the King will say to those on his right, 'Come, you who are blessed by my Father; take your inheritance, the kingdom prepared for you since the creation of the world. 35 For I was hungry and you gave me something to eat, I was thirsty and you gave me something to drink, I was a stranger and you invited me in, 36 I needed clothes and you clothed me, I was sick and you looked after me, I was in prison and you came to visit me.'

37 "Then the righteous will answer him, 'Lord, when did we see you hungry and feed you, or thirsty and give you something to drink? 38 When did we see you a stranger and invite you in, or needing clothes and clothe you? 39 When did we see you sick or in prison and go to visit you?'

40 "The King will reply, 'I tell you the truth, whatever you did for one of the least of these brothers of mine, you did for me.'

41 "Then he will say to those on his left, 'Depart from me, you who are cursed, into the eternal fire prepared for the devil and his angels. 42 For I was hungry and you gave me nothing to eat, I was thirsty and you gave me nothing to drink, 43 I was a stranger and you did not invite me in, I needed clothes and you did not clothe me, I was sick and in prison and you did not look after me.'

44 "They also will answer, 'Lord, when did we see you hungry or thirsty or a stranger or needing clothes or sick or in prison, and did not help you?'

45 "He will reply, 'I tell you the truth, whatever you did not do for one of the least of these, you did not do for me.'

46 "Then they will go away to eternal punishment, but the righteous to eternal life." Matthew 25:31-46.

His Plotting Arrest

1 When Jesus had finished saying all these things, he said to his disciples, 2 "As you know, the Passover and the Feast of Unleavened Bread are approaching and is only two days away- and the Son of Man will be handed over to be crucified." 3 Then the chief priests, the teachers of the law and the elders of the people assembled in the palace of the high priest, whose name was Caiaphas, 4 and they were looking to get rid of Jesus by plotting to arrest Jesus in some sly way and kill him. 5 "But not during the Feast," they said, "or there may be a riot among the people, for they were afraid of the people." Matthew 26:1-5. Mark 14:1-2. Luke 22:1-2.

His Betrayer

14 Then Satan entered one of the Twelve-the one called Judas Iscariot-and went to the chief priests and the officers of the temple guard and discussed with them how he might betray Jesus to them. 15 And Judas asked, "What are you willing to give me if I hand him over to you?" They were delighted to hear this; they agreed and promised to give him money. He consented, so they counted out for him thirty silver coins. 16 From then on Judas watched for an opportunity to hand him over to them when no crowd was present. Matthew 26:14-16. Mark 14:10-11. Luke 22:3-6.

His Upper Room

7 Then came the day of Unleavened Bread on which the Passover lamb had to be sacrificed. Luke 22:7.

12 On the first day of the Feast of Unleavened Bread, when it was customary to sacrifice the Passover lamb, Jesus said to his disciples, "Go and make preparations for us to eat the Passover." Peter and John came and asked him, "Where do you want us to go and make preparations for you to eat the Passover?" 13 So he sent two of his disciples, telling them, "As you enter and go into the city, and a certain man carrying a jar of water will meet you. Follow him, 14 and say to the owner of the house he enters, 'The Teacher says and asks: My appointed time is near. I am going to celebrate the Passover with my disciples at your house. Where is my guest room, where I may eat the Passover with my disciples?' 15 He will show you a large upper room, all furnished and ready. Make preparations for us there." 16 So the disciples left and did

as Jesus directed them. They went into the city and found things just as Jesus had told them. So they prepared the Passover. Mark 14:12-16. Matthew 26:17-19. Luke 22:8-13.

His Love

1 It was just before the Passover Feast. Jesus knew that the time had come for him to leave this world and go to the Father. Having loved his own who were in the world, he now showed them the full extent of his love.

2 The evening meal was being served, and the devil had already prompted Judas Iscariot, son of Simon, to betray Jesus. 3 Jesus knew that the Father had put all things under his power, and that he had come from God and was returning to God;

4 so he got up from the meal, took off his outer clothing, and wrapped a towel around his waist. 5 After that, he poured water into a basin and began to wash his disciples' feet, drying them with the towel that was wrapped around him.

6 He came to Simon Peter, who said to him, "Lord, are you going to wash my feet?" 7 Jesus replied, "You do not realize now what I am doing, but later you will understand." 8 "No," said Peter, "you shall never wash my feet." Jesus answered, "Unless I wash you, you have no part with me." 9 "Then, Lord," Simon Peter replied, "not just my feet but my hands and my head as well!"

10 Jesus answered, "A person who has had a bath needs only to wash his feet; his whole body is clean. And you are clean, though not every one of you." 11 For he knew who was going to betray him, and that was why he said not every one was clean.

12 When he had finished washing their feet, he put on his clothes and returned to his place. "Do you understand what I have done for you?" he asked them. 13 "You call me 'Teacher' and 'Lord,' and rightly so, for that is what I am. 14 Now that I, your Lord and Teacher, have washed your feet, you also should wash one another's feet. 15 I have set you an example that you should do as I have done for you. 16 I tell you the truth, no servant is greater than his master, nor is a messenger greater than the one who sent him. 17 Now that you know these things, you will be blessed if you do them.

18 "I am not referring to all of you; I know those I have chosen. But this is to fulfill the scripture: 'He who shares my bread has lifted up his heel against me.'

19 "I am telling you now before it happens, so that when it does happen you will believe that I am He.

20 I tell you the truth, whoever accepts anyone I send accepts me; and whoever accepts me accepts the one who sent me." John 13:1-20.

His Crucifixion Passover

17 When evening and the hour came, Jesus arrived with the Twelve. 18a While he and his apostles were reclining at the table eating, he said to them, "I have eagerly desired to eat this Passover with you before I suffer. For I tell you, I will not eat it again until it finds fulfillment in the kingdom of God. Mark 14:17-18a. Luke 22:14-16. Matthew 26:20-21a.

18b I tell you the truth, one of you will betray me-one who is eating with me." 19 They were very saddened, and began one by one they said to him after the other, "Surely not I, Lord?" 20 "It is one of the Twelve," Jesus replied, "The hand of the one who dips his hand and bread into the bowl with me; is going to betray me, is with mine on the table. 21 The Son of Man will go just as it has been decreed and written about him. But woe to that man who betrays the Son of Man! It would be better for him if he had not been born." Mark 14:18b-21. Matthew 26:21b-24. Luke 22:21-22.

23 They began to question among themselves which of them it might be who would do this.

24 Also a dispute arose among them as to which of them was considered to be greatest. 25 Jesus said to them, "The kings of the Gentiles lord it over them; and those who exercise authority over them call themselves Benefactors.

26 But you are not to be like that. Instead, the greatest among you should be like the youngest, and the one who rules like the one who serves. 27 For who is greater, the one who is at the table or the one who serves? Is it not the one who is at the table? But I am among you as one who serves.

28 You are those who have stood by me in my trials. 29 And I confer on you a kingdom, just as my Father conferred one on me, 30 so that you may eat and drink at my table in my kingdom and sit on thrones, judging the twelve tribes of Israel. Luke 22:23-30.

21 After he had said this, Jesus was troubled in spirit and testified, "I tell you the truth, one of you is going to betray me." 22 His disciples stared at one another, at a loss to know which of them he meant. 23 One of them, the disciple whom Jesus loved, was reclining next to him. 24 Simon Peter motioned to this disciple and said, "Ask him which one he means." 25 Leaning back against Jesus, he asked him, "Lord, who is it?" 26 Jesus answered, "It is the one to whom I will give this piece of bread when I have dipped it in the dish." Then, dipping the piece of bread, he gave it to Judas Iscariot, son of Simon. John 13:21-26.

25 Then Judas, the one who would betray him, said, "Surely not I, Rabbi?" Jesus answered, "Yes, it is you." 26 While they were eating, Jesus took bread, gave thanks and broke it, and gave it to his disciples, saying, "Take it and eat; this is my body given for you; do this in remembrance of me." Matthew 26:25-26. Mark 14:22. Luke 22:19.

27 As soon as Judas took the bread, Satan entered into him. "What you are about to do, do quickly," Jesus told him, 28 but no one at the meal understood why Jesus said this to him. 29 Since Judas had charge of the money, some thought Jesus was telling him to buy what was needed for the Feast, or to give something to the poor. 30 As soon as Judas had taken the bread, he went out. And it was night. John 13:27-30.

31 When he was gone, Jesus said, "Now is the Son of Man glorified and God is glorified in him. 32 If God is glorified in him, God will glorify the Son in himself, and will glorify him at once. John 13:31-32.

27 Then in the same way, after super he took the cup, he gave thanks and offered it to them, saying, "This cup is the new covenant in my blood, which is poured out for you. Take this, divide it among you and drink from it, all of you. 28 This is my blood of the covenant, which is poured out for many for the forgiveness of sins. 29 For I tell you the truth; I will not drink again of this fruit of the vine from now on until the kingdom of God comes; that day when I drink it anew with you in my Father's kingdom." And they all drank from it. Matthew 26:27-29. Mark 14:23-25. Luke 22:17-18, 20.

His Simon Peter

31 "Simon, Simon, Satan has asked to sift you as wheat. 32 But I have prayed for you, Simon that your faith may not fail. And when you have turned back, strengthen your brothers." Luke 22:31-32

33 "My children, I will be with you only a little longer. You will look for me, and just as I told the Jews, so I tell you now: Where I am going, you cannot come. 34 "A new command I give you: Love one another. As I have loved you, so you must love one another. 35 By this all men will know that you are my disciples, if you love one another." John 13:33-35.

36 Simon Peter asked him, "Lord, where are you going?" Jesus replied, "Where I am going, you cannot follow now, but you will follow later." 37 Peter asked; "Lord, why can't I follow you now? I will lay down my life for you. I am ready to go with you to prison and to death" John 13:36-37. Luke 22:33.

38 Then Jesus answered, "Will you really lay down your life for me? I tell you the truth, Peter, before the rooster crows today; you will disown me and deny three times that you know me! John 13:38. Luke 22:34.

35 Then Jesus asked them, "When I sent you without purse, bag or sandals, did you lack anything?" "Nothing," they answered. 6 He said to them, "But now if you have a purse, take it, and also a bag; and if you don't have a sword, sell your cloak and buy one. 37 It is written: 'And he was numbered with the transgressors'; and I tell you that this must be fulfilled in me. Yes, what is written about me is reaching its fulfillment." 38 The disciples said, "See, Lord, here are two swords." "That is enough," he replied. Luke 22:35-38.

His Place

1 "Do not let your hearts be troubled. Trust in God; trust also in me. 2 In my Father's house are many rooms; if it were not so, I would have told you. I am going there to prepare a place for you. 3 And if I go and prepare a place for you, I will come back and take you to be with me that you also may be where I am. 4 You know the way to the place where I am going."

5 Thomas said to him, "Lord, we don't know where you are going, so how can we know the way?" 6 Jesus answered, "I am the way and the truth and the life. No one comes to the Father except through me. 7 If you really knew me, you would know my Father as well. From now on, you do know him and have seen him." John 14:1-7.

His Philip

8 Philip said, "Lord, show us the Father and that will be enough for us."

9 Jesus answered: "Don't you know me, Philip, even after I have been among you such a long time? Anyone who has seen me has seen the Father. How can you say, 'Show us the Father'? 10 Don't you believe that I am in the Father, and that the Father is in me? The words I say to you are not just my own. Rather, it is the Father, living in me, who is doing his work. 11 Believe me when I say that I am in the Father and the Father is in me; or at least believe on the evidence of the miracles themselves. 12 I tell you the truth, anyone who has faith in me will do what I have been doing. He

will do even greater things than these, because I am going to the Father. 13 And I will do whatever you ask in my name, so that the Son may bring glory to the Father. 14 You may ask me for anything in my name, and I will do it. John 14:8-14.

His Counselor

15 "If you love me, you will obey what I command. 16 And I will ask the Father, and he will give you another Counselor to be with you forever- 17 the Spirit of truth. The world cannot accept him, because it neither sees him nor knows him. But you know him, for he lives with you and will be in you. 18 I will not leave you as orphans; I will come to you. 19 Before long, the world will not see me anymore, but you will see me. Because I live, you also will live.

20 On that day you will realize that I am in my Father, and you are in me, and I am in you. 21 Whoever has my commands and obeys them, he is the one who loves me. He who loves me will be loved by my Father, and I too will love him and show myself to him."

22 Then Judas (not Judas Iscariot) said, "But, Lord, why do you intend to show yourself to us and not to the world?"

23 Jesus replied, "If anyone loves me, he will obey my teaching. My Father will love him, and we will come to him and make our home with him. 24 He who does not love me will not obey my teaching. These words you hear are not my own; they belong to the Father who sent me. 25 "All this I have spoken while still with you. 26 But the Counselor, the Holy Spirit, whom the Father will send in my name, will teach you all things and will remind you of everything I have said to you. 27 Peace I leave with you; my peace I give you. I do not give to you as the world gives. Do not let your hearts be troubled and do not be afraid. 28 "You heard me

say, 'I am going away and I am coming back to you.' If you loved me, you would be glad that I am going to the Father, for the Father is greater than I. 29 I have told you now before it happens, so that when it does happen you will believe. 30 I will not speak with you much longer, for the prince of this world is coming. He has no hold on me, 31 but the world must learn that I love the Father and that I do exactly what my Father has commanded me. "Come now; let us leave. John 14:15-31.

His Vine

1 "I am the true vine, and my Father is the gardener. 2 He cuts off every branch in me that bears no fruit, while every branch that does bear fruit he prunes so that it will be even more fruitful. 3 You are already clean because of the word I have spoken to you. 4 Remain in me, and I will remain in you. No branch can bear fruit by itself; it must remain in the vine. Neither can you bear fruit unless you remain in me. 5 "I am the vine; you are the branches. If a man remains in me and I in him, he will bear much fruit; apart from me you can do nothing. 6 If anyone does not remain in me, he is like a branch that is thrown away and withers; such branches are picked up, thrown into the fire and burned. John 15:1-6.

His Father's Glory

7 If you remain in me and my words remain in you, ask whatever you wish, and it will be given you. 8 This is to my Father's glory, that you bear much fruit, showing yourselves to be my disciples.

9 "As the Father has loved me, so have I loved you. Now remain in my love. 10 If you obey my commands, you will remain in my love, just as I have obeyed my Father's commands and remain in his love. 11 I have told you this so that my joy may be in you and that your joy may be complete. 12 My command is this: Love each other as I have loved you. 13 Greater love has no one than this, that he lay down his life for his friends. 14 You are my friends if you do what I command.

15 I no longer call you servants, because a servant does not know his master's business. Instead, I have called you friends, for everything that I learned from my Father I have made known to you. 16 You did not choose me, but I chose you and appointed you to go and bear fruit-fruit that will last. Then the Father will give you whatever you ask in my name. John 15:7-16.

17 This is my command: Love each other. John 15:17.

His Chosen

18 "If the world hates you, keep in mind that it hated me first. 19 If you belonged to the world, it would love you as its own. As it is, you do not belong to the world, but I have chosen you out of the world. That is why the world hates you.

20 Remember the words I spoke to you: 'No servant is greater than his master.' If they persecuted me, they will persecute you also. If they obeyed my teaching, they will obey yours also. 21 They will treat you this way because of my name, for they do not know the One who sent me. 22 If I had not come and spoken to them, they would not be guilty of sin. Now, however, they have no excuse for their sin.

23 He who hates me hates my Father as well. 24 If I had not done among them what no one else did, they would not be guilty of sin. But now they have seen these miracles, and yet they have hated both me and my Father. 25 But this is to fulfill what is written in their Law: 'They hated me without reason.'

26 "When the Counselor comes, whom I will send to you from the Father, the Spirit of truth who goes out from the Father, he will testify about me. 27 And you also must testify, for you have been with me from the beginning. John 15:18-27.

His Told You So

1 "All this I have told you so that you will not go astray.

2 They will put you out of the synagogue; in fact, a time is coming when anyone who kills you will think he is offering a service to God. 3 They will do such things because they have not known the Father or me. John 16:1-3.

4 I have told you this, so that when the time comes you will remember that I warned you. I did not tell you this at first because I was with you. John 16:4.

His Spirit of Truth

5 "Now I am going to him who sent me, yet none of you asks me, 'Where are you going?' 6 Because I have said these things, you are filled with grief. 7 But I tell you the truth: It is for your good that I am going away. Unless I go away, the Counselor will not come to you; but if I go, I will send him to you. 8 When he comes, he will

convict the world of guilt in regard to sin and righteousness and judgment: 9 in regard to sin, because men do not believe in me; 10 in regard to righteousness, because I am going to the Father, where you can see me no longer; 11 and in regard to judgment, because the prince of this world now stands condemned.

12 "I have much more to say to you, more than you can now bear. 13 But when he, the Spirit of truth, comes, he will guide you into all truth. He will not speak on his own; he will speak only what he hears, and he will tell you what is yet to come. 14 He will bring glory to me by taking from what is mine and making it known to you. 15 All that belongs to the Father is mine. That is why I said the Spirit will take from what is mine and make it known to you.

16 "In a little while you will see me no more; and then after a little while you will see me." John 16:5-16.

His Speaking

17 Some of his disciples said to one another, "What does he mean by saying, 'In a little while you will see me no more, and then after a little while you will see me,' and 'Because I am going to the Father'?" 18 They kept asking, "What does he mean by 'a little while'? We don't understand what he is saying."

19 Jesus saw that they wanted to ask him about this, so he said to them, "Are you asking one another what I meant when I said, 'In a little while you will see me no more, and then after a little while you will see me'? 20 I tell you the truth, you will weep and mourn while the world rejoices. You will grieve, but your grief will turn to joy. 21 A woman giving birth to a child has pain because her time has come; but when her baby is born she forgets the anguish because of her joy that a child is born into the world.

22 So with you: Now is your time of grief, but I will see you again and you will rejoice, and no one will take away your joy. 23 In that day you will no longer ask me anything. I tell you the truth, my Father will give you whatever you ask in my name. 24 Until now you have not asked for anything in my name. Ask and you will receive, and your joy will be complete. 25 "Though I have been speaking figuratively, a time is coming when I will no longer use this kind of language but will tell you plainly about my Father. 26 In that day you will ask in my name. I am not saying that I will ask the Father on your behalf. 27 No, the Father himself loves you because you have loved me and have believed that I came from God. 28 I came from the Father and entered the world; now I am leaving the world and going back to the Father."

29 Then Jesus' disciples said, "Now you are speaking clearly and without figures of speech. 30 Now we can see that you know all things and that you do not even need to have anyone ask you questions. This makes us believe that you came from God."

31 "You believe at last!" Jesus answered. 32 "But a time is coming, and has come, when you will be scattered; each to his own home. You will leave me all alone. Yet I am not alone, for my Father is with me. 33 "I have told you these things, so that in me you may have peace. In this world you will have trouble. But take heart! I have overcome the world." John 16:17-33.

His Strike

30 When they had sung a hymn, Jesus went out as usual to the Mount of Olives, and his disciples followed him. Matthew 26:30. Mark 14:26. Luke 22:39.

31 Then Jesus told them, "This very night you will all fall away on account of me," Jesus told them, "for it is written: "'I will strike

the shepherd, and the sheep of the flock will be scattered.' 32 But after I have risen, I will go ahead of you into Galilee." 33 Peter declared, "Even if all fall away on account of you, I never will." 34 "I tell you the truth," Jesus answered, "this very day tonight-yes, before the rooster crows twice, you yourself will disown me three times." 35 But Peter insisted emphatically, "Even if I have to die with you, I will never disown you." And all the other disciples said the same. Matthew 26:31-35. Mark 14:27-31.

40 On reaching the place, he said to them, "Pray that you will not fall into temptation." Luke 22:40.

His Eternal Life

1 After Jesus said this, he looked toward heaven and prayed: "Father, the time has come. Glorify your Son, that your Son may glorify you. 2 For you granted him authority over all people that he might give eternal life to all those you have given him. 3 Now this is eternal life: that they may know you, the only true God, and Jesus Christ, whom you have sent. 4 I have brought you glory on earth by completing the work you gave me to do. 5 And now, Father, glorify me in your presence with the glory I had with you before the world began. John 17:1-5.

His Unity Prayer

6 "I have revealed you to those; whom you gave me out of the world. They were yours; you gave them to me and they have obeyed your word. 7 Now they know that everything you have given me comes from you. 8 For I gave them the words you gave

me and they accepted them. They knew with certainty that I came from you, and they believed that you sent me.

9 I pray for them. I am not praying for the world, but for those you have given me, for they are yours. 10 All I have is yours, and all you have is mine. And glory has come to me through them. 11 I will remain in the world no longer, but they are still in the world, and I am coming to you. Holy Father, protect them by the power of your name-the name you gave me-so that they may be one as we are one.

12 While I was with them, I protected them and kept them safe by that name you gave me. None has been lost except the one doomed to destruction so that Scripture would be fulfilled.

13 "I am coming to you now, but I say these things while I am still in the world, so that they may have the full measure of my joy within them. 14 I have given them your word and the world has hated them, for they are not of the world any more than I am of the world.

15 My prayer is not that you take them out of the world but that you protect them from the evil one. 16 They are not of the world, even as I am not of it. 17 Sanctify them by the truth; your word is truth. 18 As you sent me into the world, I have sent them into the world. 19 For them I sanctify myself, that they too may be truly sanctified. John 17:6-19.

20 "My prayer; is not for them alone. I pray also for those who will believe in me through their message, 21 that all of them may be one, Father, just as you are in me and I am in you. May they also be in us so that the world may believe that you have sent me. 22 I have given them the glory that you gave me, that they may be one as we are one: 23 I in them and you in me. May they be brought to complete unity to let the world know that you sent me and have loved them even as you have loved me.

24 "Father, I want those you have given me to be with me where I am, and to see my glory, the glory you have given me because you loved me before the creation of the world. 25 "Righteous Father, though the world does not know you, I know you, and they know that you have sent me. 26 I have made you known to them, and will continue to make you known in order that the love you have for me may be in them and that I myself may be in them." John 17:20-26.

His Crucifixion Prayer

36 Then Jesus went with his disciples to a place called Gethsemane, and he said to his disciples, "Sit here while I go over there and pray." 37 He took Peter and the two sons of Zebedee: James and John, along with him, and he began to be deeply sorrowful, distressed and troubled. 38 Then he said to them, "My soul is overwhelmed with sorrow to the point of death," he said to them, "Stay here and keep watch with me." Matthew 26:36-38. Mark 14:32-34.

35 Going a little farther, he fell to the ground and prayed that if possible the hour might pass from him. 36 "Abba, My Father," he said, "everything is possible for you. If it is possible, take this cup from me. Yet not what I will, but as what you will." 37 Then he returned to his disciples and found them sleeping. "Simon," he said to Peter, "are you asleep? Could you men not keep watch with me for one hour? 38 Watch and pray so that you will not fall into temptation. The spirit is willing, but the body is weak." Mark 14:35-38. Matthew 26:39-41.

42 Once more he went away a second time and prayed the same thing. He withdrew about a stone's throw beyond them, knelt down and prayed, "My Father, if you are willing, take this cup from me; if it is not possible for this cup to be taken away from

me, unless I drink it; yet not my will, but may your will be done." An angel from heaven appeared to him and strengthened him. And being in anguish, he prayed more earnestly, and his sweat was like drops of blood falling to the ground. 43 When he rose from prayer and went back to his disciples, he again found them sleeping, because their eyes were heavy and exhausted from sorrow. "Why are you sleeping?" he asked them. "Get up and pray so that you will not fall into temptation." They did not know what to say to him. Matthew 26:42-43. Mark 14:39-40. Luke 22:41-46.

44 So he left them and went away once more and prayed the third time, saying the same thing. Matthew 26:44.

45 Then he returned to the disciples a third time and said to them, "Are you still sleeping and resting? Enough! Look, the hour is near and has come; the Son of Man is betrayed into the hands of sinners. 46 Rise! Let us go! Here comes my betrayer!" Matthew 26:45-46. Mark 14:41-42.

His Crucifixion Betrayer

1 When he had finished praying, Jesus left with his disciples and crossed the Kidron Valley. On the other side there was an olive grove, and he and his disciples went into it. 2 Now Judas, who betrayed him, knew the place, because Jesus had often met there with his disciples. John 18:1-2.

47 While he was still speaking, Judas, one of the Twelve, arrived and appeared. So Judas came up to the grove leading and guiding, with him was a large crowd of detachment of soldiers armed with swords and clubs as weapons, and some officials from the chief priests and Pharisees carrying torches and lanterns; sent from the

chief priest, the teachers of the law and the elders of the people. Matthew 26:47. John 18:3. Mark 14:43. Luke 22:47a.

4 Jesus, knowing all that was going to happen to him, went out and asked them, "Who is it you want?" 5 "Jesus of Nazareth," they replied. "I am he," Jesus said. (And Judas the traitor was standing there with them.) 6 When Jesus said, "I am he," they drew back and fell to the ground. 7 Again he asked them, "Who is it you want?" And they said, "Jesus of Nazareth." 8 "I told you that I am he," Jesus answered. "If you are looking for me, then let these men go." 9 This happened so that the words he had spoken would be fulfilled: "I have not lost one of those you gave me." John 18:4-9.

48 Now the betrayer had arranged a signal with them: "The one I kiss is the man; arrest him and lead him away under guard." 49 Going at once to approach Jesus to kiss him, Judas said, "Greetings, Rabbi!" and kissed him. 50a Jesus asked, "Judas, are you betraying the Son of Man with a kiss?" then replied, "Friend, do what you came for." Matthew 26:48-50a. Mark 14:44-45. Luke 22:47b-48.

50b Then the men stepped forward, seized Jesus and arrested him. When Jesus' followers saw what was going to happen, they said, "Lord, should we strike with our swords?" 51 With that, one of Jesus' companions standing near, Simon Peter who had a sword, reached for his sword, drew it out and struck the servant of the high priest, cutting off his right ear. (The servant's name was Malchus.) 52 Jesus commanded Peter and said to him, "Put your sword back in its place. For all who draw the sword will die by the sword. 53 Do you think I cannot call on my Father, and he will at once put at my disposal more than twelve legions of angels? 54 But how then would the Scriptures be fulfilled that say it must happen in this way? Shall I not drink the cup the Father has given me?" Matthew 26:50b-54. John 18:10-11. Mark 14:46-47. Luke 22:49-50.

51 But Jesus answered, "No more of this!" And he touched the man's ear and healed him. Luke 22:51.

56a But this has all taken place that the Scripture writings of the prophets might be fulfilled." Matthew 26:56a.

52 At that time, then Jesus said to the crowd of chief priests, the officers of the temple guard, and the elders, who had come for him, "Am I leading a rebellion, that you have come with swords and clubs to capture me? 53 Every day I was with you, I sat in the temple courts teaching, and you did not lay a hand on me; you did not arrest me. This has all taken place that the Scripture writings of the prophets might be fulfilled. But this is your hour-when darkness reigns." Luke 22:52-53. Matthew 26:55. Mark 14:48-49.

50 Then everyone and all the disciples deserted him and fled. Mark 14:50. Matthew 26:56b.

51 A young man, wearing nothing but a linen garment, was following Jesus. When they seized him, 52 he fled naked, leaving his garment behind. Mark 14:51-52.

His Crucifixion Arrest

12 Then the detachment of soldiers with its commander and the Jewish officials arrested Jesus. They bound him 13 and brought him first to Annas, who was the father-in-law of Caiaphas, the high priest that year. 14 Caiaphas was the one who had advised the Jews that it would be good if one man died for the people.

15 Simon Peter and another disciple were following Jesus. Because this disciple was known to the high priest, he went with Jesus into the high priest's courtyard, 16 but Peter had to wait outside

at the door. The other disciple, who was known to the high priest, came back, spoke to the girl on duty there and brought Peter in. John 18:12-16.

His Simon's First Denial

54b Peter followed at a distance. 55 But when they had kindled a fire in the middle of the courtyard below and had sat down together, Peter sat down with them. 56 A servant girl at the door of the high priest came by and saw him seated there in the courtyard firelight. When she saw Simon Peter warming himself, she came and looked closely at him and said, "This man was with him." "You also were with that Nazarene, Jesus of Galilee. You are not one of his disciples, are you?" 57 But he replied and denied it before them all. "I am not. I don't know or understand what you're talking about," "Woman, I don't know him," he said and went out into the entryway. Luke 22:54b-57. Mark 14:66-68. Matthew 26:69-70. John 18:17.

18 It was cold, and the servants and officials stood around a fire they had made to keep warm. Peter also was standing with them, warming himself. John 18:18.

His Annas

19 Meanwhile, the high priest Annas questioned Jesus about his disciples and his teaching.

20 "I have spoken openly to the world," Jesus replied. "I always taught in synagogues or at the temple, where all the Jews come

together. I said nothing in secret. 21 Why question me? Ask those who heard me. Surely they know what I said."

22 When Jesus said this, one of the officials nearby struck him in the face. "Is this the way you answer the high priest?" he demanded.

23 "If I said something wrong," Jesus replied, "testify as to what is wrong. But if I spoke the truth, why did you strike me?"

24 Then Annas sent him, still bound; to Caiaphas the high priest. John 18:19-24.

His Caiaphas

57 Then seizing Jesus, those who had arrested Jesus led and took him into the house of Caiaphas, the high priest, where the teachers of the law, all the chief priests and the elders had came to together and assembled. Matthew 26:57. Mark 14:53. Luke 54a.

58 But Peter followed him at a distance, right up to the courtyard of the high priest. There he entered and sat down with the guards to see the outcome and warmed himself at the fire. Matthew 26:58. Mark 14:54.

55 The chief priests and the whole Sanhedrin were looking for false evidence against Jesus so that they could put him to death, but they did not find any. 56 Though many false witnesses came forward and testified falsely against him, but their statements did not agree. 57 Then finally two stood up and came forward; declared and gave this false testimony against him: 58 "We heard this fellow say, 'I am able to and will destroy this man-made temple of God and rebuild another in three days, not made by

man.'" 59 Yet even then their testimony did not agree. Mark 14:55-59. Matthew 26:59-61.

62 Then the high priest stood up before them and said to Jesus, "Are you not going to answer? What is this testimony that these men are bringing against you?" 63 But Jesus remained silent and gave no answer. Again the high priest said to him, "I charge you under oath by the living God: Tell us if you are the Christ, the Son of God the Blessed One." 64 "Yes, I am, it is as you say," Jesus replied. "But I say to all of you: In the future you will see the Son of Man sitting at the right hand of the Mighty One and coming on the clouds of heaven." Matthew 26:62-64. Mark 14:60-62.

65 Then the high priest tore his clothes and said, "He has spoken blasphemy! Why do we need any more witnesses?" he asked. "Look, now you have heard the blasphemy. 66 What do you think?" "He is worthy of death," they answered. They all condemned him as worthy of death. 67 Then some began to spit in his face; they blindfolded him and struck him with their fists, and said, "Prophesy!" Others slapped him 68 and said, "Prophesy to us, Christ. Who hit you?" And the guards took him and beat him. Matthew 26:65-68. Mark 14:63-65.

His Simon's Second Denial

71 Then Simon Peter went out to the gateway stood warming himself. When a little later; where another servant girl saw him, said to those people standing around there, "This fellow was with Jesus of Nazareth. You also are one of them." He was asked, "You are not one of his disciples, are you?" 72 He denied it again, with an oath: "Man, I am not! I don't know the man!" Matthew 26:71-72. John 18:25. Mark 14:69-70a. Luke 22:58.

His Simon's Third Denial

70b After a little while later – about an hour, those standing near there went up Peter. One of the high priest's servants, a relative of the man whose ear Peter had cut off, challenged and asserted him said, "Didn't I see you with him in the olive grove?" "Certainly this fellow was with him. Surely you are one of them, for you are a Galilean, for your accent gives you away." 71 Peter replied and denied it, "Man, I don't know what you're talking about!" Then he began to call down curses on himself, and he swore to them, "I don't know this man you're talking about!" 72a At that moment, just as he was speaking, immediately the rooster crowed the second time. Mark 14:70b-72a. Matthew 26:73-74. Luke 22:59-61. John 18:26-27.

61 The Lord turned and looked straight at Peter. Then Peter remembered the word the Lord Jesus had spoken to him: "Before the rooster crows twice today, you will disown me three times." 62 And he went outside, broke down and wept bitterly. Luke 22:61-62. Mark 14:72b. Matthew 26:75.

His Sanhedrin Beatings

63 The men who were guarding Jesus began mocking and beating him. 64 They blindfolded him and demanded, "Prophesy! Who hit you?" 65 And they said many other insulting things to him.

66 At daybreak the council of the elders of the people, both the chief priests and teachers of the law, met together, and Jesus was led before them. 67 "If you are the Christ," they said, "tell us."

Jesus answered, "If I tell you, you will not believe me, 68 and if I asked you, you would not answer. 69 But from now on, the Son of Man will be seated at the right hand of the mighty God." 70 They all asked, "Are you then the Son of God?" He replied, "You are right in saying I am." 71 Then they said, "Why do we need any more testimony? We have heard it from his own lips." Luke 22:63-71.

1 Very early in the morning, all the chief priests, with the elders of the people, the teachers of the law and the whole Sanhedrin, reached a decision to put Jesus to death. They bound Jesus, led him away and handed him over to Pilate, the governor. Mark 15:1. Matthew 27:1-2.

His Blood Money

3 When Judas, who had betrayed him, saw that Jesus was condemned, he was seized with remorse and returned the thirty silver coins to the chief priests and the elders. 4 "I have sinned," he said, "for I have betrayed innocent blood." "What is that to us?" they replied. "That's your responsibility."

5 So Judas threw the money into the temple and left. Then he went away and hanged himself.

6 The chief priests picked up the coins and said, "It is against the law to put this into the treasury, since it is blood money." 7 So they decided to use the money to buy the potter's field as a burial place for foreigners.

8 That is why it has been called the Field of Blood to this day.

9 Then what was spoken by Jeremiah the prophet was fulfilled: "They took the thirty silver coins, the price set on him by the

people of Israel, 10 and they used them to buy the potter's field, as the Lord commanded me." Matthew 27:3-10.

His Pilate

1 Then the Jews and the whole assembly rose and led Jesus off from Caiaphas to the palace of the Roman governor Pilate. By now it was early morning, and to avoid ceremonial uncleanness the Jews did not enter the palace; they wanted to be able to eat the Passover. 2 And they began to accuse him, saying, "We have found this man subverting our nation. He opposes payment of taxes to Caesar and claims to be Christ, a king." Luke 23:1-2. John 18:28.

29 So Pilate came out to them and asked, "What charges are you bringing against this man?" 30 "If he were not a criminal," they replied, "we would not have handed him over to you." 31 Pilate said, "Take him yourselves and judge him by your own law." "But we have no right to execute anyone," the Jews objected. 32 This happened so that the words Jesus had spoken indicating the kind of death he was going to die would be fulfilled. John 18:29-32.

33 Pilate then went back inside the palace, summoned Jesus and Jesus stood before the governor and the governor asked him, "Are you the king of the Jews?" 34 "Yes, it is as you say," "Is that your own idea," Jesus asked, "or did others talk to you about me?" 35 "Am I a Jew?" Pilate replied. "It was your people and your chief priests who handed you over to me. What is it you have done?" 36 Jesus said, "My kingdom is not of this world. If it were, my servants would fight to prevent my arrest by the Jews. But now my kingdom is from another place." 37 "You are a king, then!" said Pilate. Jesus answered, "You are right in saying I am a king. In fact, for this reason I was born, and for this I came into the world, to testify to the truth. Everyone on the side of truth listens

to me." 38a "What is truth?" Pilate asked. John 18:33-38a. Matthew 27:11. Mark 15:2. Luke 23:3.

38b With this he went out again to the Jews and said, "I find no basis for a charge against him. John 18:38b.

12 When he was accused of many things by the chief priests and the elders, he gave no answer. 13 So then again Pilate asked him, "Don't you hear the testimony they are bringing against you?" "Aren't you going to answer? See how many things they are accusing you of." 14 But Jesus made no reply, not even to a single charge-to the great amazement of Pilate, the governor. Matthew 27:12-14. Mark 15:3-5.

4 Then Pilate announced to the chief priests and the crowd, "I find no basis for a charge against this man." 5 But they insisted, "He stirs up he people all over Judea by his teaching. He started in Galilee and has come all the way here." Luke 23:4-5.

His Herod

6 On hearing this, Pilate asked if the man was a Galilean. 7 When he learned that Jesus was under Herod's jurisdiction, he sent him to Herod, who was also in Jerusalem at that time.

8 When Herod saw Jesus, he was greatly pleased, because for a long time he had been wanting to see him. From what he had heard about him, he hoped to see him perform some miracle. 9 He plied him with many questions, but Jesus gave him no answer.

10 The chief priests and the teachers of the law were standing there, vehemently accusing him.

11 Then Herod and his soldiers ridiculed and mocked him. Dressing him in an elegant robe, they sent him back to Pilate.

12 That day Herod and Pilate became friends-before this they had been enemies. Luke 23:6-12.

His Pilate Again

13 Pilate called together the chief priests, the rulers and the people, 14 and said to them, "You brought me this man as one who was inciting the people to rebellion. I have examined him in your presence and have found no basis for your charges against him. 15 Neither has Herod, for he sent him back to us; as you can see, he has done nothing to deserve death. 16 Therefore, I will punish him and then release him." Luke 23:13-16.

15 Now it was the governor's custom at the Feast to release a prisoner whom chosen by the crowd of people. 16 At that time they had a notorious prisoner, a man called Barabbas, with the insurrectionists who had committed murder in the uprising. 17 So when the crowd had came up and gathered; asked Pilate to do for them what he usually did, Pilate said and asked them, "But it is your custom for me to release to you one prisoner at the time of the Passover. Which one do you want me to release to you: Barabbas, or Jesus who is called Christ, the king of the Jews?" 18 For he knew it was out of envy that the chief priests had handed Jesus over to him. Matthew 27:15-18. Mark 15:6-10. John 18:39.

19 While Pilate was sitting on the judge's seat, his wife sent him this message: "Don't have anything to do with that innocent man, for I have suffered a great deal today in a dream because of him." Matthew 27:19.

20 But the chief priests and the elders persuaded and stirred up the crowd to have Pilate release Barabbas instead by asking for Barabbas and to have Jesus executed. 21 "Which of the two do you want me to release to you?" asked the governor. "Barabbas," they answered. 22 "What shall I do, then, with Jesus who is called Christ, the one you call the king of the Jews?" Pilate asked them. They all answered and shouted, "Crucify him!" Matthew 27:20-22. Mark 15:11-13.

18 Then with one voice they shouted and cried out back, "No, not him! Away with this man! Release and give Barabbas to us!" 19 (Barabbas had been thrown into prison for taking part in an insurrection in the city, for rebellion and for murder.) Luke 23:18-19. John 18:40.

20 Wanting to release Jesus, Pilate appealed to them again. 21 But they kept shouting, "Crucify him! Crucify him!" Luke 23:20-21.

23 For the third time he spoke to them: "Why? What crime has he committed? I have found in him no grounds for the death penalty. Therefore I will have him punished and then release him," asked Pilate. But they shouted all the louder and insistently demanded that he be crucified, "Crucify him!" And their shouts prevailed. 24 When Pilate saw that he was getting nowhere, but that instead an uproar was starting, he took water and washed his hands in front of the crowd. "I am innocent of this man's blood," he said. "It is your responsibility!" 25 All the people answered, "Let his blood be on us and on our children!" Matthew 27:23-25. Mark 15:14. Luke 23:22-23.

24 So then Pilate wanting to satisfy the crowd, decided to grant their demand. 25 Then he released Barabbas to them; the man who had been thrown into prison for insurrection and murder, the one they asked for, and surrendered Jesus to their will. Then Pilate took Jesus and had him flogged. So the soldiers took charge of Jesus. Luke 23:24-25. Matthew 27:26a. Mark 15:15a. John 19:1.

His Praetorium

27 Then the governor's soldiers took and led Jesus into the Praetorium Palace and called and gathered the whole company of soldiers around him. 28 They stripped him and clothed him in a purple scarlet robe, 29 and then twisted together a crown of thorns and set it on his head. They put a staff in his right hand and knelt in front of him and began to call out to him and mocked him. "Hail, king of the Jews!" they said. 30 They spit on him, and took the staff and struck him on the head and in the face, again and again. Falling on their knees, they paid homage to him. Matthew 27:27-30. Mark 15:16-19. John 19:2-3.

4 Once more Pilate came out and said to the Jews, "Look, I am bringing him out to you to let you know that I find no basis for a charge against him." 5 When Jesus came out wearing the crown of thorns and the purple robe, Pilate said to them, "Here is the man!"

6 As soon as the chief priests and their officials saw him, they shouted, "Crucify! Crucify!" But Pilate answered, "You take him and crucify him. As for me, I find no basis for a charge against him."

7 The Jews insisted, "We have a law, and according to that law he must die, because he claimed to be the Son of God."

8 When Pilate heard this, he was even more afraid, 9 and he went back inside the palace. "Where do you come from?" he asked Jesus, but Jesus gave him no answer. 10 "Do you refuse to speak to me?" Pilate said. "Don't you realize I have power either to free you or to crucify you?" 11 Jesus answered, "You would have no

power over me if it were not given to you from above. Therefore the one who handed me over to you is guilty of a greater sin."

12 From then on, Pilate tried to set Jesus free, but the Jews kept shouting, "If you let this man go, you are no friend of Caesar. Anyone who claims to be a king opposes Caesar."

13 When Pilate heard this, he brought Jesus out and sat down on the judge's seat at a place known as the Stone Pavement (which in Aramaic is Gabbatha). 14 It was the day of Preparation of Passover Week, about the sixth hour. "Here is your king," Pilate said to the Jews. 15 But they shouted, "Take him away! Take him away! Crucify him!" "Shall I crucify your king?" Pilate asked. "We have no king but Caesar," the chief priests answered. John 19:4-15.

31 After they had mocked him, they took off the purple robe and put his own clothes on him. Then they led him away out to crucify him. Matthew 27:31, 26b. Mark 15:20, 15b. Luke 23:26a. John 19:16.

His Golgotha

17 Carrying his own cross, he went out to the place of the Skull (which in Aramaic is called Golgotha). John 19:17.

32 As they were going out, they met a certain man from Cyrene, named Simon, the father of Alexander and Rufus, was passing by on his way in from the country, and they seized and forced him put the cross on and made him to carry the cross behind Jesus. A large number of people followed him, including women who mourned and wailed for him. Jesus turned and said to them, "Daughters of Jerusalem, do not weep for me; weep for yourselves and for your children. For the time will come when you will say, 'Blessed are the barren women, the wombs that never bore

and the breasts that never nursed!' Then "'they will say to the mountains, "Fall on us!" and to the hills, "Cover us!" 'For if men do these things when the tree is green, what will happen when it is dry?" 33 They came and brought Jesus to a place called Golgotha (which means The Place of the Skull). Two other men, both criminals, were also led out with him to be executed. 34 Then there they offered Jesus wine to drink, mixed with gall/ myrrh; but after tasting it, he refused to drink it. Matthew 27:32-34. Mark 15:21-23. Luke 23:26b-33a.

Chapter Five

HIS DEATH

His Crucifixion

33a It was in the third hour when there they crucified him, along with him the two robbers - one on his right, the other on his left and Jesus in the middle. 34a Jesus said, "Father, forgive them, for they do not know what they are doing." Luke 23:33a-34a. John 19:18. Matthew 27:35a, 38. Mark 15:24a, 25, 27.

23 When the soldiers crucified Jesus, they took his clothes into four shares, one for each of them, with the undergarment remaining. This garment was seamless, woven in one piece from top to bottom. 24 "Let's not tear it," they said to one another. "Let's decide by lot who will get it." This happened that the scripture might be fulfilled which said, "They divided my garments among them and cast lots for my clothing." So this is what the soldiers did. They divided up his clothes by casting lots to see what each would get. John 19:23-24. Matthew 27:35b. Luke 23:34b. Mark 15:24b.

36 And sitting down, they kept watch over him there. Matthew 27:36.

35 The people stood watching, and the rulers even sneered at him. They said, "He saved others; let him save himself if he is the Christ of God, the Chosen One." 36 The soldiers also came up and mocked him. They offered him wine vinegar 37 and said, "If you are the king of the Jews, save yourself." Luke 23:35-37.

37 There above his head they placed the written notice of the charge against him, which read: THIS IS JESUS, THE KING OF THE JEWS. Matthew 27:37. Mark 15:26. Luke 23:38.

19 Pilate had a notice prepared and fastened to the cross. It read: JESUS OF NAZARETH, THE KING OF THE JEWS. 20 Many of the Jews read this sign, for the place where Jesus was crucified was near the city, and the sign was written in Aramaic, Latin and Greek. 21 The chief priests of the Jews protested to Pilate, "Do not write 'The King of the Jews,' but that this man claimed to be king of the Jews." 22 Pilate answered, "What I have written, I have written." John 19:19-22.

39 Those who passed by hurled insults at him, shaking their heads 40 and saying, "So! You who are going to destroy the temple and build it in three days, save yourself! Come down from the cross, if you are the Son of God!" 41 In the same way the chief priests, the teachers of the law and the elders mocked him among themselves. 42 "He saved others," they said, "but he can't save himself! Let this Christ, this King of Israel! Let him come down now from the cross, and we may see and will believe in him. 43 He trusts in God. Let God rescue him now if he wants him, for he said, 'I am the Son of God.'" 44 In the same way the robbers who were crucified with him also heaped insults on him. Matthew 27:39-44. Mark 15:29-32.

39 One of the criminals who hung there hurled insults at him: "Aren't you the Christ? Save yourself and us!" 40 But the other criminal rebuked him. "Don't you fear God," he said, "since you are under the same sentence? 41 We are punished justly, for we are getting what our deeds deserve. But this man has done nothing wrong." 42 Then he said, "Jesus, remember me when you come into your kingdom." 43 Jesus answered him, "I tell you the truth, today you will be with me in paradise." Luke 23:39-43.

His Disfigured Appearance

13 See, my servant will act wisely; he will be raised and lifted up and highly exalted. 14 Just as there were many who were appalled at him — His appearance was so disfigured beyond that of any man and his form marred beyond human likeness — 15 so will he sprinkle many nations, and kings will shut their mouths because of him. For what they were not told, they will see, and what they have not heard, they will understand. Isaiah 52:13-15.

10 He was in the world, and though the world was made through him, the world did not recognize him. 11 He came to that which was his own, but his own did not receive him. 12 Yet to all who received him, to those who believed in his name, he gave the right to become children of God- 13 children born not of natural descent, nor of human decision or a husband's will, but born of God. John 1:10-13

His Crucifixion Ending

25 Near the cross of Jesus stood his mother, his mother's sister, Mary the wife of Clopas, and Mary Magdalene. 26 When Jesus saw his mother there, and the disciple whom he loved standing nearby, he said to his mother, "Dear woman, here is your son," 27 and to the disciple, "Here is your mother." From that time on, this disciple took her into his home. John 19:25-27.

45 From now at the sixth hour until the ninth hour darkness came over all the whole land, for the sun stopped shinning. 46 And at about the ninth hour Jesus cried out in a loud voice, "Eloi, Eloi,

lama sabachthani?"-which means, "My God, my God, why have you forsaken me?" 47 When some of those standing there heard this, they said, "Listen, he's calling Elijah." Later, knowing that all was now completed, and so that the Scripture would be fulfilled, Jesus said, "I am thirsty." A jar of wine vinegar was there. 48 Immediately one man ran and got a sponge. He soaked a sponge with wine vinegar, put it on a stalk of the hyssop plant, lifted it to Jesus' lips and offered it to Jesus to drink. 49 The rest said, "Now leave him alone. Let's see if Elijah comes to save and take him down." 50 And when Jesus had received the drink, he cried out again in a loud voice, "It is finished. Father, into your hands I commit my spirit." When he had said this, Jesus breathed his last, bowed his head and gave up his spirit. Matthew 27:45-50. Mark 15:33-37. Luke 23:44-45a, 46. John 19:28-30.

51 At that moment the curtain of the temple was torn in two from top to bottom. The earth shook and the rocks split. Matthew 27:51. Mark 15:38. Luke 23:45b.

54 And when the centurion, who stood there in front of Jesus, heard his cry and saw how he died; and those with him who were guarding Jesus saw the earthquake and all that had happened, they were terrified. Praised God and exclaimed, "Surely this was a righteous man, the Son of God!" 55 When all the people who had gathered to witness this sight saw what took place, they beat their breasts and went away. But all those who knew him, including many women were there, stood watching these things from a distance. They had followed Jesus from Galilee to care for his needs. 56 Among them were Mary Magdalene, Mary the mother of James the younger and Joses, and Salome and the mother of Zebedee's sons. In Galilee these women had followed him and cared for his needs. Many other women who had come up with him to Jerusalem were also there. Matthew 27:54-56. Mark 15:39-41. Luke 23:44-49.

31 Now it was the day of Preparation (that is, the day before the Sabbath), and the next day was to be a special Sabbath; was

about to begin. Because the Jews did not want the bodies left on the crosses during the Sabbath, they asked Pilate to have the legs broken and the bodies taken down. 32 The soldiers therefore came and broke the legs of the first man who had been crucified with Jesus, and then those of the other. 33 But when they came to Jesus and found that he was already dead, they did not break his legs. 34 Instead, one of the soldiers pierced Jesus' side with a spear, bringing a sudden flow of blood and water. 35 The man who saw it has given testimony, and his testimony is true. He knows that he tells the truth, and he testifies so that you also may believe. 36 These things happened so that the scripture would be fulfilled: "Not one of his bones will be broken," 37 and, as another scripture says, "They will look on the one they have pierced." John 19:31-37. Mark 15:42a. Luke 23:54.

His Tomb

42b So now as evening approached, there came a rich man from the Judean town of Arimathea, named, 43 Joseph of Arimathea who had himself become a disciple of Jesus but secretly because he feared the Jews, a prominent member of the Council, a good and upright man, who had not consented to their decision and action, who was himself waiting for the kingdom of God, went boldly going to Pilate and he asked for Jesus' body. 44 Pilate was surprised to hear that he was already dead. Summoning the centurion, he asked him if Jesus had already died. 45 When he learned from the centurion that it was so, and Pilate ordered with permission that the body to be given to Joseph. 46 So Joseph bought some linen cloth, he took down the body, wrapped it in a clean linen cloth, and placed it at the place where Jesus was crucified, there was a garden, and in the garden Joseph's own new tomb that he had cut out of rock; one in which no one had yet been laid. Because it was the Jewish day of Preparation and since the tomb was nearby, they laid Jesus there. The women who had come with Jesus from Galilee followed Joseph and saw the tomb and how his body was laid in it. He was accompanied by Nicodemus, the man who earlier had visited Jesus at night. Nicodemus brought a mixture of myrrh and aloes, about seventy-five pounds. Taking Jesus' body, the two of them wrapped it, with the spices, in strips of linen. This was in accordance with Jewish burial customs. Then he rolled a big stone against the front of the entrance of the tomb and went away. 47 Mary Magdalene and Mary the mother of Joses saw where he was laid and were sitting there opposite of the tomb. Then they went home and prepared spices and perfumes. But they rested on the Sabbath in obedience to the commandment. Mark 15:42b-47. Matthew 27:57-61. Luke 23:50-53, 55-56. John 19:38-42.

His Secured Tomb

62 The next day, the one after Preparation Day, the chief priests and the Pharisees went to Pilate.

63 "Sir," they said, "we remember that while he was still alive that deceiver said, 'After three days I will rise again.' 64 So give the order for the tomb to be made secure until the third day. Otherwise, his disciples may come and steal the body and tell the people that he has been raised from the dead. This last deception will be worse than the first."

65 "Take a guard," Pilate answered. "Go; make the tomb as secure as you know how."

66 So they went and made the tomb secure by putting a seal on the stone and posting the guard. Matthew 27:62-66.

Chapter Six

HIS RESURRECTION

His Raised Again

1 In my former book, Theophilus, I wrote about all that Jesus began to do and to teach 2 until the day he was taken up to heaven, after giving instructions through the Holy Spirit to the apostles he had chosen. 3 After his suffering, he showed himself to these men and gave many convincing proofs that he was alive. Acts 1:1-3a.

1 After the Sabbath was over, at very early dawn on the first day of the week, just after sunrise while it was still dark, Mary Magdalene and the other Mary (Mother of James), and Salome brought spices they had prepared so that they might go to anoint Jesus' body, were on their way to look at the tomb and they asked each other, "Who will roll the stone away from the entrance of the tomb?" Matthew 28:1. Mark 16:1-3. Luke 24:1. John 20:1a.

52 There was a violent earthquake, the tombs broke open and the bodies of many holy people who had died were raised to life. 53a They came out of the tombs after Jesus' resurrection, for an angel of the Lord came down from heaven and, going to Jesus' tomb, rolled back the stone and sat on it. Matthew 27:52-53a. Matthew 28:2.

3 The angel's appearance was like lightning, and his clothes were white as snow. Matthew 28:3.

4 The guards were so afraid of him that they shook and became like dead men. Matthew 28:4.

4 But when they looked up, they found and saw that the stone, which was very large, had been rolled away from the tomb. 5 But as they entered the tomb, they did not find the body of the Lord Jesus. While they were wondering about this, suddenly they saw a young man dressed in a white robe sitting on the right side, and two men in clothes that gleamed like lightening stood beside them and they were alarmed. Mark 16:4-5. Luke 24:2-4. John 20:1b.

5 In their fright the women bowed down with their faces to the ground, but the men and the angel said to the women, "Do not be alarmed or afraid," they said. "Why do you look for the living among the dead? For I and we know that you are looking for Jesus the Nazarene, who was crucified. 6 He is not here; he has risen, just as he said. Come and see the place where they laid him. Remember how he told you, while he was still with you in Galilee: 'The Son of Man must be delivered into the hands of sinful men, be crucified and on the third day be raised again." Then they remembered his words. Matthew 28:5-6. Mark 16:6. Luke 24:5-8.

7 Then go quickly and tell his disciples and Peter: 'He has risen from the dead and is going ahead of you into Galilee. There you will see him.' Just now I have told you." Matthew 28:7. Mark 16:7

8 Trembling and bewildered, the women hurried and went out and fled away from the tomb. They said nothing to anyone, because they were afraid yet filled with joy, and ran to tell his disciples. Mark 16:8. Matthew 28:8.

9 So when they came back from the tomb, Mary Magdalene came running to Simon Peter and the other disciple, the one Jesus loved, and said, "They have taken the Lord out of the tomb, and we don't know where they have put him!" They told all these things to the Eleven and to all the others. 10 It was Mary Magdalene, Joanna, Mary the mother of James, and the others with them who told this to the apostles. 11 But they did not believe the women, because their words seemed to them like nonsense. Luke 24:9-11. John 20:2.

3 So Peter, however, got up and ran to the tomb, and the other disciple started for the tomb. 4 Both were running, but the other disciple outran Peter and reached the tomb first. 5 He bent over and looked in at the strips of linen lying there but did not go in. 6 Then Simon Peter, who was behind him, arrived. Bending over, he saw the strips of linen lying there by themselves, 7 as well as the burial cloth that had been around Jesus' head and went into the tomb. The cloth was folded up by itself, separate from the linen. He went away, wondering to himself what had happened. 8 Finally the other disciple, who had reached the tomb first, also went inside. He saw and believed. 9 (They still did not understand from Scripture that Jesus had to rise from the dead.) John 20:3-9. Luke 24:12.

His Greetings

9 When Jesus rose early on the first day of the week, he appeared first to Mary Magdalene, out of whom he had driven seven demons. Mark 16:9. [The most reliable early manuscripts and other ancient witnesses do not have Mark 16:9-20.]

10 Then the disciples went back to their homes, John 20:10.

11 but Mary stood outside the tomb crying. As she wept, she bent over to look into the tomb 12 and saw two angels in white, seated where Jesus' body had been, one at the head and the other at the foot. 13 They asked her, "Woman, why are you crying?" "They have taken my Lord away," she said, "and I don't know where they have put him." John 20:11-13.

14 Suddenly at this, Jesus met them. She turned around and saw Jesus standing there, but she did not realize that it was Jesus. 15 "Greetings woman," he said, "why are you crying? Who is it you are looking for?" Thinking he was the gardener, she said,

"Sir, if you have carried him away, tell me where you have put him, and I will get him." 16 Jesus said to her, "Mary." She turned toward him and cried out in Aramaic, "Rabboni!" (which means Teacher). They came to him, clasped his feet and worshiped him. 17 Then Jesus said to them, "Do not hold on to me, for I have not yet returned to the Father. Do not be afraid. Go instead to my brothers and tell them to go to Galilee; there they will see me. 'I am returning to my Father and your Father, to my God and your God.'" 18 Mary Magdalene went to the disciples with the news: "I have seen the Lord!" And she told them that he had said these things to her. John 20:14-18. Matthew 28:9-10.

10 She went and told those who had been with him and who were mourning and weeping. 11 When they heard that Jesus was alive and that she had seen him, they did not believe it. Mark 16:10-11. [The most reliable early manuscripts and other ancient witnesses do not have Mark 16:9-20.]

His False Report

11 While the women were on their way, some of the guards went into the city and reported to the chief priests everything that had happened.

12 When the chief priests had met with the elders and devised a plan, they gave the soldiers a large sum of money, 13 telling them, "You are to say, 'His disciples came during the night and stole him away while we were asleep.' 14 If this report gets to the governor, we will satisfy him and keep you out of trouble."

15 So the soldiers took the money and did as they were instructed. And this story has been widely circulated among the Jews to this very day. Matthew 28:11-15.

His Different Form

13 Now that same day two of them were going to a village called Emmaus, about seven miles from Jerusalem. 14 While they were walking in the country and talking with each other about everything that had happened. 15 As they talked and discussed these things with each other, Jesus himself came up and walked along with them; 16 but they were kept from recognizing him; he appeared in a different form to two of them. Luke 24:13-16. Mark 16:12. [The most reliable early manuscripts and other ancient witnesses do not have Mark 16:9-20.]

17 He asked them, "What are you discussing together as you walk along?" They stood still, their faces downcast. 18 One of them, named Cleopas, asked him, "Are you only a visitor to Jerusalem and do not know the things that have happened there in these days?" 19 "What things?" he asked. "About Jesus of Nazareth," they replied. "He was a prophet, powerful in word and deed before God and all the people. 20 The chief priests and our rulers handed him over to be sentenced to death, and they crucified him; 21 but we had hoped that he was the one who was going to redeem Israel. And what is more, it is the third day since all this took place. 22 In addition, some of our women amazed us. They went to the tomb early this morning 23 but didn't find his body. They came and told us that they had seen a vision of angels, who said he was alive. 24 Then some of our companions went to the tomb and found it just as the women had said, but him they did not see." 25 He said to them, "How foolish you are, and how slow of heart to believe all that the prophets have spoken! 26 Did not the Christ have to suffer these things and then enter his glory?" 27 And beginning with Moses and all the Prophets, he explained to them what was said in all the Scriptures concerning himself.

28 As they approached the village to which they were going, Jesus acted as if he were going farther. 29 But they urged him strongly, "Stay with us, for it is nearly evening; the day is almost over." So he went in to stay with them.

30 When he was at the table with them, he took bread, gave thanks, broke it and began to give it to them. 31 Then their eyes were opened and they recognized him, and he disappeared from their sight. 32 They asked each other, "Were not our hearts burning within us while he talked with us on the road and opened the Scriptures to us?" Luke 24:17-32.

33 They got up and returned at once to Jerusalem. There they found the Eleven and those with them, assembled together 34 and saying, "It is true! The Lord has risen and has appeared to Simon." 35 Then the two reported and told it to the rest, what had happened on the way, and how Jesus was recognized by them when he broke the bread; but they did not believe them either. Luke 24:33-35. Mark 16:13. [The most reliable early manuscripts and other ancient witnesses do not have Mark 16:9-20.]

His Touch Me

19a On the evening of that first day of the week, when the disciples were together, with the doors locked for fear of the Jews, John 20:19a.

36 Later while they were still talking about this, Jesus himself came, appeared and stood among the Eleven as they were eating; and said to them, "Peace be with you." Luke 24:36. John 20:19b. Mark 16:14a. [The most reliable early manuscripts and other ancient witnesses do not have Mark 16:9-20.]

37 They were startled and frightened, thinking they saw a ghost. 38 He said to them, "Why are you troubled, and why do doubts rise in your minds? Luke 24:37-38.

14b he rebuked them for their lack of faith and their stubborn refusal to believe those who had seen him after he had risen. Mark 16:14b. [The most reliable early manuscripts and other ancient witnesses do not have Mark 16:9-20.]

39 After he said this, he showed them his hands and side. Look at my hands and my feet. It is I myself! Touch me and see; a ghost does not have flesh and bones, as you see I have." 40 When he had said this, he showed them his hands and feet. 41 And while the disciples still did not believe it because they were overjoyed and amazed when they saw the Lord; he asked them, "Do you have anything here to eat?" 42 They gave him a piece of broiled fish, 43 and he took it and ate it in their presence. Luke 24:39-43. John 20:20.

21 Again Jesus said, "Peace be with you! As the Father has sent me, I am sending you." 22 And with that he breathed on them and said, "Receive the Holy Spirit. 23 If you forgive anyone his sins, they are forgiven; if you do not forgive them, they are not forgiven." John 20:21-23.

24 Now Thomas (called Didymus), one of the Twelve, was not with the disciples when Jesus came. 25 So the other disciples told him, "We have seen the Lord!" But he said to them, "Unless I see the nail marks in his hands and put my finger where the nails were, and put my hand into his side, I will not believe it." John 20:24-25.

His Thomas

26 A week later his disciples were in the house again, and Thomas was with them. Though the doors were locked, Jesus came and stood among them and said, "Peace be with you!" 27 Then he said to Thomas, "Put your finger here; see my hands. Reach out your hand and put it into my side. Stop doubting and believe." 28 Thomas said to him, "My Lord and my God!" 29 Then Jesus told him, "Because you have seen me, you have believed; blessed are those who have not seen and yet have believed." 30 Jesus did many other miraculous signs in the presence of his disciples, which are not recorded in this book. 31 But these are written that you may believe that Jesus is the Christ, the Son of God, and that by believing you may have life in his name. John 20:26-31.

His Third Appearance

1 Afterward Jesus appeared again to his disciples, by the Sea of Tiberias. It happened this way: 2 Simon Peter, Thomas (called Didymus), Nathanael from Cana in Galilee, the sons of Zebedee, and two other disciples were together. 3 "I'm going out to fish," Simon Peter told them, and they said, "We'll go with you." So they went out and got into the boat, but that night they caught nothing.

4 Early in the morning, Jesus stood on the shore, but the disciples did not realize that it was Jesus.

5 He called out to them, "Friends, haven't you any fish?" "No," they answered.

6 He said, "Throw your net on the right side of the boat and you will find some." When they did, they were unable to haul the net in because of the large number of fish.

7 Then the disciple whom Jesus loved said to Peter, "It is the Lord!" As soon as Simon Peter heard him say, "It is the Lord," he wrapped his outer garment around him (for he had taken it off) and jumped into the water. 8 The other disciples followed in the boat, towing the net full of fish, for they were not far from shore, about a hundred yards. 9 When they landed, they saw a fire of burning coals there with fish on it, and some bread.

10 Jesus said to them, "Bring some of the fish you have just caught."

11 Simon Peter climbed aboard and dragged the net ashore. It was full of large fish, 153, but even with so many the net was not torn. 12 Jesus said to them, "Come and have breakfast." None of the disciples dared ask him, "Who are you?" They knew it was the Lord.

13 Jesus came, took the bread and gave it to them, and did the same with the fish. John 21:1-13.

4 while he was eating with them, he gave them this command: "Do not leave Jerusalem, but wait for the gift my Father promised, which you have heard me speak about. 5 For John baptized with water, but in a few days you will be baptized with the Holy Spirit." Acts 1:4-5.

14 This was now the third time Jesus appeared to his disciples after he was raised from the dead. John 21:14.

His Do You Love Me

15 When they had finished eating, Jesus said to Simon Peter, "Simon son of John, do you truly love me more than these?" "Yes, Lord," he said, "you know that I love you." Jesus said, "Feed my lambs."

16 Again Jesus said, "Simon son of John, do you truly love me?" He answered, "Yes, Lord, you know that I love you." Jesus said, "Take care of my sheep."

17 The third time he said to him, "Simon son of John, do you love me?" Peter was hurt because Jesus asked him the third time, "Do you love me?" He said, "Lord, you know all things; you know that I love you." Jesus said, "Feed my sheep.

18 I tell you the truth, when you were younger you dressed yourself and went where you wanted; but when you are old you will stretch out your hands, and someone else will dress you and lead you where you do not want to go."

19 Jesus said this to indicate the kind of death by which Peter would glorify God. Then he said to him, "Follow me!"

20 Peter turned and saw that the disciple whom Jesus loved was following them. (This was the one who had leaned back against Jesus at the supper and had said, "Lord, who is going to betray you?") 21 When Peter saw him, he asked, "Lord, what about him?"

22 Jesus answered, "If I want him to remain alive until I return, what is that to you? You must follow me."

23 Because of this, the rumor spread among the brothers that this disciple would not die. But Jesus did not say that he would not die; he only said, "If I want him to remain alive until I return, what is that to you?"

24 This is the disciple who testifies to these things and who wrote them down. We know that his testimony is true. John 21:15-24.

His Other Appearances

52b and the bodies of many holy people who had died that were raised to life, after Jesus' resurrection, went into the holy city and appeared to many people, Matthew 27:Repeat 52b, 53b.

3b He appeared to them over a period of forty days and spoke about the kingdom of God. Acts 1:3b.

Chapter Seven

His Witnesses

16 Then the eleven disciples went to Galilee, to the mountain where Jesus had told them to go. 17 When they saw him, they worshiped him; but some doubted.

18 Then Jesus came to them and said, "All authority in heaven and on earth has been given to me. Matthew 28:16-18.

6 So when they met together, they asked him, "Lord, are you at this time going to restore the kingdom to Israel?" Acts 1:6.

7 He said to them: "It is not for you to know the times or dates the Father has set by his own authority. 8 But you will receive power when the Holy Spirit comes on you; and you will be my witnesses in Jerusalem, and in all Judea and Samaria, and to the ends of the earth." Acts 1:7-8.

44 He said to them, "This is what I told you while I was still with you: Everything must be fulfilled that is written about me in the Law of Moses, the Prophets and the Psalms." 45 Then he opened their minds so they could understand the Scriptures. 46 He told them, "This is what is written: The Christ will suffer and rise from the dead on the third day, 47 and repentance and forgiveness of sins will be preached in his name to all nations, beginning at Jerusalem. Luke 24:44-47.

15 He said to them, "Therefore go into all the world and preach the good news to all creation. Make disciples of all nations, baptizing

them in the name of the Father and of the Son and of the Holy Spirit. 16 Whoever believes and is baptized will be saved, but whoever does not believe will be condemned; and teaching them to obey everything I have commanded you. Mark 16:15-16. [The most reliable early manuscripts and other ancient witnesses do not have Mark 16:9-20.] Matthew 28:19-20a.

His Witnesses' Signs

17 And these signs will accompany those who believe: In my name they will drive out demons; they will speak in new tongues; 18 they will pick up snakes with their hands; and when they drink deadly poison, it will not hurt them at all; they will place their hands on sick people, and they will get well." Mark 16:17-18. [The most reliable early manuscripts and other ancient witnesses do not have Mark 16:9-20.]

48 You are witnesses of these things. 49 I am going to send you what my Father has promised; but stay in the city until you have been clothed with power from on high." Luke 24:48-49.

20b And surely I am with you always, to the very end of the age." Matthew 28:20b.

His Taken Up

19a After the Lord Jesus had spoken to them, Mark 16:19a. [The most reliable early manuscripts and other ancient witnesses do not have Mark 16:9-20.] Acts 1:9a.

50 When he had led them out to the vicinity of Bethany, he lifted up his hands and blessed them. 51 While he was blessing them, he was taken up before their very eyes, and a cloud hid him from their sight; Luke 24:50-51. Acts 1:9b.

10 They were looking intently up into the sky as he was going, when suddenly two men dressed in white stood beside them. 11 "Men of Galilee," they said, "why do you stand here looking into the sky? This same Jesus, who has been taken from you into heaven, will come back in the same way you have seen him go into heaven." Acts 1:10-11.

19b he was taken up into heaven and he sat at the right hand of God. Mark 16:19b. [The most reliable early manuscripts and other ancient witnesses do not have Mark 16:9-20.]

52 Then they worshiped him and returned to Jerusalem with great joy. 53 And they stayed continually at the temple, praising God. Luke 24:52-53.

20 Then the disciples went out and preached everywhere, and the Lord worked with them and confirmed his word by the signs that accompanied it. Mark 16:20. [The most reliable early manuscripts and other ancient witnesses do not have Mark 16:9-20.]

His Saul

1 Meanwhile, Saul was still breathing out murderous threats against the Lord's disciples. He went to the high priest 2 and asked him for letters to the synagogues in Damascus, so that if he found any there who belonged to the Way, whether men or women, he might take them as prisoners to Jerusalem.

3 As he neared Damascus on his journey, suddenly a light from heaven flashed around him. 4 He fell to the ground and heard a voice say to him, "Saul, Saul, why do you persecute me?" 5 "Who are you, Lord?" Saul asked. "I am Jesus, whom you are persecuting," he replied. 6 "Now get up and go into the city, and you will be told what you must do."

7 The men traveling with Saul stood there speechless; they heard the sound but did not see anyone.

8 Saul got up from the ground, but when he opened his eyes he could see nothing. So they led him by the hand into Damascus. 9 For three days he was blind, and did not eat or drink anything.

10 In Damascus there was a disciple named Ananias. The Lord called to him in a vision, "Ananias!" "Yes, Lord," he answered. 11 The Lord told him, "Go to the house of Judas on Straight Street and ask for a man from Tarsus named Saul, for he is praying. 12 In a vision he has seen a man named Ananias come and place his hands on him to restore his sight." 13 "Lord," Ananias answered, "I have heard many reports about this man and all the harm he has done to your saints in Jerusalem. 14 And he has come here with authority from the chief priests to arrest all who call on your name." 15 But the Lord said to Ananias, "Go! This man is my chosen instrument to carry my name before the Gentiles and their kings and before the people of Israel. 16 I will show him how much he must suffer for my name."

17 Then Ananias went to the house and entered it. Placing his hands on Saul, he said, "Brother Saul, the Lord-Jesus, who appeared to you on the road as you were coming here-has sent me so that you may see again and be filled with the Holy Spirit." 18 Immediately, something like scales fell from Saul's eyes, and he could see again. He got up and was baptized, 19 and after taking some food, he regained his strength. Acts 9:1-19.

His Angel

19b Then Herod went from Judea to Caesarea and stayed there a while. 20 He had been quarreling with the people of Tyre and Sidon; they now joined together and sought an audience with him. Having secured the support of Blastus, a trusted personal servant of the king, they asked for peace, because they depended on the king's country for their food supply.

21 On the appointed day Herod, wearing his royal robes, sat on his throne and delivered a public address to the people. 22 They shouted, "This is the voice of a god, not of a man." 23 Immediately, because Herod did not give praise to God, an angel of the Lord struck him down, and he was eaten by worms and died.

24 But the word of God continued to increase and spread. Acts 12:19b-24.

His Revelation

1 The revelation of Jesus Christ, which God gave him to show his servants what must soon take place. He made it known by sending his angel to his servant John, 2 who testifies to everything he saw- that is, the word of God and the testimony of Jesus Christ.

3 Blessed is the one who reads the words of this prophecy, and blessed are those who hear it and take to heart what is written in it, because the time is near.

4 John, to the seven churches in the province of Asia: Grace and peace to you from him who is, and who was, and who is to come, and from the seven spirits before his throne,

5 and from Jesus Christ, who is the faithful witness, the firstborn from the dead, and the ruler of the kings of the earth. To him who loves us and has freed us from our sins by his blood, 6 and has made us to be a kingdom and priests to serve his God and Father- to him be glory and power for ever and ever! Amen.

7 Look, he is coming with the clouds, and every eye will see him, even those who pierced him; and all the peoples of the earth will mourn because of him. So shall it be! Amen. Revelation 1:1-7.

His Who

8 "I am the Alpha and the Omega," says the Lord God, "who is, and who was, and who is to come, the Almighty." Revelation 1:8.

His Scroll

9 I, John, your brother and companion in the suffering and kingdom and patient endurance that are ours in Jesus, was on the island of Patmos because of the word of God and the testimony of Jesus. 10 On the Lord's Day I was in the Spirit, and I heard behind me a loud voice like a trumpet, 11 which said: "Write on a scroll what you see and send it to the seven churches: to Ephesus, Smyrna, Pergamum, Thyatira, Sardis, Philadelphia and Laodicea." Revelation 1:9-11.

His Appearance

12 I turned around to see the voice that was speaking to me. And when I turned I saw seven golden lampstands, 13 and among the lampstands was someone "like a son of man," dressed in a robe reaching down to his feet and with a golden sash around his chest. 14 His head and hair were white like wool, as white as snow, and his eyes were like blazing fire. 15 His feet were like bronze glowing in a furnace, and his voice was like the sound of rushing waters. 16 In his right hand he held seven stars, and out of his mouth came a sharp double-edged sword. His face was like the sun shining in all its brilliance.

17 When I saw him, I fell at his feet as though dead. Then he placed his right hand on me and said: "Do not be afraid. I am the First and the Last. 18 I am the Living One; I was dead, and behold I am alive for ever and ever! And I hold the keys of death and Hades.

19 "Write, therefore, what you have seen, what is now and what will take place later.

20 The mystery of the seven stars that you saw in my right hand and of the seven golden lampstands is this: The seven stars are the angels of the seven churches, and the seven lampstands are the seven churches. Revelation 1:12-20.

Chapter Eight

His Ephesus Angel

1 "To the angel of the church in Ephesus write: These are the words of him who holds the seven stars in his right hand and walks among the seven golden lampstands:

2 I know your deeds, your hard work and your perseverance. I know that you cannot tolerate wicked men, that you have tested those who claim to be apostles but are not, and have found them false. 3 You have persevered and have endured hardships for my name, and have not grown weary.

4 Yet I hold this against you: You have forsaken your first love.

5 Remember the height from which you have fallen! Repent and do the things you did at first. If you do not repent, I will come to you and remove your lampstand from its place.

6 But you have this in your favor: You hate the practices of the Nicolaitans, which I also hate.

7 He who has an ear, let him hear what the Spirit says to the churches. To him who overcomes, I will give the right to eat from the tree of life, which is in the paradise of God. Revelation 2:1-7.

His Smyrna Angel

8 "To the angel of the church in Smyrna write: These are the words of him who is the First and the Last, who died and came to life again.

9 I know your afflictions and your poverty-yet you are rich! I know the slander of those who say they are Jews and are not, but are a synagogue of Satan. 10 Do not be afraid of what you are about to suffer. I tell you, the devil will put some of you in prison to test you, and you will suffer persecution for ten days. Be faithful, even to the point of death, and I will give you the crown of life.

11 He who has an ear, let him hear what the Spirit says to the churches. He who overcomes will not be hurt at all by the second death. Revelation 2:8-11.

His Pergamum Angel

12 "To the angel of the church in Pergamum write: These are the words of him who has the sharp, double-edged sword.

13 I know where you live-where Satan has his throne. Yet you remain true to my name. You did not renounce your faith in me, even in the days of Antipas, my faithful witness, who was put to death in your city-where Satan lives.

14 Nevertheless, I have a few things against you: You have people there who hold to the teaching of Balaam, who taught Balak to entice the Israelites to sin by eating food sacrificed to idols and by

committing sexual immorality. 15 Likewise you also have those who hold to the teaching of the Nicolaitans.

16 Repent therefore! Otherwise, I will soon come to you and will fight against them with the sword of my mouth.

17 He who has an ear, let him hear what the Spirit says to the churches. To him who overcomes, I will give some of the hidden manna. I will also give him a white stone with a new name written on it, known only to him who receives it. Revelation 2:12-17.

His Thyatira Angel

18 "To the angel of the church in Thyatira write: These are the words of the Son of God, whose eyes are like blazing fire and whose feet are like burnished bronze.

19 I know your deeds, your love and faith, your service and perseverance, and that you are now doing more than you did at first.

20 Nevertheless, I have this against you: You tolerate that woman Jezebel, who calls herself a prophetess. By her teaching she misleads my servants into sexual immorality and the eating of food sacrificed to idols. 21 I have given her time to repent of her immorality, but she is unwilling. 22 So I will cast her on a bed of suffering, and I will make those who commit adultery with her suffer intensely, unless they repent of her ways. 23a I will strike her children dead.

23b Then all the churches will know that I am he who searches hearts and minds, and I will repay each of you according to your deeds.

24 Now I say to the rest of you in Thyatira, to you who do not hold to her teaching and have not learned Satan's so-called deep secrets (I will not impose any other burden on you): 25 Only hold on to what you have until I come.

26 To him who overcomes and does my will to the end, I will give authority over the nations- 27 'He will rule them with an iron scepter; he will dash them to pieces like pottery'-just as I have received authority from my Father. 28 I will also give him the morning star.

29 He who has an ear, let him hear what the Spirit says to the churches. Revelation 2:18-29.

His Sardis Angel

1a "To the angel of the church in Sardis write: These are the words of him who holds the seven spirits of God and the seven stars.

1b I know your deeds; you have a reputation of being alive, but you are dead. 2 Wake up! Strengthen what remains and is about to die, for I have not found your deeds complete in the sight of my God.

3 Remember, therefore, what you have received and heard; obey it, and repent. But if you do not wake up, I will come like a thief, and you will not know at what time I will come to you.

4 Yet you have a few people in Sardis who have not soiled their clothes. They will walk with me, dressed in white, for they are worthy.

5 He who overcomes will, like them, be dressed in white. I will never blot out his name from the book of life, but will acknowledge his name before my Father and his angels.

6 He who has an ear, let him hear what the Spirit says to the churches. Revelation 3:1-6.

His Philadelphia Angel

7 "To the angel of the church in Philadelphia write: These are the words of him who is holy and true, who holds the key of David. What he opens no one can shut, and what he shuts no one can open.

8 I know your deeds. See, I have placed before you an open door that no one can shut. I know that you have little strength, yet you have kept my word and have not denied my name. 9 I will make those who are of the synagogue of Satan, who claim to be Jews though they are not, but are liars-I will make them come and fall down at your feet and acknowledge that I have loved you. 10 Since you have kept my command to endure patiently, I will also keep you from the hour of trial that is going to come upon the whole world to test those who live on the earth.

11 I am coming soon. Hold on to what you have, so that no one will take your crown.

12 Him who overcomes I will make a pillar in the temple of my God. Never again will he leave it. I will write on him the name of my God and the name of the city of my God, the new Jerusalem, which is coming down out of heaven from my God; and I will also write on him my new name.

13 He who has an ear, let him hear what the Spirit says to the churches. Revelation 3:7-13.

His Laodicea Angel

14 "To the angel of the church in Laodicea write: These are the words of the Amen, the faithful and true witness, the ruler of God's creation.

15 I know your deeds, that you are neither cold nor hot. I wish you were either one or the other! 16 So, because you are lukewarm-neither hot nor cold-I am about to spit you out of my mouth.

17 You say, 'I am rich; I have acquired wealth and do not need a thing.' But you do not realize that you are wretched, pitiful, poor, blind and naked.

18 I counsel you to buy from me gold refined in the fire, so you can become rich; and white clothes to wear, so you can cover your shameful nakedness; and salve to put on your eyes, so you can see. 19 Those whom I love I rebuke and discipline. So be earnest, and repent.

20 Here I am! I stand at the door and knock. If anyone hears my voice and opens the door, I will come in and eat with him, and he with me.

21 To him who overcomes, I will give the right to sit with me on my throne, just as I overcame and sat down with my Father on his throne.

22 He who has an ear, let him hear what the Spirit says to the churches." Revelation 3:14-22.

His Throne

1 After this I looked, and there before me was a door standing open in heaven. And the voice I had first heard speaking to me like a trumpet said, "Come up here, and I will show you what must take place after this."

2 At once I was in the Spirit, and there before me was a throne in heaven with someone sitting on it. 3 And the one who sat there had the appearance of jasper and carnelian. A rainbow, resembling an emerald, encircled the throne.

4 Surrounding the throne were twenty-four other thrones, and seated on them were twenty-four elders. They were dressed in white and had crowns of gold on their heads.

5 From the throne came flashes of lightning, rumblings and peals of thunder. Before the throne, seven lamps were blazing. These are the seven spirits of God.

6 Also before the throne there was what looked like a sea of glass, clear as crystal. In the center, around the throne, were four living creatures, and they were covered with eyes, in front and in back. 7 The first living creature was like a lion, the second was like an ox, the third had a face like a man, the fourth was like a flying eagle. 8 Each of the four living creatures had six wings and was covered with eyes all around, even under his wings. Day and night they never stop saying: "Holy, holy, holy is the Lord God Almighty, who was, and is, and is to come."

9 Whenever the living creatures give glory, honor and thanks to him who sits on the throne and who lives for ever and ever, 10 the twenty-four elders fall down before him who sits on the

throne, and worship him who lives for ever and ever. They lay their crowns before the throne and say: 11 "You are worthy, our Lord and God, to receive glory and honor and power, for you created all things, and by your will they were created and have their being." Revelation 4:1-11.

His Worthy

1 Then I saw in the right hand of him who sat on the throne a scroll with writing on both sides and sealed with seven seals. 2 And I saw a mighty angel proclaiming in a loud voice, "Who is worthy to break the seals and open the scroll?"

3 But no one in heaven or on earth or under the earth could open the scroll or even look inside it. 4 I wept and wept because no one was found who was worthy to open the scroll or look inside.

5 Then one of the elders said to me, "Do not weep! See, the Lion of the tribe of Judah, the Root of David, has triumphed. He is able to open the scroll and its seven seals."

6 Then I saw a Lamb, looking as if it had been slain, standing in the center of the throne, encircled by the four living creatures and the elders. He had seven horns and seven eyes, which are the seven spirits of God sent out into all the earth. 7 He came and took the scroll from the right hand of him who sat on the throne.

8 And when he had taken it, the four living creatures and the twenty-four elders fell down before the Lamb. Each one had a harp and they were holding golden bowls full of incense, which are the prayers of the saints. 9 And they sang a new song: "You are worthy to take the scroll and to open its seals, because you were slain, and with your blood you purchased men for God from every tribe and language and people and nation. 10 You have

made them to be a kingdom and priests to serve our God, and they will reign on the earth."

11 Then I looked and heard the voice of many angels, numbering thousands upon thousands, and ten thousand times ten thousand. They encircled the throne and the living creatures and the elders. 12 In a loud voice they sang: "Worthy is the Lamb, who was slain, to receive power and wealth and wisdom and strength and honor and glory and praise!"

13 Then I heard every creature in heaven and on earth and under the earth and on the sea, and all that is in them, singing: "To him who sits on the throne and to the Lamb be praise and honor and glory and power, for ever and ever!"

14 The four living creatures said, "Amen," and the elders fell down and worshiped. Revelations 5:1-14.

His Rest

15 Therefore, "they are before the throne of God and serve him day and night in his temple; and he who sits on the throne will spread his tent over them. 16 Never again will they hunger; never again will they thirst. The sun will not beat upon them, nor any scorching heat. 17 For the Lamb at the center of the throne will be their shepherd; he will lead them to springs of living water. And God will wipe away every tear from their eyes." Revelation 7:15-17.

His Reign Forever

15 The seventh angel sounded his trumpet, and there were loud voices in heaven, which said: "The kingdom of the world has become the kingdom of our Lord and of his Christ, and he will reign for ever and ever." Revelation 11:15.

Chapter Nine

His Bride

4 The twenty-four elders and the four living creatures fell down and worshiped God, who was seated on the throne. And they cried: "Amen, Hallelujah!"

5 Then a voice came from the throne, saying: "Praise our God, all you his servants, you who fear him, both small and great!"

6 Then I heard what sounded like a great multitude, like the roar of rushing waters and like loud peals of thunder, shouting: "Hallelujah! For our Lord God Almighty reigns. 7 Let us rejoice and be glad and give him glory! For the wedding of the Lamb has come, and his bride has made herself ready. 8 Fine linen, bright and clean, was given her to wear." (Fine linen stands for the righteous acts of the saints.)

9 Then the angel said to me, "Write: 'Blessed are those who are invited to the wedding supper of the Lamb!'" And he added, "These are the true words of God."

10 At this I fell at his feet to worship him. But he said to me, "Do not do it! I am a fellow servant with you and with your brothers who hold to the testimony of Jesus. Worship God! For the testimony of Jesus is the spirit of prophecy."

11 I saw heaven standing open and there before me was a white horse, whose rider is called Faithful and True. With justice he judges and makes war. 12 His eyes are like blazing fire, and on

his head are many crowns. He has a name written on him that no one knows but he himself. 13 He is dressed in a robe dipped in blood, and his name is the Word of God.

14 The armies of heaven were following him, riding on white horses and dressed in fine linen, white and clean.

15 Out of his mouth comes a sharp sword with which to strike down the nations. "He will rule them with an iron scepter." He treads the winepress of the fury of the wrath of God Almighty.

16 On his robe and on his thigh he has this name written: KING OF KINGS AND LORD OF LORDS. Revelation 19:4-16.

His New Heaven New Earth

1 Then I saw a new heaven and a new earth, for the first heaven and the first earth had passed away, and there was no longer any sea.

2 I saw the Holy City, the new Jerusalem, coming down out of heaven from God, prepared as a bride beautifully dressed for her husband.

3 And I heard a loud voice from the throne saying, "Now the dwelling of God is with men, and he will live with them. They will be his people, and God himself will be with them and be their God. 4 He will wipe every tear from their eyes. There will be no more death or mourning or crying or pain, for the old order of things has passed away."

5 He who was seated on the throne said, "I am making everything new!" Then he said, "Write this down, for these words are trustworthy and true."

6 He said to me: "It is done. I am the Alpha and the Omega, the Beginning and the End. To him who is thirsty I will give to drink without cost from the spring of the water of life. 7 He who overcomes will inherit all this, and I will be his God and he will be my son. Revelations 21:1-7.

His Legacy

25 Jesus did many other things as well. If every one of them were written down, I suppose that even the whole world would not have room for the books that would be written. John 21:25.

His Invitation

12 "Behold, I am coming soon! My reward is with me, and I will give to everyone according to what he has done. 13 I am the Alpha and the Omega, the First and the Last, the Beginning and the End. 14 "Blessed are those who wash their robes, that they may have the right to the tree of life and may go through the gates into the city. Revelations 22:12-14.

Index